TO

THE

LAST

BREATH

TO
THE
LAST
BREATH

THREE WOMEN FIGHT

FOR THE TRUTH BEHIND

A CHILD'S TRAGIC MURDER

CARLTON STOWERS

ST. MARTIN'S PRESS ≋ NEW YORK

Design by MAUREEN TROY

ISBN 0-312-16981-7

First Edition: February 1998

For Brandon...
who will one day want to know.

Acknowledgments

The task of explaining the inexplicable is a challenge which stubborn writers of nonfiction have taken on for decades, some with greater success than others. The drive to solve such puzzles—to lend some degree of sense and reason to an occurrence both senseless and unreasonable—can be an exercise of such futility as to cause one to throw up his hands and consider a search for some new and easier line of work.

I know: I've been there. The book you're now holding is a blue-ribbon, twenty-four-karat case in point.

I would, then, be remiss if I did not mention the names of a number of people who not only provided insight and support but quietly guarded the back door against my escape. Their favors, hospitality, and gentle urgings were endless.

To say that Sharon Couch, Detective Sue Dietrich, Brazoria County Assistant District Attorney Jeri Yenne, Dr. Linda Norton, and Annette Campise are simply women of rare strength and dedication is to shortchange them individually and collectively. The truth of the matter is that this book would not exist were it not for their courage and willing, generous help.

Additionally, there were those who patiently offered help on matters both legal and medical: Brazoria County District Attorney Jerome Aldrich, Assistant D.A. Tony Latino, lawyers Joanne Chadderdon,

Skip Cornelius, and Sam Adamo; Drs. William Anderson, Hugh Burris, John Long, Gary Bender, Dorothy Kelley, Eduardo Bellas, Charles Petty, Cecil Wingo, and John Bright; Alvin Police Chief Mike Merkel and officers Terry Earl, Howard Duckworth, and Todd Arendell.

Observations, recollections, and suggestions of so many provided pieces to the story: Vince Campise, Sunny Bradley, Priscilla Campise, Gerald Philpott, Donna Kinsel, Donna Hunt, P. G. Walls, Robert Kubena, Charles Nawrocki, Bill Crider, Bill Gray, and Paul Gauskow. Others who wished to remain anonymous won't be named but their help is greatly appreciated nonetheless.

The excellent work of fellow journalists helped provide a valuable map in the early goings of my research. Steve McVicker of the *Houston Press*; Mike Drago of the Associated Press; *Houston Chronicle* staffers Joe Stinebaker, Eric Hanson, Jerry Urban, Steve Olafson, and Patti Muck; Marty Graham of the *Houston Post*; and Kristie Watthuber of the *Alvin Advertiser* all reported admirably on the case. And a grateful nod is due Ida M. Blanchette's *Babe on the Bayou*, a charming history of the first one hundred years of Alvin, Texas.

That Janet Wilkens Manus is willing to go miles beyond the traditional function of an agent has always been an immeasurable plus. And sincere thanks is due to editor Charlie Spicer for giving this project a receptive home. Thanks, too, for the encouraging words and courtroom company provided by Dan Witt.

And, nothing of any real worth that I've ever accomplished is without the imprint of Pat Stowers: wife, friend, helpful critic, and damn fine photographer.

Finally, there was a little girl named Renee, who looked down on me daily from a photograph positioned on my bookshelf, lending silent encouragement more valuable than I'll ever be able to explain.

*Blessed be childhood, which brings down something
of heaven into the midst of our rough earthliness...*

—HENRI FREDERIC AMIEL, *JOURNAL*

*Who takes the child by the hand,
takes the mother by the heart.*

—DANISH PROVERB

TO THE LAST BREATH

Prologue

October 1994

The tiny caravan made its way northward along Interstate 90, headlights cutting into the dusk of the damp, overcast Friday evening. Through the Texas Gulf Coast communities of Subline, Rock Island, and Eagle Lake, the hearse and two accompanying police cars were never separated, linked together by some invisible tether. The passengers inside the vehicles, officers of the Alvin Police Department and a funeral home attendant, rode in silence, as if in a show of respect for the cargo being transported, their faces reflections of the grimness of the task.

It had been so since they had pulled away from the City Cemetery located on the eastern edge of the tiny community of Hallettsville.

Their destination was the Alvin Community Hospital where two other police officers awaited, having been assigned unusual guard duty. They were to stand sentry at the door of the room where, they had been informed, a casket would be kept overnight. "If you need to relieve yourself," a cautious assistant district attorney had told them, "do it before you go on duty. Once the casket is delivered and locked in the room, you don't move from your post—for any reason."

Such was the caution, the attention to the most minute detail, attached to the unprecedented event.

Earlier in the day the first exhumation of a body ever conducted in Brazoria County had occurred. A funeral home director had stood anxiously by, feeling very little comfort from the court order that had been presented him, as workers opened the grave, retrieved the casket, and placed it into the back of the waiting hearse. In his decade of death-related services, it was the first such exercise he'd ever witnessed.

As he stood there, a gentle breeze rustled through a stand of nearby cedars and across the manicured, headstone-dotted landscape. It was, he thought, as though he were watching a video rewind, repeating the somber motions of a graveside funeral service conducted eight months earlier, only this time in reverse.

///

As hospital officials in Alvin made preparations for the arrival, a nervous grandmother in her mid-forties was driving through the always heavy Houston traffic toward Intercontinental Airport, her mind racing. She had selected a silk print dress for the occasion and had her auburn hair pulled tightly back at the nape of her neck. It was foolish, she thought, to be so concerned over her appearance. Still, she felt it important to make a good impression. And so she had spent more time with her hair and makeup than she had in months, eagerly anticipating her meeting with the Florida doctor who, up until now, had been only a pleasant voice on the phone.

She had left home early enough to stop by an ATM machine for cash. In her last telephone conversation with the doctor she had urged him to forego the airline's in-flight meal and let her take him to one of Houston's acclaimed steak restaurants. There they could talk, get better acquainted, before she drove him the final forty-five miles to Alvin where his hotel reservations had been arranged.

Turning off Interstate 45 toward the airport entrance as a gentle rain began to fall, the woman felt a sudden chilling awareness sweep through her body. It had been with her throughout the day, hidden away in the back of her mind, but now it burst forward, causing her knuckles to turn white as she gripped the steering wheel of her pickup. The man she would soon meet, a highly regarded forensic pathologist, would answer the question that had haunted her, had invaded her sleep and occupied every waking moment, for such a long time. Every ounce of hope to which she had wearily clung rested in the medical abilities of someone she didn't even know, and the realization frightened her.

Rolling down her window, she took a series of deep breaths, urging the crisp night air to calm her as she made her way into the airport parking lot.

And for a moment, her thoughts turned from the doctor's arrival to the casket she knew should already have arrived at the hospital.

Feeling anxious and fragile, she found her confidence shaken by even the slightest flaw in planning. For the woman assigned to greet the pathologist and see him safely to his destination, details that would usually be considered trivial suddenly seemed to warn of impending disaster. Leaving the airport, despite her intimate knowledge of the city and its freeways, she had somehow managed to lose her way, reaching the outskirts of suburban Jersey City before realizing she was driving in the wrong direction. Then, after finally reaching the restaurant and enjoying a leisurely, conversation-filled meal of prime rib, the bill left by the waiter brought the embarrassing realization that she did not have enough cash to pay the tab and would have to ask her guest to assist.

Small things of no real consequence, but unsettling nonetheless to one whose apprehension was now bordering on paranoia.

And the difficult part still lay ahead. The next day, the woman knew, the tension level was certain to reach heights she'd never before experienced. Long after bidding the visiting doctor goodnight at his hotel and returning to her Houston home, she counted the slowly passing hours with a sleepless mixture of fear and hope.

By the time the gray prelude to the new day filtered through her kitchen window, a very real physical pain had attached itself to the woman's anxiety. Her entire body ached as if invaded by some angry virus.

Though she was not a deeply religious person, she whispered a prayer for strength.

. . .

The woman sitting at her kitchen table, awaiting the Saturday morning sunrise, was not the only one nervously anticipating the events of the day.

In Alvin, a veteran female homicide detective who, months earlier, had gone to her superiors and asked to be assigned to a case she'd long been watching from a distance, had wakened to an overwhelming feeling of dread.

That she had witnessed the aftermath of death more times than she cared to remember should, she knew, be adequate preparation for what lay ahead. The blood and carnage, while always troubling, had long since become a routine part of her job. So had attendance at autopsies.

Never before, however, had she watched over the forensic examination of a body which had been exhumed, and she found her mind playing ugly, horror-movie games. Though she would share her concern with no one, the detective was apprehensive about what she would see when the casket was finally opened.

Only the knowledge that the grim process was the final chance to move the case toward the resolution she had sought with such determination would provide her the strength necessary to get through the ordeal.

///

For a half hour the gentle hum of an air purifier and ceiling exhaust fan pulled the sick, sweet odor from the room where the body lay on a portable gurney made of yellowed fiberglass. Harsh fluorescent lighting reflected against stark white walls so bright as to be discomforting until the eyes could adjust. On one side of the room sterile cabinets housed instruments, gowns, and a variety of cleaning fluids. Attached to the opposite wall were two stainless-steel sinks.

The blinds covering the small window at the opposite end of the room in which the doctor would perform his work were closed, adding to the claustrophobic atmosphere.

It was shortly after 10:00 A.M. when the doctor drained the final sip of coffee from a styrofoam cup, aimed it at a nearby wastebasket, and gave a slight nod to the woman who had picked him up at the airport the previous evening. She forced a nervous acknowledgment, then settled on a nearby couch to begin the wait as he disappeared into the examining room.

The wary detective, suddenly aware that her hands were shaking, followed the doctor silently.

For the next four and one-half hours she watched as the pathologist worked. When it became difficult for her to look upon the body any longer, she directed her attention to the man standing over the gurney, and studied the meticulous manner in which he was conducting the examination: taking photographs, probing, making incisions, preparing slides, recording his every move and observation into a nearby tape recorder. He was younger-looking than his fifty-two years, despite the salt-and-pepper hair. The horn-rimmed glasses he wore gave his round, pleasant face a studious appearance.

But what impressed her most was the gentleness with which he approached his work.

It was 2:30 in the afternoon when he finally removed his surgical gloves, raised his head, and wearily looked across the gurney.

"Detective," he said, "you now have a homicide investigation on your hands."

One

This is how it began: with warm sun and cool Gulf Coast waters gently splashing against the Galveston beach. There was infectious laughter everywhere as young voices, most of them belonging to college students, celebrated the intoxicating freedom of the annual ritual known as spring break. They came for the beer parties and the pot, or simply to kick back and enjoy the freedom from parental watch, classroom lectures, and boring jobs back home.

They got drunk and high, a lot of them got sick, and a few were even arrested. Some fell in love. . . .

There had been a time when the Galveston Island spring break festivities were sole property of college students—young men and women, single and carefree, who came to spend Daddy's money, flash their fraternity pins, and put aside the mysteries of calculus or introductory tort law for a few glorious, fun-filled days.

By the spring of 1987, however, the caravan of students from the University of Texas and SMU and even Bible-thumping Baylor University had been joined by an increasingly large number of party-crashers. There were the high-school kids, wide-eyed and impressionable, who had grown up with the legend of sun-and-sex fun the event promised and simply had to get an early preview of its magic. Though more spectators than participants, they could be counted on to return home with wild good-time stories generally woven of pure sideline fantasy.

Then there were those of college age but no college affiliation, young people whose academic pursuits had come to a screeching halt on high school graduation night. They worked the graveyard shift at local refineries or in secretarial pools, part of a generation already enslaved to the two-dollar woes and second-lien mortgages of adulthood. They had begun trekking to the Galveston beaches in greater numbers, mingling with the Sigma Nus and Tri Delts, partying away precious vacation time or manufactured sick days in an attempt to recapture the delights of fun and freedom.

To those who studied the social makeup of the annual gathering, the latter group was judged the saddest. They called them the "wannabes," outsiders peering through a window at lost youth and missed opportunity.

Tanned and athletic-looking, Michael Shane Goode—he preferred that his friends call him Shane—could have easily passed for a collegian. His dark hair was razor cut and, though alone, he moved about the beach as if there was purpose to his presence.

In truth he was neither collegian nor man on any specific mission. Shane Goode, a postal worker in the nearby Houston suburb of Clear Creek, married but separated from his wife, had made the trip to Galveston on his motorcycle, hoping to restore some excitement to a life that had grown increasingly boring. Since his 1979 graduation from Pasadena High School, his life had followed a routinely flat-line path: a couple of years in the army spent stateside, marriage to his high-school sweetheart, fatherhood, and a going-nowhere job as a Westinghouse salesman before his dad had helped him get a job with the post office.

Shane Goode was a walking definition of the spring break wannabe, cruising the beach in hopes of getting in on the action.

Annette Tollett, meanwhile, had somewhat reluctantly joined a visiting cousin who had insisted they drive down from Houston and see what the spring break phenomenon was all about. Shy and generally uncomfortable in crowds, Annette was a pretty girl, tall and brunette. Divorced and working as a bookkeeper for a car rental agency, she felt out of place among those traveling to the historic Gulf Coast island.

Even before striking up a conversation with her, Shane Goode would make note of what he determined to be an endearing vulnerability in her face. And it pleased him greatly that she seemed genuinely flattered that he had singled her out. The Shane Goode charm, though maybe a little rusty, still worked.

Before the day ended he had entertained her with stories of his exploits in the military, soothed her concerns about his impending divorce, and had asked for her phone number. To her surprise, Annette readily provided it.

Almost giddy during the return home that evening, she and her cousin talked at length about the concept of love at first sight.

The following day Shane phoned and they talked late into the evening. Soon he was stopping by every afternoon after work. They went out to dinner and movies. He took her dancing. And he began to send roses so regularly that the ones previously delivered were still fresh when another dozen arrived. She would find notes (". . . hope you have a great day . . . find time to think of me . . .") in his familiar handwriting waiting beneath the windshield of her car when she left for work.

Annette was, for the first time in her life, the object of an old-fashioned courtship and she delighted in it. Her relationship with this well-mannered, funny, caring new man in her life was light-years removed from previous experiences. The husband whom she had finally divorced a year earlier had become so abusive that she had finally taken her year-old daughter and moved out. The display of violent anger had made Annette skeptical of trusting another man anytime soon.

Yet Shane was different. There was a warmth and gentleness to him which she had to admit was disarming. He spoke lovingly of his own daughter, vowing that he would make every human effort to see to it that his divorce did not damage their relationship. Annette liked the fact that he showered her child with attention on every visit to the house. He loved kids, he said, and it showed.

Even if she had been determined to detect flaws, she was convinced she could not have found them. Unlike her ex-husband, Shane wasn't a drinker, didn't spend long nights out in the company of buddies, prowling the Houston strip joints. Shane had a good job which he obviously took very seriously and talked optimistically of a bright future he had planned for himself. In a word, he was more mature than any man she'd ever met.

They had been seeing each other on a daily basis for almost three weeks before he kissed her. And even then it was accompanied with an apology. He didn't want to rush things, he said; didn't want to scare her away by moving their relationship ahead at a speed that might make her uncomfortable.

In truth, Annette was feeling no discomfort at all. She was already in love with Shane Goode.

By May, she and two-year-old Michelle had moved from their duplex into Shane's mobile home in the nearby suburb of Pasadena. He had seemed almost giddy with excitement on the day they arrived. It was good, he said, to have a family again.

Soon they were talking of marriage.

///

It pleased Sharon Couch to see her daughter happy again. The long-absent sparkle had returned to Annette's eyes, the lethargy that had set in during the aftermath of her failed first marriage was replaced with new energy and optimism. As do all caring parents, Sharon, herself a divorcée, quietly shared in her child's newfound happiness. It was something that had been, for her and her family, in short supply for far too long.

In truth, Sharon knew little about this man who had swept into her daughter's life. On those occasions when she had been around him he had appeared painfully shy, the complete opposite of the gregarious, fun-loving person whom Annette had described to her mother. Attempts to lure him into conversation were met with short replies. *"Shane, have you decided where you're going on your vacation?"* *"Don't know yet."* *"How's work?"* *"Okay."* He never made eye contact, even when they did have their brief, one-sided talks. Sharon eventually joked that her future son-in-law seemed to have a remarkable fascination with her living-room floor.

None of which caused her undue concern. It was no business of hers to pick at the personality traits of others. That Shane seemed to make Annette happy and treated her well, that her granddaughter liked him and had quickly forged a strong bond with his daughter was more than enough. When Annette announced that Shane's divorce was final and he had asked her to marry him, Sharon was pleased. Given time, she was sure, Shane would warm to her and the rest of the family.

Her first real doubts formed as the planned October wedding date neared. Annette had, for months, been spending every spare minute in preparation for the event, shopping for her gown, choosing brides-maids, writing and rewriting her list of those who would be invited.

It wasn't until after all the plans were set and the invitations had gone out that Shane Goode got cold feet. Two days before the wedding he told Annette that he was not ready to get married.

"I love you and don't want to lose you," he said, "but it is too soon for us to be married. We've got to be sure—both of us—because I want us to be together forever. Let's just give things a little time."

Annette was perplexed by the turn of events. If Shane loved her so much and wanted to "be together forever," why had the idea of marriage—his idea to begin with—suddenly become so frightening? The signals he'd been sending out were, at best, confusing. Since she and Michelle had moved in with him he had constantly talked of how much he enjoyed being in a family setting. His single-minded devotion to Annette had, in fact, seemed to border on the obsessive: On those rare occasions when one of Annette's girlfriends would stop by for a visit and still be there when Shane returned home from work, the routine would always be the same. He would disappear into the bed-room to sulk until the visitor had left, then later would remind An-nette how precious he viewed their time together. "I work all day, thinking about nothing but getting home so I can spend time with you," he would say. "I just hate the idea of anyone taking that time away from us." Annette had never before encountered this kind of jealousy, and at first, she found it flattering. Avoiding her friends in order to spend more time with the man she hoped to soon marry seemed a logical and worthwhile trade-off. There would be plenty of time for friends after she and Shane became more comfortable and confident in their relationship.

But Annette's mother, a cut-to-the-chase, bottom-line kind of per-son, found that the issue of the canceled wedding posed a big problem. Her fear was that Shane, for all his charm and the lavish attention he showered on her daughter, might not be what he seemed. But she also knew that it would be futile to suggest this to her daughter. Annette was blindly in love and motherly advice would only cause damage to a mother-daughter relationship already marked by a history of stubborn disagreement.

Sharon's relationships with her children had, in fact, always perplexed her. From childhood, Annette, her oldest, had been the headstrong one, quietly determined to chart her own course, quick to rebel against rules and motherly advice. Sharon's son Steven, meanwhile, had been easygoing and demonstrative with his affection.

Annette and her mother, friends had often observed, were simply too much alike to get along.

And so Sharon remained silent on the matter, resigned to keeping her concerns private. It is unlikely she would have been able to maintain that silence had she known that Shane, after announcing he was not ready to marry, refused to call any of the invited guests to inform them of the change in plans. That responsibility fell to an embarrassed and confused Annette.

Two months later, as the family gathered at Sharon's home for Thanksgiving dinner, Annette told her mother that the wedding was back on.

"When?"

She was taken aback when Annette told her it would take place the following day.

Instead of the long-planned ceremony with dozens of friends as guests, Annette and Shane Goode were married on November 27, 1987, with only Annette's daughter Michelle and Sharon in attendance.

Sharon thought it strange that no one from Shane's family was present.

///

For the first few months of their marriage, Shane and Annette Goode blended into that melting pot of young couples starting new lives together, both working, keeping tight rein on their budget in hopes of soon moving from the trailer park into a house. Young Michelle looked forward to those times when Shane's daughter Tiffany came to visit. On weekends, Sharon routinely volunteered to baby-sit so the newly married couple might get out for a movie or an evening of dancing.

Actually, what she saw during the brief periods of time she was around her daughter and new son-in-law pleased her. They seemed happy and eagerly looking ahead to the future.

Sharon had no idea that a dark and troubling side to the relationship had already begun to develop. She saw only signs of a happy relationship and heard only positive comments from a daughter who had always been reluctant to share even the most trivial of personal details with her. Annette, her mother knew, had, since childhood, suffered her personal anguishes, large and small, in private.

Among the things Annette did not reveal to her mother was her growing concern over the changes she had seen in Shane in recent days. Without provocation he would fall into a sullen mood that would last for days before finally exploding in anger. Annette would ask repeatedly what was troubling him, only to learn after his mood developed into an angry outburst, that the cause was some obscure event that had taken place days, sometimes weeks, earlier. She was quickly learning that her husband kept things bottled up inside, allowing them to fester until they had grown completely out of proportion before exploding to the surface. When Annette suggested they talk things out, Shane would abruptly end the conversation. After he had had his say, had vented whatever anger he harbored, the discussion was over.

And though he was never physically abusive, he seemed to relish the exercise of mental cruelty. As their first Christmas together neared, he arrived home from work one evening with a large, gaily wrapped box. Placing it under the tree with great fanfare, he assured Annette that she was going to be really surprised when she opened it. Excited, she could only hope that the sports jacket, slacks, and tie she had selected as his gift would match up to what he had purchased for her.

When, on Christmas morning, she expectantly ripped into the package, she found that it contained nothing but a pair of old black pumps that Shane had obviously taken from her closet. Laughing heartily at his "joke," he said her stunned expression was even better than the one he'd seen on his first wife's face when she had opened a gift of what he had promised her was a string of cultured pearls. What she had found instead was a cheap dimestore necklace.

Later, when Annette's birthday neared, Shane would make mention of it almost daily. *"You've got a birthday coming up . . . just a few more days until the big day . . . birthday's tomorrow . . ."* She could only interpret his constant reminders as hints of some special plan he had for the occasion. Then, on the day, this same man, who once showered her with flowers and loving notes, would avoid even the slightest mention of it. There would be no gift, no trip out for a romantic dinner. Nothing.

One evening at a popular Pasadena country-western dance club, things had started off well—until one of Annette's friends from work and her husband arrived. Annette had been talking with the woman for only a few minutes when Shane excused himself to go to the men's room. When he did not return after a reasonable period of time, Annette began looking for him, finally going into the parking lot to find that his pickup was gone. Embarrassed, she had to ask her friend for a ride home.

When she arrived the pickup was parked in front and the lights inside were out. Her purse, locked in the truck, contained her key and she had to knock for some time before Shane finally answered the door. He explained that he had already gone to bed and hadn't heard her knocking.

When Annette pressed for an explanation for his strange behavior, he only shrugged and said it had been clear to him she was more interested in talking with her friends than spending the evening with him, so he'd left.

It was a devious, childish form of behavior with which Annette had no previous experience, and not the slightest idea how to handle.

In time she reached the decision that had always been her way of dealing with turmoil. She blindly hoped the problems would magically go away, that some fairy-tale solution waited in the days ahead.

Meanwhile, she would simply do the best she could to keep her husband happy.

Two

The Shane Goode seen by his mother-in-law was still quiet, almost withdrawn—a man who never seemed altogether comfortable in the company of others. The only family member with whom he seemed to share any common interests was Annette's rebellious teenage brother, Steven. A troubled youngster who had begun to experiment with drugs and test his independence at every opportunity, he seemed to delight in his new brother-in-law's attention. To Shane's new wife, the warm and gentle man she had fallen in love with had become a moody and demanding ruler of his domain. And to friends and coworkers he displayed yet another personality: self-assured to the point of cockiness, attaching an unwarranted importance to his job as a letter carrier and his membership in the National Guard. At work he had no supervisory authority but was quick to criticize the performance of others and offer unsolicited advice. And while most of his Guard contemporaries viewed themselves as "weekend warriors," content to address their military obligation on a part-time basis, Goode thrived on the meetings and the training, loved dressing in his fatigues, and assured all who would listen that he was a deeply committed patriot, fully prepared and eager to go to battle for his country if called.

Many of the stories he relished telling had a certain Walter Mitty ring to them. He was, he said, trained to survive in the most severe locales, was an expert marksman, and was well schooled in the art of hand-to-hand combat. And he knew, he insisted, how to kill without leaving the slightest trace.

To some people, Michael Shane Goode seemed quiet, reserved, thoughtful, and confident; others found him a tense, angry young man, constantly wrestling with his own low self-esteem.

Among those who had seen Shane's dark side was his first wife. Chandra Kaye Goode—called Kaye by her friends—had been a student at Houston's Milby High School when they had first met. She, too, was immediately drawn to the handsome senior from nearby Pasadena High who showered her with attention. After only a few dates, she was convinced he was the man she wanted as her husband. They married in February of 1981 and during the next six years, Kaye Goode became one of the few to see all his faces. The quicksilver mood swings, which became increasingly frequent, had at first puzzled her, then became frightening. His mean-spirited sense of humor became impossible to understand.

Then there were the bizarre, off-putting stories he often told.

As a youngster, he bragged, one of his most enjoyable forms of summer recreation was to catch the stray cats which often wandered the neighborhood. He would then dig holes in the backyard and bury the animals, leaving only their heads exposed above ground. That part of his meticulous game accomplished, he would then decapitate them with a power lawnmower.

Kaye never knew whether to believe such stories or not but found the zest which he applied to their telling chilling.

Finally, on an early June evening in 1987, an argument between her and Shane escalated into physical violence. As they stood in the parking lot of a local convenience store having a shouting match, Shane suddenly slammed his fist against the left side of his wife's head. As she tried to turn and run he grabbed at her, tearing away an earring.

Calm was restored only when the store manager raced into the parking lot and threatened to summon the police. Glaring at Shane, the manager, a hard-muscled young man who easily outweighed

Goode by a hundred pounds, threatened to "kick his cowardly ass" before Kaye stepped forward to assure him that everything was under control.

Reluctantly, the manager watched as the couple got into their car. Before Shane could pull away, however, the man tapped against the driver's window. Goode rolled it down only a few inches as the manager leaned forward and again glared at him. "You take her straight to a hospital, asshole," he said in a stern, commanding voice.

Shane Goode was still nodding as he backed from the parking lot.

At Pasadena's Bayshore Medical Center emergency room, doctors determined that Kaye's left eardrum had been perforated and applied medication to her still-bleeding right ear.

Kaye realized that it was time to get out. After filing assault charges, she and three-year-old Tiffany moved into an apartment. And, despite Shane's tearful apologies and pleas that she return and give him another chance, Kaye hired a divorce lawyer.

Even before the final decree, Shane Goode had been sentenced to a year's deferred adjudication probation for the assault. Additionally, the divorce court had ruled that Kaye would serve as managing conservator of their daughter and that her ex-husband would pay $480 per month in child support.

For Goode, the latter demand was devastating. Putting a pencil to his dismal financial situation, he found that his net monthly income would be reduced to only $1,425. His expenses, including such bare essentials as rent, utilities, car, insurance, and loan payments, amounted to almost $1,700.

He would, he realized, soon be drowning in red ink.

///

To Annette, much of her husband's past remained secret—or if not secret, it was shaded by the versions Shane chose to share with her. His ex-wife had caused their marriage to fail, he was quick to point out. Kaye's constant attempts to block him from spending time with his daughter were, he suggested, but a continuing example of the hell she had put him through when they were husband and wife.

Annette innocently accepted Shane's word and viewed his ex-wife as the vengeful, self-centered person he described. Because of the drain of child support payments and Kaye's seemingly endless need for additional money to pay for Tiffany's doctor bills or some other unexpected expense, their budget was tight. But neither was it impossible, Annette thought.

Shortly after they married, in fact, they had purchased a new Pontiac Trans Am which would serve as Annette's car. In budgeting for the new expense, they agreed that the monthly payments to the finance company would come from her paycheck.

In time, however, Shane realized that even their combined income would not provide the financial comfort zone he wished for. Arguments over money became routine. Shane criticized Annette's spending habits and told her to look for something that paid better than her bookkeeping job. When she suggested that the best long-term solution to their financial problems would be for her to take nursing courses in the evenings—something she'd long wanted to do—he balked. The concept of spending money to make money eluded him.

Growing more and more impatient with his darkening financial situation, Shane was looking for a quick fix.

Before leaving for work on the morning of May 20, 1988, he invited his wife out for dinner and dancing that evening. In light of his recent concerns over money, Annette was somewhat surprised but readily agreed. She phoned her mother to ask if she would baby-sit Michelle and was pleased by Sharon Couch's eager response. It would be good to get out of the house. Shane had even picked the club they would go to, a trendy place called J. Larkins located on the bayou out near NASA.

For the remainder of the day, Goode went about his routine in unusually good spirits, leaving work in the afternoon to return home only long enough to change into his jogging suit before driving over to a Pasadena public-school track for a lengthy workout.

By eight o'clock he was showered, dressed, and urging Annette and his stepdaughter to hurry up. He was starving.

After a hurried dinner at Grandy's, they dropped Michelle off, and arrived at J. Larkins shortly after nine. Though there was ample parking near the entrance, Shane steered the red Trans Am into one of the spaces facing the bayou, almost a hundred yards from the club. "Less chance of some drunk banging into a fender or scratching up one of the doors," he explained as he locked the car, pocketed the keys in his jacket, and escorted Annette toward the front door.

It was a pleasant evening. The band was good and the dance floor wasn't too crowded. Annette couldn't remember the last time she'd seen her husband so relaxed and carefree. He sang along with the music and kissed her on several occasions as he seemed swept up in the romantic atmosphere of the club. It was, Annette found herself thinking, suddenly like old times.

It was one in the morning when they walked into the parking lot, arm in arm, their laughter echoing into a thin fog which had begun rolling in from the bayou. Though she had had very little to drink, Annette was feeling a warm sense of intoxication brought on by the fun-filled evening.

Suddenly, however, the laughter died. The spot where Shane had parked the car was empty.

Goode's mood immediately turned foul. Angrily pacing the dimly lit parking lot, he cursed, waving his arms in frustration. "Some son-uvabitch stole it," he repeated over and over. "Stole the goddamn car." Stunned by the turn of events, Annette stood silently, arms folded across her chest, watching her husband's tirade.

Such was the scene Nassau Bay Police patrolman Elbert Love saw as he began a routine drive through the nightclub parking lot. As he turned into the isolated area where Goode had parked, his headlights caught a young man waving to get his attention.

"My car's been stolen," Shane shouted at the patrolman.

Officer Love quickly took a description of the car, wrote down the license plate number, and called in a report to his dispatcher. He then launched into a rote speech which he made to all car-theft victims. If the thief was off on a joyride, there was a chance that it might be found abandoned in a brief period of time. "They get their jollies for a while, then panic," he said. That was the optimistic scenario. If it was professionals—and the pros, he emphasized, had a particular liking for the sporty Trans Ams—Goode's automobile could already be in some chop shop or en route to Mexico.

Still cursing his misfortune, Shane assured the officer that he'd locked the car and had left no keys in it. Speaking up for the first time, Annette confirmed her husband's statement.

The patrolman completed his investigation by taking down Goode's phone number and address, then asked a final, routine question. "Sir, do you know the approximate value of the vehicle?"

"Fifteen thousand," Shane replied.

"We'll be in touch," Officer Love said.

Seated in the back of a cab that would deliver them home, Annette was relieved to note that the anger her husband had displayed in the parking lot had subsided. "All we can do is wait and see," he told her with a shrug, then smiled for the first time since they'd left the club.

///

The Trans Am was never found. Once police had assured him there was little hope of its recovery, Goode filed a claim with his insurance company. The check he received from Allstate not only cleared the burdensome $12,000 bank note but provided him with an extra $1,745 which he deposited in his checking account.

Rather than grief, Shane expressed great relief that the Trans Am and the payments attached to it were history.

What he never bothered to tell Annette was that, according to her younger brother, Steven, Shane had arranged for him to steal the car from the nightclub parking lot that evening. Steven, in turn, would sell it to an aquaintance who dealt in hot cars, then split the profit with his brother-in-law.

While he would later deny it, Shane Goode had solved his financial problems for the time being.

///

Sharon Couch, eager to see her daughter's second marriage work and not wanting to interfere, kept her distance. She was ready to care for Michelle whenever asked and she occasionally invited Shane and Annette to her house for dinner, but she made a point of never attempting to intrude on their private lives.

Aside from Shane's occasional offhand remarks about his wife's spending habits, usually made in a half-joking, half-sarcastic manner, Sharon had no indication of the tension that had begun to pervade the relationship.

When Annette announced that she was pregnant, her mother was pleased. And the fact that Shane and Annette had decided to move from his cramped trailer into a house they had rented in Pasadena seemed to be a positive move forward.

On the weekend the move was scheduled, Sharon was quick to volunteer her help. Despite the fact that she was five months pregnant, Annette lifted furniture and heavy boxes throughout the day without the slightest show of concern from Shane. Sharon, on the other hand, had repeatedly urged her daughter to let her and her son-in-law load and unload the heavy objects. Only when Annette became testy, assuring her that she felt fine, did Sharon drop the subject. She knew that her daughter was energized by the excitement of the move into the more spacious and comfortable house and eager to get settled in. To that end, Sharon opted to silently hurry along her own lifting and carrying.

Just a few weeks later, however, Annette phoned her mother, sobbing. She had suffered a miscarriage, she said.

For Sharon, the compassion she felt for her daughter instantly mixed with a growing anger directed at Shane. His nonchalant attitude in allowing Annette's physical exertion during the move had, Sharon was convinced, contributed to the miscarriage. Sharon found it impossible to like her son-in-law.

Soon she began to see signs that the marriage was not going well. During visits to her grandmother, Michelle began to innocently mention that her mother and Shane were arguing more and more. "They make me go to my room when they're mad at each other," she said, "but I can still hear them yelling."

By the fall of 1988 Shane had begrudgingly agreed to Annette's idea of returning to school to pursue pre-med studies. In keeping with his pattern of picking special dates for playing out his mind games, he waited until the day before Annette was to take her semester final exams to announce that he was thinking about moving out. His only explanation: "This fucking marriage was a big mistake."

Distraught, Annette performed poorly on her tests and saw her grades slide to a barely passing level. The day after, Shane apologized for having upset her.

His cruel game, however, was not over. A week later on Thanksgiving morning, they argued again before he stormed from the house, slamming the door behind him. He drove to his aunt's house where the Goode family had gathered for the traditional noon meal of turkey and dressing. Annette telephoned, tearfully begging that he return home and pick her up. Shane refused. "I just don't know about all this," he said. "I think the best thing is for me to leave."

Annette spent the lonely holiday agonizing over the latest turn of events in her life, swallowed up by self-pity and the conviction that whatever problems had caused her husband to consider leaving were of her making. When Shane did return late that evening, acting as if nothing untoward had occurred, it was Annette who apologized. The stress of school had been greater than she'd expected, she insisted. She would be a more attentive, better wife, she promised. Things would improve if he would only give her the chance to prove it to him.

When Shane held his ground she desperately took another tack. If, in fact, he was determined to move out of the house, what harm could be done by his postponing it until after the holiday season? "That way," she pleaded, "Michelle can at least have a good Christmas."

Leaning against a doorway, his hands shoved into the hip pockets of his jeans, Shane pondered the suggestion, then shrugged. "Sure," he replied, "Why not?"

Annette felt a wave of relief at having bought herself and her marriage more time, and set about to create the idyllic home environment that would convince Shane to stay. She kept the house spotless, cooked his favorite meals, and began making plans to decorate for the season.

On a Friday morning, a week before Christmas, she had to visit the dentist for an abcessed tooth that had become unbearably painful. Shane agreed to accompany her since she had been told that oral surgery would be necessary and the sedation required would make it unsafe for her to drive afterward.

Groggy from the ordeal, Annette had little recollection of the drive home from the dentist's office or of her husband helping her into bed. Gently tucking the covers over her and kissing her on the forehead, Shane urged her to get some sleep while he went out to have her pain medication prescription filled.

Throughout the afternoon Annette woke from her sedated state several times and called out to her husband, each time only to realize he'd not yet returned. The trip to the drugstore had taken from shortly after noon until almost six in the evening.

The following Monday, after Shane had left for the post office, she realized why.

While looking for the mail that had arrived over the weekend, she found an envelope which contained a lease agreement for a one-bedroom apartment he had rented. It was dated the previous Friday.

She was seated on the couch, in tears and still clutching the lease papers when Shane arrived home from work. "Why?" she wanted to know. "And why now?"

"Hey, we've already discussed this, remember," he shot back. "I told you I was going to leave. Goddammit, I thought you understood."

Annette hugged her knees to her chest and buried her face in the cradle of her arms as she let out a pained groan that sounded as if it came from some dark and hidden depth inside her. Her shoulders seemed to convulse as she sobbed uncontrollably.

Suddenly, she was surprised to feel Shane's hand gently massaging the back of her neck. His voice was soothing, almost lyrical, as he urged her to stop crying. "It's Christmas," he said. "Let's go get a tree."

With those few words Annette's roller-coaster life took another upward turn. And before the evening was over she, Shane, and Michelle had selected a tree after visiting several lots where sweet-smelling pines and cedars stood waiting for a holiday home. Showing no outward sign of the nightmare that had enveloped them, the young family wandered through mall department stores in search of new lights and ornaments. Annette carefully selected each brightly colored ball, each porcelain angel in the silent hope that their presence on the tree might signal some new beginning.

Finally trimmed in the early morning hours, it was the most beautiful Christmas tree Annette had ever seen. Turning out the lights, she and Shane sat silently in the darkness of their living room, staring at the warm twinkle of lights and reflections from the ornaments.

But the day after Christmas, the holiday fantasy ended. While his wife and stepdaughter were away, Shane Goode packed his things and left. When Annette and Michelle returned home, they found only the bare tree, stripped of the newly purchased lights and ornaments.

Shane Goode reasoned that since he had paid for them, they belonged to him.

///

Angry and confused, Annette quickly spiraled into a deep depression. Sleep was impossible and she ate only when daughter Michelle or her mother coaxed her with warnings that she was in danger of making herself physically ill.

Friends who were aware of her torment could not understand her determined refusal to see her husband for what he was. Why was she unable to summon the strength to walk away?

Annette had gathered all blame for the breakup of her marriage onto her own shoulders, blind to any fault that should have been assigned to Shane. She ignored his cruelty, both subtle and blatant, because she was still very much in love with him.

Three

Historians are quick to argue that there was, in the beginning, no logical reason for the city of Houston to exist, much less thrive. The natural resources of the region were limited and the brain-baking summer heat and humidity assured no bountiful crops would ever grow. Built on foul-smelling swampland, it grew up fifty miles inland from the Gulf of Mexico, too landlocked ever to hope to benefit from the rich shipping trade. Even when a collection of farsighted city fathers posed the idea of floating a bond issue to have a gigantic channel dredged, in effect bringing the Gulf inland to Houston, it was viewed by many as a financial folly even more absurd than the idea of digging something called the Panama Canal.

The Houston project, however, had moved forward with all the bullheaded optimism for which the city would become famous. Houston was launched into a new age, on a fast-track course to becoming one of the most prosperous, most heavily populated cities in the United States. Millionaires built mansions in the silk-stocking River Oaks and Bellaire areas, while dock workers and refinery employees settled into the subdivisions, apartments, and trailer parks of sprawling suburbs like Channelview, Galena Park, and Pasadena.

Though it may have been a city without aesthetic appeal or much social charm, it was a city graced by the presence of big bucks. If you wanted to become a millionaire, Houston was the place to be. If you already had millions and still wanted more, the opportunities were endless. At the peak of its boom, it was a city of dreams.

Never mind that the crime rate soared, political scandals were routine, and the bayou stench and August heat waves kept most residents constantly in a short-tempered frame of mind. The wheels of Houston spun on money.

Those who didn't have it spent great amounts of time in search of the office promotion, the investment, the windfall inheritance, or, in many cases, the illegal scheme that would somehow allow them to share in the wealth.

It was in this atmosphere that Shane and Annette Goode had grown up. And it was, friends quickly assumed, the cause of their separation. Like so many young couples desperate to sip wine on a six-pack budget, the romance and high expectations of married life had given way to the ever-present disappointments and frustrations that routinely destroyed Houston families like some dark sweeping plague.

For Annette, however, the explanation was not so simple.

In the weeks after Shane moved out she functioned by rote, caring for her daughter, working, continuing to attend classes, always carrying with her the hope that some magic might cause her husband to return to her. The love she felt for Shane, her dependence on him, masked all pain resulting from his cruel behavior. In her selective memory, the good times were all that counted, and she willingly bore the blame for his decision to leave.

A month passed before he finally telephoned. With no preamble or explanation or apology he told Annette he would like to come over. "I've been thinking," he said. "Maybe we ought to sit down and talk."

Anxiously, Annette agreed.

Seated at the kitchen table, Shane and Annette had a conversation that was at first tentative. Both felt uncomfortable after Shane's lengthy absence. It was Shane who finally moved the discussion past trivialities. "I've missed you," he said.

It was a statement that unleashed a flood of emotion from his estranged wife. She had missed him, too, she said. Things had been so difficult without him: the bills which she was trying to keep up with on her modest salary, the pressures of being a single mother trying to juggle the responsibilities of work and school and still attend to Michelle's needs. The hardest part, she said, was understanding why he'd left. What had she done that was so wrong? Why had he refused to give her the slightest hint as to what he believed caused the problems in their relationship?

The questions poured out in an honest, desperate plea for understanding that might help them reach a new starting point.

Shane's expression turned sullen as he listened, folding his arms across his chest. Finally he began to slowly shake his head and rose to his feet. "I was thinking about moving back in," he said, "before you started talking like that."

"Like what?" Annette replied. "My God, Shane, I'm just trying to tell you how things are. I'm doing my best to understand all this. What am I doing wrong? Please, you've got to tell me."

Now standing, ready to leave, he glared at her. "It's your lousy fucking attitude," he said. "I'm not coming back."

Even before he began walking toward the front door, Annette was in tears. Shane Goode had played out another of his games and declared himself the winner.

By February of 1989 Annette realized she could no longer keep up payments on the house. Placing her furniture in storage, she and Michelle moved in with her mother. The pain Sharon Couch saw in her daughter's eyes was heartbreaking.

In the months that followed Sharon would rise from her bed, weary of fighting sleeplessness long into the dark hours of night, and sit alone on the patio of her backyard while her troubled daughter and grandchild slept inside. She tended her grief in private, trying to recall a time when her life had not been such a windstorm of angst and grief.

On those nights when even the stars were smudged by the haze that hung over Houston like a suffocating canopy, Sharon would question her own shortcomings as mother and advisor. But always, before returning to the house for one last attempt at sleep, she would somehow summon the courage and resolve to move forward. It was, she had long ago decided, the only way some degree of control and happiness might be restored.

Sharon Couch did not realize it, but she was a woman of remarkable inner strength and resolve.

/ / /

It had been years since her own marriage to a Greek nightclub entertainer had ended in divorce, leaving her to raise two small children on her own while their father continued touring from city to city, continent to continent, more concerned with his music career than family. Rarely, over the years, had he ever contacted the children to see how they were or to lend some manner of fatherly support.

Even as his daughter and son grew older and more curious about him, he had kept his distance. Remarried and settled in Florida, it was as if that part of his previous life which had included a wife and children had been completely erased.

When Michelle was born, Annette had seen the event as an opportunity to try once more to establish some kind of relationship with a father she hardly knew. Yet when she phoned him at his home to tell him that he was a grandfather, he demonstrated no interest at all in seeing the baby.

It had not been until the children grew into their rebellious teenage years that Sharon actually felt any real resentment for the absence of an adult male figure in the family. As her rules were ignored and her attempts at discipline failed miserably, she discovered long unresolved angers surfacing. Had the children's father remained, he might have helped avert troubles that had worsened as Sharon watched helplessly.

The ongoing friction between Sharon and Annette resulted in her daughter spending more time at the house of her nearby grandparents than she did at home. Still, it was young Steven who had begun to worry his mother most.

In the spring of 1986, as he was nearing his sixteenth birthday, he instigated a prank that would result in consequences far more serious than anyone could have imagined.

On a May afternoon, while Sharon was still at work, Steven and a friend invited two teenage girls over to listen to music and share the marijuana which Steven had begun using on a regular basis.

As the impromptu party went on, the girls excused themselves to the bathroom. When they did so, Steven took the car keys from the purse of one of his guests, went out front, and placed them on the front floorboard of the girl's car, which was parked at the curb. Giggling as he returned to the house, he then phoned Mark Adams* another of his friends who lived nearby, and told him to come get the car.

"No fucking way, man," the youngster had at first argued.

Steven laughed at his friend's concern. "Hey, it's cool," he said. "We're just playing a little joke."

The girl to whom the car belonged found nothing funny about it. When she and her friend prepared to leave and saw that the car was gone she became hysterical, then called a friend to come and pick them up. Forcing a look of concern until they drove away, Steven burst into laughter as soon as they were gone. Sobered by the potential trouble the prank might cause and wanting no part in it, his friend also left.

Later that evening, with the buzz of his afternoon pot party gone, Steven was sitting on the front porch when Mark pulled up in the girl's car. Amid laughter and loud music that boomed from the radio, they set off for an evening of joyriding.

They had gone only a few blocks down the access road that led to a freeway entrance when Mark stopped for a red light, paying no attention to a black tow truck parked beneath the underpass. Nor did they see the figure jump from the truck and begin running in their direction.

Even before reaching the access road the young man—the boyfriend of the girl who owned the car—began yelling, "Hey, that's my girlfriend's car. . . . You assholes got my girlfriend's car."

Behind the wheel, Mark turned to see the boy approaching and saw that he had a knife in his hand. Frozen and locked in traffic, he could do nothing but duck away from the window as the enraged pursuer lashed at him with the knife. "Get the fuck out of here," Steven yelled.

Mark quickly put the car in gear, swerved past stunned drivers

*Pseudonym

waiting for the light to turn green, and roared down the access road. In the rearview mirror he could see that the black tow truck was already in pursuit.

"Who the fuck is this guy?" he said. "He's crazy."

Steven, whose face had lost all color, said nothing.

The high-speed chase continued along the access road, then twisted and turned through a residential neighborhood until Mark lost control attempting to make a sharp turn. The car careened into a drainage ditch, its wheels burrowing into the mud. Mark and Steven jumped out and ran toward the safety of darkness, leaving the car behind.

Not until the early morning hours did the frightened and exhausted youngsters leave a nearby park where they had been hiding and make their way home.

The ordeal, however, was not over.

The following afternoon Mark looked up from his job as a sacker at a local grocery store to see the same angry face he'd looked into at the stoplight the night before. Ignoring the customer to whom Mark was attending, the visitor stood near the checkout counter, glaring. "Why did you steal my girlfriend's car?"

Working hard to remain calm, Mark shook his head and forced a smile. "I don't know what you're talking about," he replied. "Who are you?"

The teenager identified himself as Rodney Richards.

"Sorry, man, I don't know anything about anybody's car being stolen," Mark said, returning to the customer's groceries.

Richards didn't move. "Like hell," he said. "Lift up your shirt. Last night I cut the sonuvabitch that was driving. And he looked a helluva lot like you." With that he reached out and tore open Mark's shirt, surprised to see no wound.

As the store manager escorted him out, Richards was shaking his head. Certain he would find the injury that he had inflicted during the confrontation, Richards was unaware that the switchblade he'd swung at Mark the night before had malfunctioned. The blade had folded harmlessly when it impacted against the back of the driver's seat.

Almost a week later, Steven became the focus of Richards's rage.

Sharon Couch had just returned home from work when the phone rang and she overheard her son's part of the conversation. "I didn't have anything to do with it," he said. "Why are you calling me? She got her car back, right?" Then she heard the all-too-familiar anger exploding in his voice: "Look, why don't you just come on over here and we'll settle this. No knives, no guns—just you and me, okay?"

Sharon did not hear Rodney Richards's threatening reply. "I know you were in the car," he said in a low, guttural voice. "You and your buddy did this and I'm going to get your ass for it. You can count on it." With that, he hung up.

Standing by the phone for several seconds, Steven finally replaced the receiver.

"What is it?" his mother asked. "Steven, what's going on?"

"He's crazy."

"Who?"

As if he'd not heard the question, Steven's only reply was to repeat his observation. "The guy's crazy."

Despite his mother's frantic pleas, he would say no more. Agitated and nervous, Steven paced the house and made several phone calls to friends. During each conversation he alluded to the mental state of the person who had called him earlier.

Finally, just after dark, he told his mother he was going out. "Stay in the house, Mom," he yelled as he walked onto the front porch.

By then concerned that her son might be in some kind of real danger, Sharon begged him to stay at home.

"Just get back in the house," he screamed. It was, however, not anger she heard in his voice. It was the sound of stark fear.

From the porch she watched her son walk hurriedly down Ogden Street to the corner where a car was parked. Squinting into the darkness, Sharon saw a figure emerge from the car and approach her son. What she was not able to see was that Rodney Richards had pulled a gun from his boot, aimed it in Steven's direction, and fired. Her hands flew to her face and she screamed at the sound of the shot and watched as Richards raced back to his car and sped away. Steven, who had felt the bullet breeze past his ear, ran toward home.

As soon as he was safely inside, Sharon dialed 911. "Somebody just shot at my son," she screamed into the phone, her hands shaking so badly she had difficulty holding the receiver.

In a city where drive-by shootings and honky-tonk hitmen had become commonplace, where lives were routinely taken over a new pair of name-brand sports shoes and where the disappointed mother of a shunned cheerleader candidate opted for murder-for-hire to settle the score, the occurrence on Ogden Street would not even make the ten-o'clock news.

"Ma'am," asked the dispatcher, "is your son injured? Do you need an ambulance?"

"No."

"Do you know the name of the person who shot at him?"

"No, I don't."

"Did you get a license number of the car?"

"No."

"Then," the dispatcher said in a dispassionate voice, "I'm afraid there isn't much we can do." Though Sharon offered her address, there was never even a patrol car visit to the Couch home.

/ / /

No amount of argument could persuade Steven to admit to his mother the car theft that had prompted the threatening phone call and gunfire. "Hey, it was all over nothing," he said. "Don't worry about it."

"Who was the boy who shot at you?"

Steven shrugged. "Just some guy named Rodney. He's a nutcase. But, it's over."

He was wrong. Eighteen-year-old Rodney Richards had fixated on Steven, his single-minded goal: revenge for the theft of his girlfriend's car.

During the next eighteen months he pursued it with a vengeance.

On an August evening in 1986, Steven rode with Annette and Michelle to a nearby convenience store where his sister planned to make a withdrawal from an ATM machine. The transaction completed, Annette had just returned to the car when a young man jumped from an old pickup and ran toward her car.

Bending to look into the backseat where Steven was sitting, he said, "You're Steve, aren't you?"

Even before Steven could reply, Richards pulled a knife from his hip pocket and began yelling, "You sonuvabitch, you stole my girl-friend's car . . ."

Stunned by the sudden encounter, Annette instinctively pulled her child close to her and hurriedly started the car. "Go," Steven said. "Get us the hell out of here." Even as he shouted his demand, Annette was backing away, leaving the cursing Richards standing in the parking lot.

Only when certain they were not being followed did Annette break the silence, looking at her younger brother through the rearview mirror. "What," she asked, "was that all about?"

"Nothing."

Annette said no more until she pulled into her mother's driveway and shut off the engine. Then, turning to face Steven, she demanded a better answer. "We're not getting out of the car until you tell me what's going on," she said.

Finally, after considerable urging, her frightened brother confided to her the chain of events that had begun with his drug-clouded decision to have his friend take the car.

"This is stupid," Annette responded. "Can't you talk to him and get it settled? Maybe you should go to the police."

Steven slumped in the backseat and shook his head. "The guy's crazy," he said.

Keeping her promise not to mention the incident to their mother, Annette did, however, tell her husband what had occurred and the story Steven had related. Shane Goode's reaction was disturbingly nonchalant. If anything, he seemed to find it amusing.

Richards, meanwhile, continued his harassment. Steven would answer the phone to hear a now familiar voice, low and menacing. "I'm going to kick your ass," the caller would say, then quickly hang up.

In mid-January of 1987, Sharon was awakened by the popping sound of a gunshot, followed by breaking glass. Racing into the living room, she found that the window directly behind the couch had been shattered.

She went immediately into Steven's bedroom and found him awake, sitting on the side of his bed, shivering. Though neither spoke his name, both were certain the drive-by shooter had been Rodney Richards.

Steven decided it was time to explain to his mother the cause of the nightmare she'd been drawn into.

Sharon again phoned the police. And again she was told that without some kind of proof any investigation would be fruitless. Her only comfort came when the next three months passed without incident. She began to believe that the matter had run its insane course and simply faded from memory, the grudge finally laid to rest.

Such was not to be the case.

One spring afternoon, as Steven sat on the front porch talking with several friends, Richards suddenly appeared at the end of the sidewalk, knife in hand. Immediately upon seeing him Steven had retreated into the house while the others tried to persuade Rodney to leave by assuring him that the police were being called even as they talked. Finally, without having ever said a word, he turned and slowly walked away.

A month later, Sharon received a call at work from a man who identified himself as a Houston police officer. He said he was investigating the matter of a car that had been stolen by her son.

Perplexed by his interest after the passage of so much time, she recounted her previous calls to the authorities, explaining their lack of interest. "And," she finally said, "didn't the girl get her car back the very same day?"

The caller's explanation became increasingly jumbled and confused until finally Sharon began to suspect that she was not, in fact, talking to a police officer. "Sir," she said politely, "I wonder if I might have your badge number." With that the line went dead.

It was a week later that she answered a late-night knock at the door to find Rodney Richards on her porch, eyes glazed, a crooked smile on his face. "I want to see Steve," he said.

Though she'd never before seen the tall, lanky young man standing in the yellow glow of her porch light, Sharon knew immediately who he was.

"I know he lives here," Rodney said.

Frightened, Sharon checked the latch on her screen to be certain it was secured. "He's not at home," she said, not mentioning that her son had been in New Orleans for almost a week, visiting friends. "He's out of town."

Richards nodded but made no move to leave. Finally, just before Sharon closed the door, he spoke again. "He stole my girlfriend's car, you know. He shouldn't have done that. And I'm going to get him for it. You tell him that."

Sharon slammed the door and quickly locked it. For the remainder of the long night she sat alone in her living room, her teeth chattering from the cold wave of fear that swept over her. The bizarre ritual being played out defied logic or explanation, but she realized that it was serious. She knew that something terrible was going to happen if she didn't get some help in resolving the problem before it escalated further. But where? From whom?

The only thing she knew for certain was that Steven's words, first spoken over a year earlier, had the loud and clear ring of truth: This young man bringing terror into their lives had to be mentally unstable.

///

Whether affected by the constant pressure of knowing that Richards remained determined to settle their score or the drugs he had begun to use more and more frequently, Steven's own behavior was a growing concern for Sharon. The smiling, good-natured youngster she'd watched grow into his teen years had become increasingly sullen and incommunicative. He was rarely at home and he frequently ran around with new friends to whom he'd never bothered to introduce her.

It puzzled her that the only member of the family with whom he seemed to communicate was her son-in-law. Never close before, Steven and Shane began spending a good deal of time together.

The troubled mother had no way of knowing that from the relationship between brother and brother-in-law would come Steven's involvement in Shane Goode's plot to have his car stolen.

Nor did she have any idea that her son had begun carrying a gun. "For protection," he explained to friends.

. . .

On the evening of June 12, 1988, less than a month after Shane and Annette's Trans Am had disappeared off the J. Larkin parking lot, Steven and his date were stopped at a red light while on their way to pick up another couple with whom they planned to attend a party. In celebration of what was to be a special occasion, the girl's grandmother had rented a Lincoln Town Car for Steven to drive for the evening.

As they waited at the light, Rodney Richards pulled alongside them in his pickup, rolled down his window, and began shouting his familiar accusations.

At first ignoring him, Steven finally looked in Richards's direction and yelled back. "Look," he said, "I'm sick and tired of this shit."

"Fuck you," Rodney replied. "You stole my girlfriend's—"

Steven didn't allow him to finish. "Look," he said, "I've had it with all this. Follow me and we'll settle it." With that the light turned green and Steven sped off, Rodney's pickup pulling in behind him.

Turning into a convenience store parking lot, Steven quickly got out of the car and saw that his pursuer was about to pull in nearby. "Pop the trunk," Steven told his date.

"Why?" she asked. "What's happening?"

"Just pop the trunk," he shouted. "Do it. *Now.*"

Before he could reach the rear of the car, however, the pickup turned in and headed toward him. Steven lunged out of the way just before it collided into the back of the Lincoln.

Suddenly the scene turned to bedlam. In the car, Steven's date began to scream hysterically.

Steven glared at Rodney. "You crazy sonuvabitch."

Rodney yelled back. "Fuck you . . . fuck you . . . fuck you," he chanted. "I got you now."

As the exchange took place, Steven eased his way back to the trunk of the car and was reaching inside as he saw Rodney lean down in the cab of the pickup.

Certain that Richards was reaching for a weapon, Steven pulled a shotgun into view and fired into the passenger window of the pickup.

No sooner had the blast shattered glass and sent the padding of the truck seat flying than Rodney was out the door and running, crossing the street in the direction of a Dairy Queen. Reaching the curb, he stopped and turned. Steven fired a second shot and Rodney clutched at his abdomen before falling to the pavement.

A crowd was already gathering as Steven tried unsuccessfully to start the damaged rental car. "I just shot a guy," he said in a voice filled with disbelief. "Jesus, I just shot him."

///

It was not until early the next morning that Sharon Couch learned of the tragic event. Having called a friend to pick him and his girl-friend up, Steven was in hiding.

Sharon knew there was something wrong the moment she heard his voice on the phone. She felt her legs go weak as her frightened son told her what had occurred.

"Maybe he's not dead," she finally offered.

Steven was silent for what seemed like an eternity. "Mom, he's dead," he finally said. "I had a friend drive back over there later and he said there was a sheet over the body."

Sharon Couch was unable to keep her fragile emotions in check. She braced herself against the wall, afraid that her legs would no longer support her.

"Oh, God," she yelled, her pained cry echoing through the empty house.

Four

The marital problems of Annette and Shane suddenly seemed less important as Sharon Couch struggled to deal with the troubles of her son. Nothing in her life had prepared her for a crisis of such magnitude and she felt a numbing helplessness unlike anything she'd ever before experienced. On the phone, Steven was no longer the rebellious, argumentative teenager determined to assert his manhood. Rather, he sounded like a little boy again, scared, confused, and wanting his mother to make everything right.

Sharon knew it was an impossible task. Though he would not tell her where he was, Steven stayed in touch, gradually telling her the full story of his almost two-year feud with Rodney Richards. He convinced his mother that he had actually been afraid for his life. He told his mother that he was certain that Rodney had a gun on the night he had fired the fatal shotgun blast.

Sharon contacted a lawyer who advised Steven to immediately turn himself in to the authorities because there was a good chance that a self-defense plea might be embraced by the district attorney's office. But when she suggested it to her frightened son, he balked, saying he'd have to think about it.

When a homicide investigator visited her house in search of Steven, Sharon honestly said that she had no idea where her son might be. And her attempt to explain the sequence of events which had led to the shooting seemed to be of little interest to the detective.

All Sharon could do was to continue to urge her son to come forward and face his problem. "Just tell me where you are," she pleaded, "and I'll come get you and go to the police station with you. I've talked to a lawyer. . . ."

For the first time in days she heard a new strength, a rebirth of determination, in Steven's voice. "I don't want a lawyer," he said. "I'm not going to jail."

However, his tone began to change in a matter of days. "I just want to get it over with," he said to his mother. "I'm so tired." He would turn himself in, he told her, but first he needed a little more time to think it through.

Soon, he again changed his mind.

Steven had telephoned his father in Florida and together they had come up with a plan: He would slip away to Greece and live in an apartment his dad owned in the northern coastal city of Thessaloniki. Members of his father's family had agreed to look after him.

For the youngster's confused and frightened mother, the plan seemed to have little merit at first. She knew that Steven could not spend the remainder of his life in hiding and on the run. He would find no happiness in a foreign country, living among virtual strangers. And the idea of his being so far away, essentially on his own at age seventeen, concerned her greatly.

But he refused to listen to reason.

Resigned to the inevitable, Sharon gave the plan her blessing. On one hand, she began to think that Steven's being out of the country might work to her advantage. The lawyer she'd spoken with had told her that her son's defense would carry a $25,000 price tag. Before even taking the case, he would require a $10,000 retainer. For her to raise that kind of money would take time.

Still, she wanted to see him before he left, to hold him in her arms, to assure him that she loved him, and to make one last plea that he reconsider. A small family reunion had been planned and she urged him to attend, if only for a few minutes. No one there, she assured him, had been told of his problem. And there seemed little likelihood that the police, even if they were trying to locate him, would be monitoring every family gathering in a metropolitan area the size of Houston's.

A friend drove Steven to the isolated city park where the gathering was to be held and as women laid out home-cooked food on the concrete tables and men mingled nearby, renewing acquaintances and swapping stories, Sharon Couch and her son met beneath the canopy of a sprawling oak tree and embraced.

Nervously looking around, he listened as she promised to somehow find the money to pay a lawyer. As soon as she did so, she would contact him and he could return and face the charges against him.

Looking pale and thinner than she'd ever seen him, Steven nodded his head in agreement, then hugged her. "I gotta go," he said.

It would be the last time Sharon Couch would see her son for almost a year.

Meanwhile, the pressures of living in her mother's house were becoming unbearable for Annette. While she, too, was concerned over Steven's troubles, there was little she could do to help resolve the problem or even make it better. And she was still fighting her own private battles, searching for some way to get on with her life and put her feelings for Shane behind her.

If she was to move forward with her life, she would have to move out.

Her studies, at least, were beginning to pay off. She got a job as a chemical analyst for a medical firm in the suburb of Clear Lake and by early December had saved enough money to lease a small condominium near her work.

It had been a difficult year, but finally Annette was beginning to feel the gentle tingle of a newfound optimism.

The winter darkness had fallen by the time she packed the last of her belongings into a box and prepared to load it into the car. As she walked toward the front door the phone rang.

"What are you doing?" It was Shane, his voice casual and cheerful. No one would have guessed that he'd not spoken to his wife in several months.

Annette composed herself with a deep breath before answering. "I was just going out," she said.

"Oh, sorry. Be okay if I call you later?"

"I guess so."

A week would pass before she heard from him again. Work and settling into her new home had kept her busy, pushing thought of Shane's earlier call to the back of her mind. This time she could not come up with an excuse for not talking with him.

"I hear you've moved," he said. It was an observation that lent validity to a feeling Annette had experienced for several weeks. Although she had not actually seen Shane, she had the distinct impression that he'd been watching her, keeping some distant vigil over her comings and goings. She knew her mother would not have told him of her move. And her phone number was not new, simply transferred from the line she'd had installed in her bedroom when she moved in with Sharon. Annette was convinced he had followed her on one of her numerous moving trips. How else could he have known that she was now living in Clear Lake?

Still, the conversation was pleasant enough. Shane asked about Michelle and pointed out that he and Tiffany missed seeing her, talked of how busy he'd been with work and National Guard duties, and seemed eager to know how she was doing in school. When Annette told him about her new job he was quick to offer congratulations.

Even as they talked, Annette waited expectantly to learn the real reason for the call. After all this time, had he finally decided to proceed with a divorce? Was he just trying to find the right moment to tell her? For a second she considered asking him about it, then decided not to. Neither did she ask if he had been following her.

"I just wanted to say hello and see how you are doing," he said before hanging up. Annette sat in her new dining room for several minutes, replaying the conversation in her mind. There had been no angry outbursts, no threats or blame-placing, not the slightest hint of cruel intent. It had been nice. Shane had sounded much like the man she'd met on the Galveston beach in a time that seemed so long ago.

Annette, however, was determined not to let down her fragile guard. She still loved her husband and at times entertained fantasies of their resolving their differences and reuniting as a family. Such thoughts, however, had come less often as time passed and she found herself able to look back on their difficulties in a more dispassionate way. For all her secret hopes, she saw no way their lives would ever work together.

Instead, Annette concentrated on building a life for herself and her daughter. She had made friends at school and on her job, inviting them over for weekend dinners so she might show off her new home. When she went out socially, it was generally in the company of female friends from school or a group from the office.

Money was still tight, her work and school schedule were at times exhausting, and there was the constant concern for the fate of her younger brother, now hiding away in Greece. But, all in all, Annette's life was gradually becoming less complicated. Even her mother, with whom she spent time every weekend, made note of the fact that she had begun to smile more often.

Shane had not called again and, despite nagging suspicions that he might still be watching her, Annette began to consider accepting the repeated offers for dinner or a movie extended by several of the men with whom she worked.

It was on Valentine's Day, 1989, that she was preparing dinner for a coworker named Jeff whom she had begun to see casually. Though she had told him of her separation from her husband and emphasized that she was not interested in developing a serious relationship, Annette had attended a couple of movies with him and they had occasionally joined others from the office for a drink after work. When he had invited her out to celebrate the holiday, she had suggested instead that she cook a meal at her home.

Jeff had arrived with flowers for Annette and helium-filled balloons for Michelle.

He had been there only a short time when the doorbell rang. Annette answered it to find Shane standing on her porch. Smiling, he did not wait for an invitation before making his way into the house.

Annette introduced her estranged husband to Jeff, then, not really knowing how to deal with the situation, hurried back into the kitchen where her dinner preparations were under way. While Jeff remained in the living room, making small talk with Michelle, Shane followed Annette, stationing himself on the counter next to her stove.

As she continued cooking, he chatted amiably, asking how she'd been doing, praising the manner in which she'd decorated the house.

After a while, Annette excused herself and returned to the living room to whisper an apology to her invited guest. "I'm trying to get him to leave," she said with a shrug that suggested her surprise over Shane's appearance.

Jeff, too, was feeling uncomfortable. "Look," he said, "maybe you guys need to talk. Why don't I just take off?"

The idea of being left alone with Shane frightened Annette. "No," she in a pleading voice. "I've already asked him to leave."

Jeff suggested that he step out onto the patio and give her the opportunity to talk to Shane in private.

Returning to the kitchen, Annette's demeanor became less hospitable. "Shane," she said, "I've got to get dinner ready. As you can see, I've got a friend here. What is it you want?"

Shane shrugged innocently. "I miss you," he said.

Annette's response was a silent stare. "Please leave," she finally said.

His discomforting visit had lasted almost an hour. When Annette finally served dinner, Jeff ate in silence except for an occasional polite compliment on her cooking. After helping her clear the table, he told her he felt it best he also leave. "I don't think," he said, "that it is a good idea for me to be coming over if you guys are trying to work things out."

"It's not going to work out," Annette argued.

Jeff's smile did not hide his obvious disappointment at the way the evening had gone. "Oh, I think it might," he observed.

///

Annette was convinced more than ever that Shane had been keeping track of her. Had she known that he was parked just down the street when her guest arrived, watching as she had opened the door to let Jeff in, her suspicions would have been confirmed. For months, in fact, Shane had watched her from the shadows of nearby parking lots, followed at a distance as she returned home from work or drove to school. From a vantage point just around the corner he had sat in his pickup, watching as she moved her belongings from her mother's house. He knew her new address long before she had given it to him.

Why? Had he become a jealous stalker, concerned that his wife was seeing others? Were his actions the formulative stages of some evil payback plan? A secret game? Or just unexplained curiosity? Shane himself would have been hard-pressed to provide a satisfactory answer.

In time, Annette's phone would ring just minutes after her return from work or school. It would be Shane, asking how her day had gone or sharing with her some less-than-extraordinary thing that had happened that day at his work.

The emotions created by such conversations confused Annette. The pain of his cruel jokes and angry rages had lessened but still remained. She had begun to feel a quiet comfort in her life without him, but it had disappeared almost immediately when he began contacting her. Though she had tried to remind herself of the way he had treated her in those weeks before their separation, the memories would quickly be overshadowed by the empty loneliness she'd felt since the day he left.

Despite everything, Annette was still in love with her husband and willing to let bygones rest if it might restore the family life she so desperately wanted. She found herself searching for more subtle reasons for the rocky start to their marriage. Perhaps, she thought, Shane's problems with the break-up of his first marriage had not been fully resolved. Maybe the solution was as simple as awaiting the passage of time.

"All I know," Annette told her mother, "is that if I don't give him the benefit of the doubt, I won't be able to say I tried everything to save my marriage."

Soon, Shane was visiting Annette regularly, sometimes staying overnight. After he'd begun spending weekends at her house, often bringing Tiffany along to play with Michelle, Annette gave him a key.

Shane Goode was back in her life, repeatedly assuring her that he had made a big mistake when he'd decided to leave. Their problems, he admitted, were of his own making. He was certain they could make a go of it if she would only give him a second chance.

As 1990 approached, both were facing renewal of their respective leases and they began talking about living together again. In view of the fact that Annette's condo was in close proximity to her job and night classes, it was decided that Shane would move from his Pasadena apartment and they would begin their new life together in Clear Lake.

And for a time, things seemed to be working out. They fell back into an easy routine of work, weekend trips to a movie or a fast-food dinner out with the kids. Both had outside interests they pursued without pressure from the other: Shane, his Guard activities; Annette, her schoolwork. Rather than rehash old problems, they embraced the present. Each seemed eager to wipe the slate clean.

It was not until the prospects of Desert Storm began to dominate the news that Shane's moodiness returned. Annette, seeing it as an understandable anxiety caused by rumors that his unit might soon be called into battle, shared his concern.

As the military action escalated, so did Shane's mood swings. When Annette attempted to discuss the matter, he became withdrawn. "I don't want to talk about it," he said.

On the evening of November 27, Shane and Annette returned from a dinner celebrating their anniversary and turned on the ten o'clock news. Annette was on the couch and Shane stretched out on the floor, listening to the latest report from the Mideast.

Her question was innocent enough, meant only to continue the pleasant conversation of their evening out. "Have you heard anything about whether you'll have to go?"

Suddenly, Shane was on his feet, glaring down on her. "Why do you keep nagging me about it?" he yelled.

"I wasn't nagging—"

"Like hell."

The sudden tension that swept across the room stunned Annette. Speechless, she wondered what was so wrong with a wife's concern that her husband might have to put himself in harm's way.

Shane began shaking his head, a look of disgust on his face. "This isn't going to work," he said.

"What are you talking about?"

"You heard me," he shot back. "You and me. It won't work." With that, he started toward the door.

Annette had not moved from her position on the couch. "You're leaving?" she said in stunned disbelief.

"You're goddamn right."

She rose and moved quickly to the doorway, blocking his way. This time, however, the delay tactic was not intended to buy time until he calmed down. Nor was it to afford him the opportunity to apologize for whatever had caused the blowup, or to beg him to stay.

"Leave your key," Annette said. "And don't come back."

For a moment Shane seemed surprised but said nothing. He removed the house key from his key chain and dropped in into her outstretched palm.

Closing her hand around it, she looked at him, summoning a new inner strength she did not know existed. "You're right," she said as she stepped aside. "This isn't going to work."

///

As the holiday season passed Annette heard nothing from Shane and was pleasantly surprised to find that his most recent departure had not sent her into a long bout with depression. Perhaps, she decided, she had finally begun to master the art of starting her life over. Certainly, she'd had enough experience.

Shortly after Christmas, she was scheduled to take an exam in the Emergency Medical Technician training course she'd enrolled in. Running late, she was hurrying to get ready when she stepped into the shower, slipped, and fell. A blinding pain shot up her spine and it was several minutes before she could climb from beneath the warm spray and limp to the phone.

Breathing with great difficulty, she called her mother and asked if she could come over and drive her to the emergency room.

At the hospital, X rays revealed that Annette had fractured a vertebra. The attending physician explained that she would have to endure some pain for a time but the injury was not serious and would likely heal quickly. Before exposing her to the X rays, however, he had suggested performing a routine procedure of a pregnancy test.

"When was your last period?" the doctor asked.

Annette wasn't sure, explaining her history of menstrual irregularity.

Already feeling the effects of the pain medicine she'd been given,

Annette made a halfhearted attempt to argue against the waste of time. She just wanted to go home, to lie down, and sleep away the pain.

The doctor smiled, gently ignoring her plea. "It won't take but a few minutes," he assured her.

Five

The news that she was pregnant sent Annette Goode off on another emotional roller-coaster ride. On one hand, there was a warm, new excitement that accompanied the surprising announcement that she would soon have another child; on the other, the prospect of caring for two children as a single parent was unnerving.

There were days when she found herself eagerly focusing only on the birth of her baby, the anticipation sweeping away all concerns about the physical demands and financial strains it was certain to bring. Already she loved the tiny life that was growing in her womb. Still, there would be somber times of stark fear when she allowed herself to contemplate a future in which she would try to continue her education, maintain a job, and also be the mother she hoped to be.

She would, she determined, just take it one day at a time. Somehow, things would work out.

She waited several weeks before telephoning Shane to tell him about her pregnancy. "I'm not calling to ask you for anything, and I don't want us to try again to get back together," she said. "I just thought you ought to know. Nothing more."

Although he was at first taken aback by the news that he would once again be a father, Shane assured her that he would support her in every way possible. Maybe, he suggested, he should come over so they could talk. "I'm sorry about the way I acted," he said. "I don't know what gets into me—"

Annette quickly interrupted him. "Shane," she said, "I just called to tell you what the situation is. I'm not asking you to come back."

"But, don't you think . . ."

"I don't *want* you to come back."

There was a brief silence before he responded. "Okay, I understand. But I do want to help you."

By February Annette's doctor had begun warning her that the remaining months of her pregnancy might be difficult. All appeared well at the time, he said, but her medical history indicated the need to take extra precautions. He advised her to drastically cut back on her workload, take a leave of absence if possible. He urged her to consider curtailing attendance at night classes until after the baby was born. Rest, he said, was the best assurance that she would carry to term and give birth to a healthy child. Additionally there would be a routine of precautionary tests he would like to make throughout her second and third trimesters.

Annette realized that it was going to be an expensive pregnancy. Though she had vowed not to involve him, she was going to need her estranged husband's help.

She drove to his apartment late one February afternoon. She had been anxious about the meeting since a brief telephone conversation during which Shane had invited her to come to his apartment to "discuss things." She had not seen him face to face for months. And, for all her protestations to friends and family that her marriage was over, Annette was still secretly dealing with her feelings for the father of the child she carried. What was she to read into the fact that he'd still not filed for divorce? Did he, too, harbor hope that their differences might somehow be resolved and that they could resume their life together? She knew only one thing for certain: She was finding it very difficult to stop loving him, to chase away the ever-present fantasy of having a family.

The Shane Goode she encountered upon her arrival at his apartment was far from the gentle, concerned person she'd spoken with on the phone. Instead, she was confronted with Shane, the manipulator: at first smooth and soft-spoken, then mean and loud.

If she really loved him, he said, she would have an abortion. Another child could only become an additional stumbling block in their chance to ever get their lives back together. "Look," he said, "I'm just trying to be very honest with you. I don't want you to have this baby— and I don't think you do either."

"Well, you're wrong," Annette replied coldly. "You are so damn wrong." She studied his face in silence for several seconds, the real purpose of his invitation suddenly clear. "Are you telling me that if I get rid of the baby we'll get back together and everything will wonderful?"

"I just thought that—"

"—And if I don't, we won't?"

A pulsing anger quickly filled the room. As Annette rose to leave, Shane exploded in frustration. He realized that he had failed to sway his wife. He clenched his teeth and the veins in his neck bulged. "If you have this baby," he yelled, "I don't want to have anything to do with it. I don't ever want to see it. I don't want to see you. As far as I'm concerned, you might as well be pregnant with someone else's kid. That's how I feel, goddammit. If *you* want it, *you've* got it."

Annette had seen similar outbursts before, yet she once again found herself stunned by the suddenness with which this latest fit of cruel rage occurred. Saying nothing more, she quickly let herself out the door and hurried to her car.

On the way home, as she replayed the confrontation in her mind, she pounded her fist against the steering wheel and cursed. Her anger, however, was not directed at Shane Goode. Rather, she was furious at herself for the uncontrolled tears that streamed down her cheeks.

Feeling more alone than she could ever remember, and distraught in the knowledge that Shane would offer no financial help, Annette sought refuge in the one place she knew it would be offered without hesitation or question.

She and Michelle bade farewell to the condo and moved back in with Sharon Couch. For Sharon, it was a welcome distraction from the consuming worry about the fate of her fugitive son.

• • •

Almost from his arrival in Thessaloniki, Steven's letters home were filled with self-pity and disdain for the life he was living. An uncle had found him work as an apprentice welder, a job in which he had no interest. The language barrier troubled him, and he was lonely. He was, he wrote, ready to return to the United States and give himself up to the authorities.

Worried that the funds she had managed to raise would not be enough to provide him adequate counsel, Sharon was anxious to see his situation resolved. The possibility that he might be convicted of murder and sent to prison chilled her.

She wrote back to him that it would be best if he managed to tolerate his life in limbo for a while longer, at least until she had enough money to pay a worthy lawyer's retainer.

As each letter from her son became more desperate, Sharon decided the best thing would be for her to visit him in person so they could discuss his options. Paranoid that the Houston police might be keeping track of her movements in an effort to find her son, she did not book a direct flight to Greece but rather flew from Houston to Istanbul, Turkey, then on to Athens. From there she took a train northward to Thessaloniki.

Once there, she listened as he described his misery, begged for details of family and friends back home, and contemplated the bleakness of his future. For Sharon the few days spent with her son were heartbreaking and her inability to provide him immediate solution to his problem lent a sense of frustration she'd never before experienced.

Still, before leaving she had managed to accomplish one thing. Steven grudgingly agreed to remain in Greece a while longer, holding to the promise that his mother would send for him just as soon as she could make the necessary arrangements with an attorney.

She had, in fact, already been in contact with a highly regarded Houston lawyer when she received a midnight call from a representative of the State Department, informing her that Steven was being held in the Korydallos prison in Athens. He had been arrested and charged with bringing hashish into the country from Amsterdam.

Her spirits at a new low, Sharon began making plans for a return trip to Greece, this time to attend her son's trial. Only after she arrived on one of the bitterest days of the Grecian winter did she learn that the judge hearing the case had offered the equivalent of a plea bargin: If Steven admitted guilt to using the illegal drug confiscated from his apartment—and agreed to leave the country immediately—he would receive a probated sentence.

Steven needed no persuasion to agree to the deal being offered him. As the papers were being drawn up, his mother was already making arrangements for their return to the U.S.

"Even if I do have to go to jail when I get home," he told her, "it will be better than being locked up here. I'm sorry I ever came."

It was while they waited to change planes in Amsterdam that Steven heard his name being called on the airport paging system. The operator told him that he had an emergency phone call. He was surprised that anyone would know his whereabouts and fearful that some change of heart had taken place among the Greek authorities. When he answered the phone he heard the voice of his father, who was calling from his home in Florida. Steven's uncle had alerted him to the most recent turn of events and had provided him with his son's flight schedule.

Out of his mother's earshot, Stephen listened, argued mildly, then said "Okay, I'll try it," before hearing an abrupt disconnect on the other end of the line.

All enthusiasm drained from his face as he walked to where Sharon sat.

"It was Dad," he said.

"Your father called here?"

Steven nodded. "I can't go back," he said, his voice barely a whisper.

"What are you talking about? Steven, what's happened?"

"He says it's a bad idea; that I'll be sent to prison."

"We don't know that," Sharon pleaded. "That's what lawyers are for. The ones I've been talking with say there's a very good chance that . . ."

Steven raised his palms and shrugged. Arguing would not change his mind. "Dad's got a cousin in Germany who's going to let me stay with his family. There's a ticket waiting for me at the gate."

Tears began to stream down Sharon's face and her body trembled with anger. Unable to speak, her mind raced with questions. How could his father suggest such an idea? What gave him the right to propose solutions that were really no solutions at all?

Alone on her flight back to Houston, Sharon continued to cry, more fearful than ever of the uncertain future and what it held.

She was eager for something good to happen to her. She felt it was long overdue.

///

That happy event occurred on August 27, 1991, when Katherine Renee Goode was born. Sharon stood by her daughter in the delivery room as a cesarean section was performed, holding her breath as the doctor encountered difficulty in removing the tiny form from the mother's womb. When one small leg came into view, she bit into her lip. When the doctor began gently twisting the tiny torso it took all her restraint to refrain from screaming out a warning that he might injure the baby's back.

Finally, the traumatic procedure was completed and Sharon held her beautiful, healthy granddaughter in her arms while the attending nurse bathed her. Relieved and suddenly happier than she'd felt in a long time, the proud grandmother thought it almost seemed as if little Renee, now resting peacefully in her arms, had not wanted to come into the world.

There was something bordering on the magical that attended Renee's birth. The loving attention showered on her by mother and grandmother quickly chased the dark montage of family worries into a far corner. In the days immediately following the baby's homecoming from the hospital, there was little time for Sharon to worry over the well-being of her faraway son or for Annette to brood about her new child's absent father.

A fragile infant, beautiful and innocent, had restored fractured faith and hope and smiles simply by her presence.

Six weeks after returning home, Annette, her strength returned and her resolve to embrace the future restored, filed for divorce from the man who did not even know that his new daughter had been born.

. . .

The Harris County Family Law Center, a building with a glass front and pillars on the eastern end of downtown Houston, serves as an ideally situated review stand from which to observe the city's endless promenade of misery. Along its wide, echoing halls hurry dozens of well-dressed attorneys, each carrying a briefcase, their voices mingling while they outline the final battle plans for divorces and custody fights to grim-faced clients. In its small, starkly lit courtrooms, marriages end and lives dramatically change in assembly-line fashion. The only displays of emotion are reserved for the first-time visitors, husbands and wives angered or saddened by their court-ordered presence and judges' rulings.

From the Franklin Street foyer one can see the imposing Harris County Courthouse, where cases of rape and murder, armed robbery, and foiled swindles are heard. At the corner of the quadrangle arrangement is the building housing the offices of the district attorney; next door is the multi-storied county jail, linked to the halls where its residents will go to trial by a busy network of tunnels and skywalks.

It is a conveniently designed layout which allows attorneys, law enforcement officers, and devoted trial-watchers the judicial equivalent of one-stop shopping.

Getting Shane Goode to appear at the law center so that divorce proceedings initiated by Annette might move forward had been no easy task.

For Joanne Chadderdon, Annette's attorney, the simple act of serving papers turned into a quest. Goode, it was learned, had moved from his Pasadena apartment, careful to leave no forwarding address. And while she had learned that he had moved in with a new girlfriend, neither Chadderdon nor her investigator could find friend or family member willing to provide them with a name or address.

Repeated trips to the post office where Goode worked had been fruitless. As if equipped with some instinctive radar, he always seemed to have left just minutes before the divorce papers arrived. For a time, Chadderdon's process server even made slow drives along the winding mail route he knew Goode to take, yet failed to encounter the elusive carrier.

Finally, after three cat-and-mouse months, Chadderdon received the judge's blessing to serve Shane Goode by proxy, leaving the papers with his employer who, in turn, was ordered by the court to pass them along.

Chadderdon, who early in her legal career had cast aside the wishful fantasy of the "easy" divorce, could see this one would be anything but.

///

It was in January of 1992 when lawyers and their clients finally took their places at separate tables, facing a weary-looking judge who would hear preliminary arguments in Cause 91-5130-7, the number assigned to Annette's petition for divorce.

The primary purpose of the hearing, Chadderdon had explained, was to seek temporary child support from Shane. There should be no problems, she assured her client, in light of the fact that Renee's father had offered absolutely no financial assistance or shown the slightest interest in his daughter in the five months that had passed since she was born.

Annette sat silently, staring straight ahead, without looking in Shane's direction, as her attorney painted a verbal portrait of a gainfully employed spouse who had refused to address the most basic of parental responsibilities. It was an argument she had made countless times in pursuit of many other deadbeat fathers she'd encountered during her legal career; one that the judge had also heard, almost word for word, thousands of times before.

But what came next forced Annette finally to turn in Shane's direction, her eyes registering shock and anger.

"If it pleases the court, your honor," his attorney said, "my client has a good and reasonable explanation for not contributing to the support of the child in question. . . ."

From that point on Annette heard the lawyer's words as if they were being spoken from some deep, dark tunnel. ". . . It is, your honor, my client's sincere claim to this court that he is not the biological father of this child . . . that he denies paternity of Katherine Renee Goode . . ."

The judge's shoulders slumped slightly as he realized that disposition of the case would not go as swiftly as he had hoped. Having heard the arguments of both attorneys, he sat silently at the bench. In a tone that made no attempt to hide his displeasure at the unexpected delay, he ordered Shane to immediately begin making temporary child-support payments in the amount of four hundred dollars per month. Meanwhile, both parties involved in the proceeding—including the child in question—were ordered to schedule blood tests which would determine whether or not Shane Goode was the father.

The barely discernable smile that flickered across Shane's face quickly disappeared when the judge ordered that he would be responsible for the cost of the testing procedure.

By mid-March a report from the Roche Biomedical Laboratories confirmed that Shane Goode was, in fact, Renee's father. Finally, just days before Christmas, the divorce became final.

But Shane Goode threw one final curveball. "If I've got to pay child support," he angrily told his attorney after learning the results of the paternity testing, "I'm damn sure going to have visitation rights."

Annette, relieved to see the court proceedings end, viewed her now ex-husband's demands as nothing more than a way to save face. Why, after fourteen months of absolute disinterest in his child, after fighting legally to disprove that Renee was even his, would he suddenly want visitation rights?

"I've seen it time and time again," Joanne Chadderdon assured her client. "He's just doing it to get back at you the only way left to him."

Chadderdon did not believe that Goode would miraculously turn into a caring father. She was more worried about how conscientious he would be about the monthly support payments. During the time he had been ordered to pay temporary support, the checks had come at the last minute and only for the first couple of months. Then they had ceased without explanation. Only when Chadderdon filed a contempt-of-court motion did Goode resume payments. The judge had then ordered that an automatic deduction from his pay be made twice a month and deposited in Annette's account. Keenly aware that Goode was both cunning and manipulative, Chadderdon privately hoped that he would not find some way to secrete his earnings away and stop paying Annette what was owed her.

Initially, Annette spent little time contemplating such possibilities. Perhaps naively, she believed that her ex-husband had the simple choice of paying child support or going to jail, making the decision an easy one for him. And the possibility that Shane might actually ever want to be a part of his daughter's life seemed remote. If at some future date he did show interest, she would deal with it then.

For now, what mattered was the fact that Shane Goode was officially out of her life.

Six

S haron Couch was seated in an overstuffed chair in the corner of her living room as she watched her eighteen-month-old granddaughter's uncertain attempt to accomplish a somersault. Renee giggled with delight, obviously satisfied with her budding athletic prowess, and then ran to another part of the house to retrieve a toy for display.

Clearly she was doing her best to impress her audience.

Seated on the couch was Shane Goode. Just one half hour before, he had finally been introduced to his daughter.

Annette had been surprised when he called to ask to meet Renee. Though the divorce decree granted Renee's father two visits per month, he had shown no interest in exercising his parental rights during the first two months that followed the ruling. In fact, he had allowed his first opportunity to pass, choosing instead to travel to Dallas that weekend to attend the annual January Cotton Bowl football game. Annette had been more convinced than ever that Shane would continue to show no interest in seeing his child.

Then, suddenly, he was there, accompanied by his daughter Tiffany, offering neither an explanation nor an apology for past behavior.

For Annette, the visit was unsettling, an emotional mixture of rekindled anger and disappointment as she realized that her ties to her ex-husband still remained. As she sat on the couch with Shane, making small talk as the children turned the living room into part circus, part dance recital, Annette fought mightily to disguise her feelings. *Be pleasant . . . smile . . . do it for the children's sake,* she kept reminding herself.

For Sharon, a silent observer of the scene, old memories flooded back; of her own divorce, the impossible task of explaining it to children who rarely saw their father, the hollow wish that things might somehow have been different. At age forty-six, she was just beginning to accept the fact that the wounds of divorce never completely heal, that its victims survive and move on with their lives yet forever carry with them the wounds.

She knew that Annette and Shane were still too young and too close to the hurt of their breakup to look ahead. In time, and with effort, the painful memories might fade. Perhaps the vengeful remarks and bitter denials spoken by her former son-in-law had been only the angry cries of a man who had been hurt by his wife's desire for a divorce. Sharon wanted to give him some benefit of the doubt. She felt she had to for the sake of her granddaughter.

The end of her own marriage had left an emptiness in her children's lives that she did not wish her granddaughter ever to feel. Annette would have to find the strength to allow Shane room in their lives.

Perhaps, she thought, the tension-filled visit playing out before her might be the first step.

If so, it was a tentative one. In less than an hour Shane and Tiffany were gone. Renee, still full of energy, had joined Michelle in their bedroom where they continued to play while Annette and her mother sat in the silence that had fallen over the living room.

Finally, Annette began to slowly shake her head. "He didn't even touch her," she said. "No hug, no kiss. He didn't even try to pick her up and hold her. Nothing." There was a tone of genuine disappointment in her observation.

It had been as if Renee, in some innocent way, had realized the importance of the event in which she was the star attraction and had attempted everything in her youthful power—the acrobatics, the dancing, the sharing of toys—to impress her father.

"It was as if she felt she had to perform for him." Annette observed. "I thought his being here would make me angry. But instead, all it did was make me feel really sad."

Sharon rose and moved across the room to her daughter, placing an arm across her shoulders. "I know," she said. "I felt the same way. Maybe next time it will be better."

At her suggestion of a future visit from Shane, Sharon saw her daughter grow suddenly tense with dread.

///

What passes for spring along the Texas Gulf Coast is a brief period of intermission between winter's penetrating chill and summer's cloying humidity. People instinctively change gears. With the end of football season, the usual failure of the Oilers to get within smelling distance of the Super Bowl is quickly forgotten by barroom pundits as they shift focus to the guarded hopes of baseball's Astros. In the Bellaire and River Oaks sections of town, women reluctantly put away their furs and begin to concentrate on acquiring an even tan. Country club golf courses and jogging tracks fill with instant jocks bent on sweating away the extra pounds of cold weather inactivity. Even the less well-to-do get into the spirit as they tend lawns and shrubbery that have suddenly turned from harvest brown to emerald green. Barbecue grills are dusted off and flowers are planted. It is a time for new beginnings and fresh starts.

Once again, Annette began to think of leaving her mother's home and moving ahead with her own life. A girlfriend from work, also in search of new living quarters, had suggested sharing the expense of an apartment. She and Annette got along well and she enjoyed the company of Annette's children. She even volunteered to baby-sit Michelle and Renee on those evenings when their mother had night classes.

And while Annette hoped to be able once again to afford a condominium in the Clear Lake area, the idea of sharing an apartment, at least for a while, excited her. It would be another step toward the independence she wished for herself and the girls.

Though she knew she would miss having the children under her own roof, Sharon was pleased by her daughter's eagerness to venture out on her own again. She had been pleasantly surprised at the maturity she'd seen Annette display as Shane continued to occasionally stop by to see Renee. Remarkably, it had been he, not Annette, who had seemed uneasy during the brief but cordial visits.

"I'll never like it," Annette had confessed to her, "but I can live with it."

Annette began to feel hopeful about her future. She had her children, her job, and a new home. She could even cope with Shane's occasional intrusions into her life with a minimum of anxiety. After all, he was Renee's father. And, as she knew better than most, a young girl's relationship with her father was important.

With some reservations, she had even agreed to let Shane take Renee to his parents' home in nearby Alvin for an evening visit. "She needs to know her grandparents," he had urged. He occasionally volunteered to keep Michelle and Renee on Wednesday evenings while Annette attended her nursing class.

The apprehension Annette had once felt before each encounter with her ex-husband began to ease. Old pressures seemed to have disappeared as she found herself thinking of Shane only on those occasions when he called to arrange the increasingly frequent visits he was making to his daughter.

Annette's own circle of new friends had expanded to include a young man named Vince Campise, a sailboat repairman who had been introduced to her by the boyfriend of her roommate. Occasionally the foursome would get together for pizza or a cookout and a video movie and, while she was not yet ready for a serious relationship, Annette enjoyed the relaxing, fun-filled companionship such gatherings provided.

Meanwhile, Shane Goode was sharing an apartment with a new girlfriend who worked with him at the post office. On the surface, he and Annette seemed to have finally made peace and were going their separate ways, linked only by a common interest in a child who would soon be two years old. The situation, however, soon changed.

One Wednesday evening after class, Annette drove to her exhusband's apartment to pick up the girls. They greeted her eagerly as she collected toys and Renee's diaper bag at the front door.

Shane followed her to the curb, standing silently with his hands stuffed in his pockets as she secured Renee into the car seat. "You doing okay?" he asked her.

"Just fine," Annette replied.

She was behind the wheel before he spoke again. "I put something in the diaper bag for you," he said.

Annette gave it little thought on the trip home, listening instead to the happy chatter of her children. Hours later, after putting them to bed, she remembered what Shane had said. Hoping it might be an early child-support payment, she found instead a letter written to her in Shane's familiar hand.

"Everytime I see you," it began, "I want to put my arms around you and hold you." Annette read on in disbelief. "Things were so awful during the divorce . . . but that's all behind us now. I now feel so much better about myself, and about us . . ." Shane rambled through recollections of past good times they had spent together, took full blame for the bad ones, and ended the letter with a renewed profession of his love for her.

Stunned by its content, Annette stared silently at the letter. Finally, she picked up the phone and dialed Shane's number.

"I read your letter," she said.

"And?"

"Shane, there's been a lot of water under the bridge. Too much. I'm not ready for this kind of thing. I just can't handle it."

She was surprised by the gentle tone of his reply. He offered no argument nor did he display the anger she had anticipated. "I understand," he said. "I really do. I just wanted to let you know how I feel."

What he did not mention was the fact that the girlfriend with whom he'd been living had told him to move out.

///

By the end of the summer, Annette had again leased a condo in Clear Lake, determined the move would be the last in her vagabond journey from trailer house to rental home, from apartments to her mother's house. It was time to settle down.

Meanwhile, Shane's note had destroyed any feeling of ease she'd begun to feel during his sporadic visits to see Renee. Despite his announcement that he'd moved into his own apartment in nearby Pasadena, she quickly refused his repeated offers to continue caring for the children while she attended her Wednesday night class. Because of the distance to her new home, she explained to Shane, her mother had not been able to see the girls nearly as often and had offered to look after them for her.

In fact, Annette had suggested a return to the structured visitation schedule originally set out in the divorce decree. She pointed out that both their schedules were hectic—hers with work and school, his with his responsibilities at the post office and Guard duties—making his habit of spur-of-the-moment arrangements difficult on everyone. What she did not mention was her fear that the visits to Shane's apartment were becoming traumatic for her daughter. Upon her return from each visit, Renee, who was generally cheerful and exuberant, would sit quietly for several hours, showing no interest in playing with her sister or her toys, before finally returning to her normal behavior.

Though bound by the ruling of the court, Annette was determined to limit her daughter's exposure to Shane as much as possible, at least until Renee's reaction seemed more positive.

Sharon Couch eagerly looked forward to the renewed visits from her grandchildren. Their cheerful voices and innocent demands for attention provided a brief respite from her own endless parade of worries.

Months earlier her father had died, raising concerns about the care of her mother. Then there was her son, who was rarely out of mind.

///

Steven's stay in Germany had been short. When he had phoned Sharon to say he wanted to return to Houston she advised him that an attorney had been retained and was only waiting for his arrival. "He says that it is very important that you turn yourself in," Sharon explained. "He doesn't want you arrested."

"Okay," her son agreed. "I'm coming home."

She felt uneasy as they discussed plans for his return, uncomfortable in her role of co-conspirator. It had been Steven's suggestion that he take a roundabout route that would lessen the possibility of his being taken into custody by Customs officials. Instead of flying directly into Houston International, he would book a flight from Munich to Montreal where he had friends who would drive him across the Canadian border to Detroit. From there he would take a domestic flight home.

Soon after Steven arrived home, he and his mother met with his lawyer who accompanied him to the police department for his long-delayed surrender into custody.

The optimism once displayed by the attorney was soon dashed when prosecutors refused to discuss a plea bargain or sentence reduction. They were determined to go through with a jury trial. Thus Steven was tried and convicted of murder, and sentenced to ten years in state prison.

Annette shared her mother's concern for Steven and was saddened by the thought of his being sent to prison. However, there was little she could do but offer moral support and occasional visits. Seeing him in confinement always left her depressed and she soon found herself looking for excuses not to make the drive to the Harris County jail where he awaited transfer to the Texas Department of Corrections.

Her own continuing problems were enough of an emotional drain. The uneasy truce between Shane and her had ended when, after Renee's first overnight visit with her father, Annette had taken a stand against his impromptu visitation.

Feeling the economic strain of child-support payments to his first wife and now Annette, Shane had moved from his apartment and taken up residence with his father and stepmother in Alvin. Once settled in, he had taken advantage of his scheduled visitation weekend by picking Renee up on a Friday afternoon when he got off work. He promised to have her back home by midday Saturday.

Annette had been reluctant to let Renee go, even telephoning her attorney to ask if there might be some way to avoid such an extended visit. Joanne Chadderdon explained that to deny Shane's request could cause Goode to file a complaint with the courts in which he could legally argue that she was not adhering to the judge's ruling. "It's called contempt of court," the attorney said, "and he'd have a good case." She urged her client to allow the visit unless she was worried that her child might be in physical danger while away.

"Are you concerned about that?"

"No," Annette had told her. Besides, Shane's parents and Tiffany would be there as well.

However, after Renee returned home, Annette's attitude changed dramatically.

Knowing that Renee had difficulty sleeping in any bed other than her own, Annette had asked her ex-husband if he'd had any problems getting her to sleep. Yes, he had said as he stood at her front door, sliding toys and a diaper bag into her hallway. In fact, he had finally spanked her to get her to stay in bed.

Annette flew into a rage. "You spanked her? Shane, dammit, she's a two year old in a strange house, staying overnight for the first time, probably scared to death."

"There was no reason for her to be scared."

"And there was no reason—no reason whatsoever—to spank a child in that situation," Annette shouted back before slamming the door.

When her father stopped by two weeks later, Renee had clung to her mother, crying and shaking her head. She did not want to go. The strength of her reaction surprised even Annette. Her daughter had always enjoyed car rides, eager to go "bye-bye" with almost anyone who visited. Her reluctance to go with Shane was out of character.

"She doesn't want to go," Annette had said. "And I'm not going to make her."

Shane made no attempt to disguise his anger. "She's going to have to get over it," he shot back. "I'm her father and she's got to get used to it."

Reluctantly, Annette agreed to a brief visit of a few hours to be spent getting ice cream and playing in the park. Placing her daughter in the car seat, she kissed her and told her she would see her in a couple of hours. The look of sadness on Renee's face troubled her mother greatly.

Upon their return, Renee was again pensive and uncommunicative for several hours. Annette knew that somehow she would have to find a way to protect her daughter from what was clearly becoming a traumatic experience.

Annette was certain that Shane would take her to court if she refused him access to Renee, yet she could not ignore the growing discomfort that attended the visits.

When her ex-husband called again, she tried once more to explain Renee's reaction to her visits with him, hoping that he might be understanding and give Renee time to adjust to the situation. "It's not right to force her," Annette offered.

"Nobody's forcing her to do anything," Shane replied angrily. "She's my daughter, too."

Annette knew that arguing was futile yet she continued. "Look, I just don't feel comfortable with her having to go when she doesn't want to. It scares her."

"So, let Michelle come with her. She'll feel more comfortable with her sister along, right?" He would also pick up Tiffany, whose company Michelle enjoyed, so they could all play together.

She knew that it was a logical solution to the problem. Annette reluctantly agreed to give it a try.

She would probably not have agreed had she been aware of the concerns Shane's first wife was having about his relationship with their child at the same time.

An attorney for Kaye Goode had not only filed a motion to increase the amount of child support Shane was paying, but she also asked for a drastic modification of the visitation agreement. Kaye had become concerned over her eight-year-old daughter's withdrawn behavior after weekend visits with Shane.

She learned that on occasion he had allowed Tiffany to dress in clothing more suitable for an adult and to wear makeup. He then took her on visits to a local nightclub, where they were seen dancing.

Like Annette, Kaye Goode was trapped by court-order paperwork and forced to allow Tiffany to visit her father. Even when the visitation rights were modified to eliminate extended visits, Kaye's mind had not been put at ease.

Shane, meanwhile, assured all who would listen that the worries of Tiffany's mother were unfounded. So what if he had taken Tiffany out for an occasional evening of father-daughter fun? There was nothing perverted about it. What was perverted, he furiously complained, was the fact that his monthly support payment for Tiffany had increased to $480. He had been placed in a position of paying out over half his income to ex-wives.

Annette got her first inkling of the troubles that had arisen between Shane and his first wife from a remark Michelle made after she and Renee had returned from one of their visits.

"Shane had a tape recorder," Michelle said. "He was trying to get Renee to talk into it."

"About what?" Annette wanted to know.

"He was trying to get her to say that she wanted to come live with him," Michelle reported. Seeing the sudden anger that crossed her mother's face, she quickly added, "All Renee would say was 'no.' "

When Annette telephoned to confront Shane on the matter, he immediately assured her that Michelle had been mistaken. Yes, he admitted, they had been playing with a tape recorder. He'd tried to get all the girls to talk into it. But it had been Tiffany, not Renee, who he'd tried to persuade to say on tape that she wanted to come live with him. He was convinced that Kaye was trying everything in her power to turn his daughter against him.

"She's not taking care of Tiffany like she should, so I've decided I'm going to take her to court," he said. "I'm afraid she's not the good mother that you are."

///

It was not until New Year's Eve of 1993 that Shane was able to convince his former wives to allow his daughters to visit overnight. Kaye was relieved that Shane had returned home to live with his parents, thereby assuring more adult supervision while her child was away. She had finally agreed to allow Tiffany to spend the holiday evening at the Goode home in nearby Alvin, but only after Shane had promised that she could pick her up early the following day.

It had been Tiffany who phoned Annette to ask if Michelle and Renee could join her at the Goode home. After the typical childlike pleading, Shane got on the phone. "I know it is short notice," he said, "but we'd love to have them over."

"It's New Year's Eve and you don't have any plans?" Annette chided.

"No plans," Shane replied. "Can they come?"

At first, Annette was hesitant. In recent days she had been concerned over a fall Renee had taken in the living room of the apartment and had continued to watch her closely despite the doctor's assurance that her daughter was fine. She had been riding her plastic tricycle through the living room one evening and, in an effort to impress her big sister, had attempted a "wheelie." The result was a fall against a coffee table where she had hit her head. A quick trip to the Clear Lake Humana Hospital emergency room revealed no concussion, only a small laceration which had not even required stitches. Still, Annette had been worried about Renee, watching her closely for several days before she was convinced her baby was okay.

The doctor had assured her that this kind of childhood accident was part of life. It was the same lecture she'd heard several months earlier during a similar emergency-room visit after Michelle had accidently shut the car door on Renee's finger. On each occasion, she had been assured that her daughter was a perfectly healthy child.

Still, Annette had begun to feel comfortable allowing Renee to run and play normally only a few days before Tiffany called. Earlier in the week, Annette and Vince had been invited to drop by the house of some friends who lived in Alvin for a late dinner and quiet celebration of the new year. At first, they had declined, then reconsidered when they realized the drive to the Goode house would put them within a couple of miles of their friends' home. "Okay," Annette finally agreed, "I'll drop them off around eight."

"Great," Shane replied. "Tell the girls that I'm looking forward to seeing them."

"Eight o'clock," she repeated, and was about to hang up when she heard him speak her name. "Annette . . ."

"Yes?"

"I just wanted to wish you happy new year," he said. She tried hard to ignore the intimacy in his voice.

Her ex-husband had known for some time about her relationship with Vince. She'd introduced the two on one of Shane's first visits to her condo. Yet, even when he'd become aware that Vince was spending much of his time at Annette's place, Shane had surprised her by refraining from any private inquisition. Aside from a casual hello or a few minutes of small talk when he picked up Renee, he continued to act as if no other man existed in Annette's life.

Which was the way she liked it. She had confided to Vince about the failures of her past relationships long before they had moved beyond simply being friends. He knew of the difficulties she'd had with Shane, of the private fear she experienced as a result of his unpredictable behavior, his stalking, and his vengeful rages. And while he had immediately disliked Goode, he promised Annette that he would not do or say anything that might provoke additional problems. But only so long as Shane Goode treated her and her children properly. If not, he made it clear that all bets were off.

Annette appreciated his understanding. Shane, she assured him, was quite capable of building the slightest incident into some reason for launching into a bitter custody fight over Renee. He would do it, she was convinced, not because he loved his daughter but as a way of getting back at her, of inflicting a new barrage of hurt. There was in Shane Goode a mean-spiritedness which was far beyond her ability to explain.

It was for that reason that Annette guarded a tightly held secret.

She and Vince had secretly married but had told no one—not their friends, not her mother, not even Michelle—for fear of Shane's reaction. In time, she reasoned, his anger, which always hid just below the surface, had to subside. Eventually, he would come to the realization that there was no love left to be rekindled, accept it, and move ahead. Only then, she had tried desperately to explain to Vince, would she feel safe in making their marriage public.

Some of Annette's closest friends, meanwhile, continued to view the bond that remained between her and Shane as strange. A few privately held the belief that Annette had not completely accepted the fact that they were divorced and still hoped a day of reconciliation might come. Few considered the possibility that it might be Shane, not Annette, who refused to let go.

Vince knew only that her fears were real. Rather than question her, he offered unqualified support, and agreed to the request for secrecy that could only be viewed as bizarre.

///

They had arrived home shortly before 2:00 A.M. on the first day of 1994 and were preparing for bed when the ringing of the phone sent a cold, instinctive fear racing through Annette's body.

She answered quickly and heard Michelle's voice. "Mommy," her daughter said, "something's wrong with Renee."

"What's the matter?"

"She's real cranky . . . and she's got a fever."

"Where's Shane?"

"He had to go someplace," Michelle said.

Annette's fear now mingled with rage. "Let me talk with grandmother or granddaddy."

Shane's parents, she was told, were in their bedroom in the back of the house. "Shane told us we weren't supposed to wake them up," Michelle explained.

"I'm coming right now," Annette said. "Tell Renee I'll be there as quickly as I can."

///

Upon her arrival at the Goode house, Annette did not even bother to tell her former in-laws, still soundly sleeping in the back of the house, that she was taking Renee and Michelle. All she wanted was to get her children and leave as quickly as possible.

To her relief the cause of Renee's discomfort and fever had been nothing more than a slight ear infection. Cradled in her mother's arms as Vince drove them back toward home, she whimpered briefly, then fell asleep.

Once she was assured that Renee was okay, Annette began to question Michelle about the night's events.

Shane had received a call shortly after they had arrived and had left. He'd explained that a friend had some kind of car trouble and he was going to lend a hand. The girls had been given strict instructions to remain in the house and under no circumstances were they to disturb their grandparents.

As they drove through the fog that greeted the early morning hours of the new year, Annette stared silently at the road ahead for some time. Soon Michelle, too, had fallen asleep.

They were almost to Clear Lake when she turned to Vince with a look of resolve on her face he'd never before seen. "That's it," she said.

It was time to pay a visit to her attorney; time to start fighting back.

Seven

Sitting in Joanne Chadderdon's office, Annette recounted the event in a measured, controlled voice that took the attorney by surprise. Seated before her, flanked by a wall of diplomas and law books, was a young woman on a mission. There were no hysterics, no frantic pleas for impossible immediate relief the attorney was so often asked to provide.

Annette, she found herself thinking, had matured considerably since they had first met.

Chadderdon listened as Annette recounted Shane's phone call New Year's Day with his frail excuse for having left the children the night before. And she agreed that his action justified the anger her client felt.

"Unfortunately," the attorney explained, "he did nothing illegal. There were adults in the house—his parents—so, technically, there is no real basis for a claim that he abandoned the children."

Undaunted, Annette continued to list her grievances: Shane's spanking Renee to make her go to sleep, his erratic schedule of visits, the incident with the tape recorder, and, most disconcerting, Renee's withdrawn behavior following each trip to spend time with her father. "There is something wrong with their relationship," Annette insisted.

Chadderdon had a good idea what her client was intimating yet remained silent, waiting for Annette to say it: "I don't know if he's molesting her or what, but something just isn't right."

"Even if true, there is nothing we can do without proof," Chadderdon explained.

Nor, as things stood, was there any legal way by which Annette could prohibit Shane from seeing Renee. "All he would have to do would be to take you to court," she said, "and from what you've told me about this guy, he'd enjoy doing it."

"What if he is abusing her?"

"That's a different matter altogether," Chadderdon acknowledged. She advised Annette to check her daughter thoroughly before her next trip to see her father. Then, she told Annette to take Renee directly to a doctor for an examination when she returned. "If nothing else, it might give you some peace of mind."

The demeanor of the young woman seated across from her turned to one of weary disappointment. Her lawyer, rich in experience with such problems, had offered only the slightest cause to hope that hers might be solved.

She was preparing to leave when, almost as an afterthought, Annette mentioned that her ex-husband had fallen behind on the court-ordered payments on her student loan.

Chadderdon smiled and began writing herself a note on the yellow legal pad in front of her. "That," she said, "I *can* do something about."

///

As the January days passed, Annette agonized over her next phone call from Shane. Dread became her constant companion, a burning, heavy pain that lay in the pit of her stomach, refusing to go away. Her mind raced to find excuses not to allow her child to leave home, to find some way to ensure Renee's safety and happiness. But she came up with nothing that offered more than a temporary stay of the inevitable. Shane, she knew, had the law on his side, a powerful, unbending adversary that she had come to resent mightily. Annette had begun to understand the motivation that drove mothers to disappear quietly with their children—to hide them away, out of reach of those who might cause them harm. When such thoughts crossed her mind they would always be followed by a surge of stubborn anger. Why, dammit, should she allow Shane and his childish, manipulative behavior to drive her away from friends and family? From home and the new life she and Vince were working to build for themselves and the children?

She would simply have to find the strength to meet her enemies—the frustration and paranoia—on her own turf and defeat them.

On Saturday, January 22, Annette answered her phone to hear once again the cheerful, excited voice of Shane's daughter, Tiffany. "Daddy says we can have a slumber party tonight," she said. "Can Michelle and Renee come? Please . . ."

Annette asked to speak with Shane. "I'd better not get a phone call in the middle of the night," she said.

Shane dismissed the coolness in his ex-wife's voice. The girls would have fun, he said. In addition to Tiffany, Michelle, and Renee, there would be his ten-year-old niece Christine who was living with his parents.

"And you're going to be there?"

"Hey, I promise," Shane said. "I'll pick them up around six-thirty, okay?"

Before he arrived, Annette fed the girls and bathed Renee, carefully examining her for any scratches or bruises she might have recently suffered in the course of normal child's play. She methodically followed the suggestion of her attorney, checking to see that Renee's ear infection had gone away, that there was no sign of redness of the throat, no irritation of the genitals, no temperature.

An overwhelming sadness gripped Annette as she conducted her examination and made preparations for the girls' overnight stay. Michelle, she knew, looked forward to spending time with Tiffany, but Renee demonstrated not the slightest hint of enthusiasm for the proposed visit. Annette hated the idea of sending her away to a place she didn't want to be, to be cared for by a person she was convinced her child feared.

As she laid out the purple sweat pants and flower print pullover shirt Renee would wear, Annette called Michelle aside. "I want you to have fun," she said, "but you have to watch after your little sister for me, too. Okay?"

Michelle nodded.

"And, if Shane leaves," her mother added, "you call me right away."

"I will," Michelle promised.

Minutes later they were in the front yard, arranging overnight bags and Renee's car seat in Shane's pickup. Annette hugged her daughters, then helped them into the cab. Buckling Renee in, she kissed her, then Michelle. "Mommy loves you," she said.

Even before his black pickup disappeared from view Annette was aware of the warm tears that had begun to fall down her cheeks. She'd been standing at the curb for some time when Vince emerged from the apartment to place his arm around her. "It's just for the night," he said. "Everything's going to be okay."

Nothing he tried afforded relief from the worry Annette was feeling. Throughout the night she paced from room to room, seeking something to occupy her mind. Several times she considered phoning the Goode house to make sure everything was okay but decided against it. Any attempt by Vince at conversation would end with Annette crying, her hands shaking so badly she could not grip the cup of hot tea he had prepared for her.

The first gray flickers of dawn had begun to show when exhaustion finally claimed her last bit of energy. "Just lie down and take a little nap," her husband urged.

While Vince had become intimately familiar with the anxieties his wife experienced each time the children were with Shane, he'd never before seen Annette this upset. It was, he would later tell a friend, as if she'd had a sixth sense that something out of the ordinary might happen.

Annette had finally stretched out on the bed and was just drifting off into a state of half-sleep when she heard the phone ring and Vince answer. By the time she was fully awake and sitting up, he was standing at the bedroom door, his face ghostly pale.

"Something's wrong with Renee," he said. His voice trembled as he choked out the words.

Annette was quickly on her feet, racing past him toward the hallway phone where she heard Michelle's frightened voice:

"She's not breathing, Mommy. Something's wrong with her."

Annette clutched a hand to her brow and grimaced as if someone had just delivered a blow to her midsection. "Oh, God, no," she moaned. Then, attempting to compose herself she focused on Michelle. "Honey, who's there? Where's Shane? Put a grownup on the phone. Please do it . . . now . . . hurry. . . ."

She heard the receiver clank loudly against something—likely the counter in the Goode kitchen—as Michelle left in search of an adult who could speak with her mother.

Annette tried to visualize what might be happening in the Goode home. If she had, she would have seen her ex-husband in the living room, bending over Renee, while his stunned father, awakened from sleep, stood nearby as if in shock. Shane's mother, still feeling the effects of medication she had taken, had been told by her husband to remain in their bedroom.

Endless, agonizing seconds passed before Annette again heard Michelle's tiny voice. "Nobody will come to the phone," she said, as she began to cry. "Mommy, some paramedic people are here. . . . They're saying she's gone."

///

For Annette, there would be no memory of the frantic forty-five-minute drive from Clear Lake to Alvin, of the impatient running of red lights, or the numbing frustration that the miles would not pass quickly enough.

She had been in a kind of shock ever since getting Michelle's call. While quickly pulling on jeans and a T-shirt, she screamed, cursed, and then sobbed with rage. "He did something to her," she repeatedly yelled at Vince. "I know he did. I know he did."

There would be sudden moments of unexplained calm during her outbursts. It was when she had finished dressing and had grown briefly quiet that Vince had urged that they get on the way. They were walking out the front door when the rage suddenly exploded again. Annette had jerked her arm away from her husband and she turned to walk hurriedly back in the direction of the bedroom.

"Where are you going?" Vince asked.

"To get my gun," she replied.

Her grandfather had given her his .357 magnum when she'd first moved to Clear Lake, concerned that she might one day find herself in need of protection. And while she had always been fearful of it and had never even learned to fire it, she was suddenly determined to find it and take it with her. "I'm going to kill the sonuvabitch," she said.

Several minutes passed before Vince could persuade her not to take the gun.

///

They turned onto the 1800 block of Meadowview Street where the generally quiet, peaceful atmosphere of the neighborhood had become a flurry of activity. Parked in front of the Goode's home were police cars and an ambulance. Several people milled about the front yard, watched over by a uniformed officer who had stationed himself on the front porch.

As she ran toward the house the officer stepped in front of her to block her path. "I'm sorry, ma'am. No one's allowed to—"

"My baby is in there," she cried out.

The officer, moved by the pleading in the young woman's voice, pointed toward the open front door. "Through there," he said.

Her steps abruptly slowed as she entered the den. Suddenly it was as though all of her muscles had shut down, her legs heavy weights that would move only with the greatest of effort.

Shane was seated on the floor with his back to her, his body gently rocking. Cradled in his arms was the lifeless body of Renee, wrapped in a white sheet.

Annette's painful cry echoed through the house as she walked to a love seat near where Shane sat. "Give her to me," Annette said. "Give me my baby."

As though he'd not heard her, Shane continued to rock, his cold, tearless stare focused on a nearby wall. When his ex-wife repeated her plea, reaching out toward him, his only response was to slump his shoulders slightly and quicken the pace of his back-and-forth movement. "She's gone," he finally said.

Until that moment Annette had been unaware of the sizable audience assembled in the room. There were police and members of the emergency medical care unit that had been summoned; the children, her father-in-law, and Vince. No one spoke.

It was Annette who broke the silence. Looking up at an officer of the Alvin Police, her eyes filled with anger, she began shaking her head. "She was perfectly fine just a few hours ago," she began. "What are you going to do about this?"

When the officer offered no reply, she got to her feet and moved in his direction. "Something is very wrong here. Something is going on here."

Then her crazed grief exploded. She began to scream, moving about the room as though in frantic search of some escape from the nightmare, finally stopping to point an angry finger toward Shane. "He did something to my baby. She was fine . . . don't you under-stand? Can't you see? *He did something to her. . . .*"

The officer moved toward her, reaching out for her arm. "Ma'am," he said, "I realize you are upset. But if you don't calm down I'm going to have to ask you to leave."

Annette glared at him, shaking her head in disbelief. None of this could be happening. It wasn't real, just some horrible dream, her imagination playing vile, ugly tricks. She began to cry again and sud-denly her angry voice became only a painful whisper. "That's my baby. My sweet, beautiful baby," she said.

Shane was still sitting on the floor, still rocking his dead child, when Patrolman Terry Earl, the first officer to arrive at the scene, asked Annette if she would step outside with him so he could ask her some questions.

Seated on the porch, she tried determinedly to compose herself so that she might convince the officer of her suspicions. "It has," she began, "been going on for a long time."

///

As she spoke, Detective Howard Duckworth arrived and joined his fellow officer, listening to the grieving mother's tirade of accusa-tions against her ex-husband. Called by his nickname, Bodie, by all in Alvin who knew him, he was considered the premier narcotics in-vestigator in the community's small department. But on this Sunday morning it had been his lot to be the detective-on-call—therefore he was responsible for the investigation of the child's death.

Only when convinced that Annette had regained some measure of composure did the officers end their questioning. Earl excused himself to enter the house and told Shane to accompany him to another room where they might discuss the events of the previous evening.

Annette followed to help Michelle gather her things. As she waited in a doorway that led to the den, she turned to glimpse Renee's now prone body laying atop a sheet as EMS officers silently prepared to deliver her to the morgue. For a moment she felt as if she might faint.

Renee still wore the pants and shirt she'd dressed her in the previous afternoon and Annette felt a new wave of sadness crash over her. She had been so careful to pack her daughter's favorite nightgown, and Shane had not even bothered to see that she changed into it.

She fought the urge to rush to her baby, to pick her up and hold her. In her mind, the den was a crime scene. It was important, she reminded herself, that she do nothing to disrupt any evidence that could prove Renee's death had been no accident.

///

It was only after all interviews had been conducted and the child's body delivered to the coroner that Detective Duckworth returned to the Alvin Police Department to begin organizing his report.

From the information he'd gathered, it appeared that the events that had preceded Katherine Renee Goode's tragic death could have been innocently played out in half the homes in the community:

Shortly after the girls had arrived, Carolyn Goode had phoned in an order for pizza, then excused herself to her bedroom. Still feeling the effects of dental surgery she'd undergone earlier in the day, she planned to go to bed early, leaving her stepson to care for the young guests.

Throughout the evening Shane served as chaperon while the children played hide-and-seek, watched television, and snacked on marsh-mallows and lemonade. It had been shortly after eleven when he had begun to urge the girls to prepare for bed. Michelle had unrolled the pink sleeping bag she had brought, draping it across the love seat. Tiffany had chosen the couch and Christine placed her pillow and blanket across a nearby stuffed chair that was her favorite. Shane spread a pallet on the floor in the center of the room for Renee and helped her remove her shoes. Tiffany volunteered to change Renee's diaper.

No sooner had everyone taken her place, however, when Renee had moved from her spot to join her sister on the love seat, giggling as she snuggled beside Michelle.

She had curled her lips into a disappointed pout when Shane insisted that she return to her pallet, demanding that she be allowed to have a sleeping bag like her older sister. Shane brought his old army-green sleeping bag from a closet and spread it on the floor for her.

Still restless and not ready for the play to end, she was up and down, whispering to the older girls, hoping to convince someone to turn the television back on.

In an attempt to calm her, Shane had lain on the floor beside her. When she had continued to move restlessly, he lifted her onto his chest where she lay for several minutes before finally going to sleep.

With all finally quiet, Shane had retreated to his own bedroom. He'd checked in on the girls shortly before 1:00 A.M. and found that Christine had decided the chair was too uncomfortable and had moved to her own bedroom. After looking in on her, he'd gone to bed and was soon sleeping soundly.

During the night Carolyn Goode, groggy from the pain medication she'd taken, had wakened to make a trip to the bathroom for a drink of water but had not thought to check on the children in the den. Neither had her husband, who returned home from his late shift at the post office at 2:30 A.M. Upon his arrival he had entered the kitchen, placed his lunch box on the counter, had a glass of iced tea, showered, and gone to bed.

Michelle remembered being awakened by "some kind of noise" during the night. From the digital glow of the television VCR she could see that it was 3:30 A.M. Tiffany, she recalled, was asleep on the couch and Renee was on the floor, lying on her side. She had quickly fallen back to sleep.

It was not until 8:30 that Michelle woke again, roused by the sound of morning cartoons from the nearby television. Tiffany was sitting on the den floor near the set. She had already tried to wake Renee without success and was pleased to see that Michelle was up. She suggested they get a bowl of cereal from the kitchen.

Michelle's attempt at waking her little sister had also been futile. Gently shaking her shoulder and calling her name got no response. Normally a light sleeper who was awake at the slightest noise or touch, Renee, now lying on her stomach, did not respond. Michelle, still not fully awake herself, bent over her and saw that a dark liquid was oozing down her cheek.

Frightened, she called out to Tiffany. "Something's coming out of Renee's mouth," she said. "She won't wake up."

"Go get Shane," Tiffany urged.

///

Shane had hurried from his bedroom and was kneeling over the baby, calling her name, trying to shake her awake while instructing Tiffany to bring him a damp towel from the bathroom.

As he bathed Renee's face he told Tiffany to dial 911. "Give them the address and tell them she's not breathing," he said. "Tell them to hurry."

Unnerved by her adult responsibilities, Tiffany bravely followed her father's instructions and found herself in the role of go-between, relaying instructions and questions from the emergency dispatcher. "She says to clear her airway," she shouted from the kitchen.

Shane was nodding. "I've already done that."

"Daddy, she wants to know if you know how to do CPR."

"No," he said.

"She said they're on the way."

Tiffany could already hear the distant wail of a siren by the time she entered her grandparents' room to tell them what was taking place in the den. "Something's wrong with Renee," she said. "Something real bad."

Donald Goode, jolted awake by the urgency in Tiffany's voice, urged his wife to remain in the bedroom, then hurried toward the front of the house. He reached the hallway just in time to answer the urgent knocking of the emergency medical service personnel.

In a matter of minutes all urgency had drained from the efforts of the medical attendants. Renee's body was cold, without any sign of life. Rigor mortis had, in fact, already begun to set in.

She had been dead for some time, perhaps several hours.

/ / /

Detective Duckworth hunched over his desk, reviewing the tragic sequence of events in an effort to determine the pertinent information his chief would want to read when he reported to work the following morning. Observations, he knew, were sometimes as important as the factual recollections of those interviewed.

He would note that during his interview, Shane Goode had mentioned that Renee had bumped her head against the headboard while playfully jumping on his bed earlier in the evening. Had the blow been so severe that it could have ultimately caused death? Goode had insisted that he'd checked and found no indication of a laceration or bruise resulting from the accident. Renee, in fact, had been happily playing again, moments after she'd bumped her head. Could it be possible, Duckworth wondered, that such a seemingly insignificant accident had led to the child's death? That, he knew, would be for the coroner to determine.

And what of the bitter accusations of Annette Goode? The detective had heard much the same from other ex-spouses over the years as he'd been called to investigate countless domestic disturbances. In the heat of anger and pain, husbands and wives lashed out at each other with venom. He felt sympathy for Annette's pain but had dismissed much of what she had said.

Still, there had been something unusual about her ex-husband. It would be nothing the detective could put into a report; only a sense that the man he'd interviewed had been far more calm than he could have been in a similar situation. Patrolman Earl had remarked on the fact he'd not seen the father shed a single tear, even as he sat rocking the dead child in his arms.

Duckworth had, in fact, felt an unsettling coldness throughout the house as he'd carried out his investigation. Donald Goode had stood to one side, arms folded, saying nothing as the EMS personnel had gone about their work. He had insisted that his wife, still sequestered in her bedroom, had no information to offer and had refused to allow police to talk with her.

Doubtful that she could shed light on what had transpired, Duckworth had decided to wait and speak with her after things had settled down.

All that aside, there had been nothing that had set off the kind of alarm bells trained investigators often hear, urging that they look for deeper, hidden truths.

Still, the visit to 1830 Meadowview Street had been one of the most trying of Duckworth's career.

During his ten years of police work, countless death scenes had accumulated in his memory bank—highway accidents, homicides, suicides. Each was memorable for some unique aspect, yet shared a similarity that never failed to haunt him for days after an investigation. Death rarely made sense to him. That it would be visited on an innocent child was one of the mysteries he knew no amount of experience or faith would ever allow him to untangle.

The image of Renee Goode's motionless body, lying on the den floor, would be forever burned into his mind's eye.

Eight

Dreaming, theorizes Dr. Charles Fisher, director of the sleep laboratory at New York's Mount Sinai Hospital, permits one to be quietly and safely insane every night. It was not a concept Sharon Couch had ever considered, despite the fact that her sleep had been routinely interrupted in recent months. The most common night sounds—the distant barking of a dog, wind-driven tree limbs scratching against the roof—were certain to wake Sharon. And there were the agonizing dreams—nightmares, really—of her son and the myriad difficulties he was facing. At times they were disjointed and impossible to remember the following day; others were so real they would jolt her awake, triggering thoughts that would rob her of rest for hours as she lay staring at the ceiling.

Rarely, if ever, were her dreams pleasant.

Never before, however, had she experienced a moment like the one that interrupted her sleep at somewhere around 4:00 A.M. that Sunday. It was more of a physical sensation than a dream, without storyline or faces.

Suddenly, her breathing became labored as she felt something pressing down on her. She sensed something soft around her throat, applying pressure that made it increasingly difficult to fill her lungs.

She woke up gasping, frantically gulping the sweet night air of her darkened room. It was several minutes before she was able to breathe normally. Knowing that a return to sleep would be impossible, she pulled on her robe and went into the kitchen to put on coffee.

She and Gary Meaux, whom she'd been seeing for some time, had planned to meet for brunch later in the day, and by getting an early start she could accomplish some overdue housecleaning chores before meeting him at his apartment.

Gary, raised in nearby Port Arthur, gave balance to Sharon's life. She had met the quiet, introspective accountant in 1979 while working as a data process supervisor at Medical Center del Oro, a Houston rehab hospital. As she got to know him, Sharon soon learned that he had a wonderful sense of humor. That, she recognized, was something she badly needed.

During the course of their leisurely meal she mentioned her nighttime experience—"It was the weirdest feeling," she said—then dismissed it, turning the conversation to the shopping plans they had made. Renee, now growing at a rate that amazed her mother and grandmother alike, needed new shoes and Sharon had volunteered to buy them.

Yet after finding a pair she liked at a nearby department store, Sharon had second thoughts about purchasing them without having her granddaughter try them on first. She would, she decided, return the next day with Renee.

That decision made, they idled away much of the morning and early afternoon before returning to Gary's apartment. He was at his computer, eager to test a new piece of software he'd purchased, when the phone rang.

There was a puzzled look on his face as he turned to Sharon, holding out the receiver for her. "It's Annette," he said.

A moment later he saw the color drain from her face and heard her anguished cry. Sharon was shaking her head in disbelief. Gary rose from his chair to stand next to her, fearful that she might faint.

"Where are you?" she asked into the phone. Then: "We'll be right there."

Handing the phone back to Gary she stood for what seemed like several seconds with her shoulders slumped and tears filling her eyes.

"Oh, God," she said as her head shook from side to side. "God, no."

Gary gently placed his arms around her shoulder. "Sharon, what is it? What's wrong?"

She buried her face into his chest and began to sob uncontrollably. Her reply was barely coherent, muffled as if it had come from deep in her throat, but Gary understood her. A sudden chill ran through his body and he held her even tighter.

"Renee is dead," she had said.

///

Gary's residence was only a short distance from the condo where Annette lived, yet the trip seemed endless. Sharon, still pale and shaken, stared blankly out the window, deaf to the questions Gary had been repeatedly asking since they got in the car. "Are you sure?" he asked. "What happened?"

They were met at the door by a blank-faced young woman clearly in shock. Exhausted, without makeup, Annette looked as if she had suddenly aged far beyond her years.

"Where have you been?" she asked her mother. "I've been trying to reach you for hours." There was a childlike tone, a plea, to her question. Then she began to cry.

Over the next few hours, Annette's fragile emotions again hopscotched from silent devastation to screaming outrage. Slowly, carefully, her mother probed for answers to her multitude of questions. How? When? Why? Alternately staring at the carpeted floor and closing her eyes, as if to hide from the horror that had visited her life, Annette told of the early morning phone call from Michelle, of rushing to the Goode home and finding her child dead, wrapped in a sheet and cradled in Shane's arms.

Then, lifting her eyes into a fixed stare, the rage swept over her as she spoke of Shane. "He did something to her," she said. "I know he did something to my baby." Then her anger spilled over to the police officers who she felt had treated her not as a mother but as an intruder.

Sharon sat silently through her daughter's angry recollections, feeling a helplessness unlike any she had ever experienced. Only after Annette quieted and leaned her head against the back of the sofa, adrenaline drained and exhaustion setting in, did her mother speak. "Would you like for me to handle the funeral arrangements?" she volunteered.

Annette nodded ever so slightly and again began to cry. This time her tears came softly, no longer accompanied by hysterics.

The tranquilizers she'd taken were beginning to take effect.

///

Sharon Couch felt a strange calm as Gary drove her home that evening. For the past several hours there had been a caravan of friends and relatives in and out of Annette's apartment. Sharon found herself wanting out of there, wanting to be away from everything and everybody that served as a reminder of the horrible truth she knew she must somehow accept. Even with the knowledge that Vince would be there to watch over Annette, Sharon felt a sense of guilt at her overwhelming urge to get away, to run from the nightmarish tragedy. Maybe, just maybe, by distancing herself from her grieving daughter and the story she had related, the sharp, stabbing edges of reality might somehow be dulled. She strongly felt the mother's responsibility to be with her daughter yet she needed time to herself, to somehow get a grasp on what had transpired.

The excuse she had given for leaving had been both valid and logical. She volunteered to take Michelle home with her where she might get some rest, away from the tension and tears that served as constant reminders of what she'd awakened to earlier in the day.

And Sharon had to begin planning for Renee's funeral.

As Gary drove, Sharon's thoughts were absorbed with the bitter allegations Annette had made. Without a doubt, Annette was absolutely convinced that Shane Goode was somehow responsible for the death of his own daughter. She had not even responded to her mother's gentle reminder that state law demanded that an autopsy be performed or her suggestion that they wait until hearing the medical examiner's findings before placing blame. There had to be some explanation more reasonable, more satisfactory, more comforting, than what Annette was suggesting. No man, however uncaring, could purposely take the life of a beautiful, innocent child.

Annette's response was like bile erupting from deep in her soul. "He did this," she repeated. "I know him."

To Sharon Couch, the idea was inconceivable.

Late into the night she and her sister Carol, whom she had phoned from Annette's, sat talking. Always the conversation came back to the same agonizing question: How could a child so vibrant, so healthy, now be dead? Just days earlier Renee had been in her home, laughing, playing, a picture of good health.

Sharon thought back to Renee's December tricycle accident in the living room of the apartment. Was it possible, she wondered, that a blood clot might have gone undetected and ultimately led to the child's death? Carol, employed as an administrative assistant for a Houston surgeon, speculated that a seizure of some sort might have been the cause. Both were simply guessing, vainly searching for an answer.

Few chores in life are more stressful than making preparations for the funeral of a loved one. Immediate decisions are demanded at a time when the most simple mental tasks are incredibly difficult. Sharon moved about in a body drained of all energy, holding on to a faint hope that her efforts might somehow inch everyone closer to calm and peace. Yet in her heart, deep down where the most honest of truths remain guarded and private, she knew things would never again be the same.

Annette had agreed to have the funeral in nearby Hallettsville with burial in the family plot of the community's City Cemetery. Sharon asked if she wanted her to purchase a dress for Renee but Annette had opted to have her child buried in a navy blue sweater and corduroy pants that Sharon had bought her as a Christmas gift. "I want her to look like herself, like Renee," Annette said. She would, in fact, bring along her daughter's favored baseball cap to place in the casket, along with the bunny blanket and white stuffed bear Renee was seldom without.

Gary had asked if he might put a rosary in the casket.

On Monday morning he drove Sharon and Carol to Hallettsville where they selected a casket, arranged for a minister, and discussed plans for the brief, simple service Annette had requested. The funeral was scheduled for Tuesday afternoon.

Most traumatic of the preparations had been the decision regarding Shane. Annette's anger toward her ex-husband had not abated at all and she continued to adamantly insist that she did not want him attending the funeral. Still, Sharon struggled with what she viewed as a moral obligation to make him aware of the plans. Finally, she discussed it with her sister. "It seems to me," Carol said, "that he has a right to be there. Despite whatever differences he and Annette have had, Renee was his daughter, too." That said, she admitted concern over Annette's reaction should she see Shane.

"Still, I think you have to call him," she advised.

The brief conversation had been very unsettling to Sharon. She detected nothing in Shane's voice that suggested he shared the same pain she was feeling. No, he said, he had no idea what had caused Renee's death. She had seemed fine when she had finally gone to sleep. There was a whining quality to his voice which Sharon found off-putting.

Quickly changing the subject, she told him of the funeral plans. "Annette's pretty upset," she continued, explaining that her daughter had said that she didn't want him at the service. "Shane, please understand that I believe you have every right to be there. But I just hope and pray that we can avoid any kind of scene."

He understood her concern and for the first time a slight hint of emotion crept into his voice as he spoke of his daughter. "I want to see her," he said. "Do you think it would be all right if I came down early and left before the service?"

Relieved, Sharon gave him directions to the funeral home.

Carol stood across the room, waiting for her sister to hang up the receiver. "How did he sound?" she asked.

For a moment Sharon searched for an answer. "Cold," she finally replied. "Very cold."

. . .

What first struck Sharon Couch as she entered the small funeral parlor chapel in the early Monday evening hours was the absolute silence. Her footsteps made no sound against the thick carpet; her breathing seemed to echo from the paneled walls as she approached the casket. She had insisted that the funeral director contact her as soon as preparations were completed so that she might spend what she knew would be her last moments alone with her granddaughter. Soon family members would be arriving and the unsettling tradition of viewing the body would be under way. Then Sharon would have to summon strength she was not sure she possessed and turn her attention to comforting Annette.

Now, however, she needed time alone to say goodbye to the child, so tiny and innocent, who lay in the silk-lined casket.

For almost an hour she kept her quiet vigil, summoning warm memories that filled her thoughts like treasured snapshots. There had been two birthdays, three Christmases, a few trips and visits to park playgrounds, and a lot of smiles and hugs and kisses. Sharon wanted to remember them all, to mark them so indelibly that no passage of time could ever erase them. And for the moment she found comfort in the escape from the ugly questions and bitter accusations that had so poisoned her mind since learning of Renee's death.

The solitude ended with Annette's arrival. All composure the distraught mother had summoned during the day was immediately lost the minute she saw the casket. Crying uncontrollably, she wanted to lift her daughter into her arms, wanted to hold her. With no small amount of effort Sharon finally managed to calm her and the two women stood silently, arm in arm, sharing a grief unlike any either had ever known.

There was another matter—certain to add to Annette's angst— about which her mother had yet to inform her. Annette wanted Renee baptized and Sharon had spoken about it to the Lutheran minister who had agreed to conduct the funeral service. And while she had pleaded for him to understand the comfort it would afford her daughter, he had made it clear that the orders of the church forbade baptizing the deceased.

"Then would it be possible," Sharon had asked, "to have some kind of ceremony before the funeral? Isn't there something? It's very important to my daughter."

Reluctantly the minister had agreed to make a call to church authorities to see what, if anything, he might be allowed to do. Finally, he agreed to a brief blessing of the child and prayer prior to the funeral. Only the immediate family should attend, he said.

Perplexed throughout her adult life by the myriad rules and regulations of formal religion, Sharon Couch thought of herself as a Christian but for years had not been a regular churchgoer. The attitude of the minister, his unbending stance on the matter, gave her no cause to consider changing.

The news that Renee could not be baptized was an additional source of grief to her distraught mother. Annette had seen to it that Michelle was baptized when only a year old, and had joined the Mormon church two years earlier. In the aftermath of the separation and divorce from Shane, however, her faith had been shaken and visits to church had become increasingly infrequent. Now, she chastised herself: Why had she not put her own personal problems aside long enough to see to the eternal salvation of her baby?

Sitting in the pews of the dimly lit chapel, Annette said nothing for several minutes. Finally she got to her feet, inhaled a deep breath, and turned toward the door. Halfway up the aisle she stopped and turned back for a final look at the casket. "Do you think she's going to heaven?" she asked.

Sharon reached out to squeeze her daughter's hand. "Honey, she's already there. No question about it."

And with that, they walked together into the brisk Texas night, each drawing on the other's fragile strength and dreading the day that lay ahead.

///

Shane Goode arrived at the funeral home a few minutes after noon, dressed in a charcoal suit and accompanied by his father and brother.

Sharon explained to her daughter and the other family members— who had gathered at the rural farmhouse that had once been used as a weekend retreat—that she needed to leave early to oversee last-minute preparations. She was already in the chapel when her ex-son-in-law walked in.

He was pale and approached Renee's casket haltingly. Sharon was sure he had been crying. She watched as he stood at the casket for several minutes, staring silently. His hands appeared to be shaking and Sharon was certain that his teeth were chattering. It was Shane's father who finally put a hand on his shoulder and directed him to a nearby pew. Sitting there, Shane placed his hands beneath his chin and began to slowly rock back and forth. Tears streamed down his cheeks.

The young man sitting in the tiny chapel, just a few feet from his daughter, was not the cold, almost nonchalant Shane Goode with whom Sharon had spoken on the phone. His every mannerism was that of a genuinely grief-stricken father. *Maybe,* she found herself thinking, *he really did care about Renee.*

Sharon's apprehension over a possible conflict between Shane and her daughter grew as he lingered, occasionally getting to his feet to walk back to the casket. Soon his brother's girlfriend arrived, then Shane's first wife, Kaye, who had brought Tiffany.

They have a right, Sharon kept telling herself. Renee was theirs, too. But—please, God—let them leave before Annette arrives.

A sense of relief flooded over her as Shane finally walked from the chapel into the parking lot. Sharon, who had said nothing to him or his family in the chapel, followed Shane to his car where he stood, his head resting against the side door. She placed her hand on his shoulder and expressed her appreciation for the understanding he had demonstrated.

"I want to talk with Annette," he said.

"Shane," she replied, "this is not a good time. She's very upset and—"

"She thinks I had something to do with this." He again began to cry.

Sharon shook her head, surprised at the sympathy she was feeling for her former son-in-law. "I'm sure this is something that no one could have prevented. It's no one's fault. Maybe when we get the autopsy report back it will clear things up for everyone."

"I just don't understand how . . ."

"Last December Renee slipped and hit her head," Sharon said in an attempt to provide some measure of comfort. "I don't know, maybe that could have had something to do with it."

Goode lifted his head and for the first time looked at Sharon. "When?"

"I'm not sure. Sometime before Christmas. The X rays showed nothing serious."

Shane was no longer crying. Instead, he stared into the distance as if suddenly lost in thought. Across the parking lot he saw Annette's brother, free on an appellate bond, step from a car and look in his direction.

"I'd better be going," he said, the coldness which so disturbed Sharon returning to his voice. She stood alone in front of the funeral home long after the car disappeared, puzzled by his reaction, sure that she had told him something he hadn't previously known.

The sympathy she had felt for him moments earlier was quickly replaced by an emotion with which she was not at all comfortable. It was neither the time nor place to be feeling such anger.

///

The service, preceded by the finally agreed-upon blessing ceremony attended only by Annette, Michelle, and Sharon, was brief. Seated in the small flower-decorated chapel were members of the immediate family and a few friends. Among those who silently slipped in and out, their presence recorded only by a signature in the guest book, was Shane Goode's mother. Long estranged from her son and ex-husband, she had learned of Renee's death while scanning the obituaries in the Victoria paper.

The minister spoke of God's special interest in children, assuring the mourners that a glorious heavenly reunion was taking place even as they grieved. A recording of Dolly Parton's plaintive "I Will Always Love You" was played, there was a prayer, and then those in attendance began a somber parade past the casket.

In the adjoining cemetery, a sudden wind gust whipped at the blue canvas tent stretched over the gravesite as the casket was lowered into the ground.

Annette's hair, so perfectly coiffed when she arrived for the services, blew across her face, matting against her damp cheeks.

"Good-bye, baby," she said. "Mommy loves you."

Nine

In the late 1800s a man named Alvin Morgan, a Louisana
entrepreneur with equal parts vision and wanderlust, crossed over
into the Texas prairieland south of Houston, planning to establish a
town on the banks of Mustang Bayou. Officials of the Santa Fe railroad required a water stop for their steam engines, and Morgan had
quickly seen beyond the need for his wooden watering tower and hast-
ily built stock-loading pens and recognized the possibilities of expanding commerce. To accommodate the local ranchers weary of
lengthy trips to Houston and Galveston for supplies, he opened a
general store fashioned from a discarded railroad boxcar, and began
selling clothing, groceries, whiskey, and tobacco. As the community
grew, so did Alvin Morgan's fortune—and stature. When the town
reached such a size that the locals felt need of a proper name for the
place they called home, its founder got the honor.

Alvin thus began as did so many pioneer communities in Texas.
And through a century of quiet growth, a couple of destructive hur-
ricanes and one fabled fire—each causing its stubborn residents to
rebuild and start over—there has been little in its history to set it
apart.

Now that the population has reached sixteen thousand, many locals view the fact that Alvin is the home of superstar baseball-pitcher
Nolan Ryan as the town's greatest achievement.

Interstate 45 has made the city handy and attractive to NASA employees seeking a place other than Houston to raise their children. Alvin, like hundreds of other Texas communities located near thriving metropolitan areas, has greatly benefited from big-city industry while maintaining the charm and appeal of a small town. There are the church socials and rummage sales, meetings of the Rebekah Lodge and Kiwanis, pilgrimages to the high-school stadium on football Friday nights when the beloved Alvin Yellowjackets do battle, even a community college for those not inclined to leave town in pursuit of higher education.

And, in the tradition of communities of its size, Alvin has few secrets.

Word of the tragedy on Meadowview Street spread quickly, common knowledge throughout town long before the weekly edition of the *Alvin Journal* could be published.

The reaction was predictable. In coffee shops and cafeteria lines, PTA meetings and neighborhood gatherings, people spoke softly of the horrible thing that had occurred. Parents found themselves hugging their children a bit tighter, making more nighttime visits to bedrooms than usual, listening for the welcome sound of gentle breathing.

For friends and neighbors of the Goode family, the loss of Renee raised a disquieting question: Just how much pain and suffering could one family be expected to bear?

Carolyn and Donald Goode each had children by a previous marriage: She had three boys and a girl, he had four sons.

It was in 1977, while they were living in Pasadena, that Carolyn's ten-year-old daughter, Barbara, had been seriously injured when an automobile in which she was riding hit a bull that had strayed onto a farm-to-market road. The collision had thrown her through the windshield with such force that the first officer on the scene had to remove shards of glass from her mouth to allow her to breathe. She lived for six weeks following the collision before dying on the eve of stepbrother Shane's sixteenth birthday.

Then, in 1991, while the Goodes were living in Bryan, a second tragedy occurred. Carolyn's thirty-two-year-old son, Ernest, committed suicide. Apparently distraught over a separation from his wife, he hanged himself from a tree in the Goode backyard, his lifeless body discovered by his father.

And now the Goodes' granddaughter was dead.

/ / /

Late on the morning of January 31, Sharon Couch answered the phone to hear her daughter crying hysterically again. The outburst was unsettling in light of the fact that Annette had seemingly gained remarkable control of her fragile emotions in the days following the funeral. There was a lingering sadness about her and she seemed withdrawn at times, lost in thoughts she shared with no one, but she had also displayed an enviable strength in the aftermath of her child's death. After the graveside ceremony there had been no more tears, as if she simply had none left to cry.

What Sharon heard on the phone, however, was the return of heartbreaking vulnerability. Her daughter's strength had vanished in much the same way Houston's morning sun almost instantly burns off the city's predawn mist.

"I . . . I just got off the phone with Detective Duckworth," Annette said. It was necessary for her to pause and breathe deeply, summoning some degree of composure, before she could continue. "He told me . . . he told me that he'd just gotten the preliminary results from the medical examiner's office . . . and . . . and . . . they're saying that Renee died of pneumonia." Her voice became angry. "Pneumonia," she said as if spitting something distasteful from her mouth. "She wasn't even sick when she went over there that night. Not so much as a runny nose. I took her temperature before she left. How in God's name do you develop pneumonia in a matter of hours? Mother, it's impossible. . . ."

"I agree," Sharon replied. Her face felt flushed, hot, as she spoke. "What's the detective's number?"

Minutes later Bodie Duckworth was, for the second time that morning, trying to calm a woman caller who was becoming increasingly agitated as the conversation continued.

"I'd like to know who in the M.E.'s office gave you your information," Sharon demanded.

"Ma'am, I'm not allowed to give out that sort of information until the findings are official. All I can tell you is that the information is very reliable. I thought your daughter would like to know what was going—"

Sharon's voice drowned out the remainder of his sentence. "Look, I'm no doctor, but you and I both are smart enough to know that a child who has pneumonia doesn't run around the house playing, eating pizza, acting hyper, like my granddaughter did that night."

"I'm told there was congestion in the lungs," the detective offered.

"And that automatically means pneumonia?" Sharon challenged, unaware that she was now literally screaming into the phone.

It was only after she had regained some degree of composure that she mentioned Annette's accusations that Renee might have been abused. Were there, she asked, any such indications?

Detective Duckworth did not immediately reply. Annette Goode had made no mention of such suspicions to him. "Why," he finally asked, "wasn't I told about this?"

"I'm telling you now," Sharon replied.

Even as he hung up the phone, the detective was planning to call Shane Goode and ask that he stop by the police station.

/ / /

In what would become a pattern during the days to come, Sharon phoned her daughter to relay the skimpy bits of information she'd received from the the police and the M.E.'s office. Annette was no longer able to mask the anger she was feeling for those who refused to heed her urgings that the truth of Renee's death remained undiscovered. She was in no frame of mind to discuss such matters as autopsy findings. Thus it fell to her mother to seek the answers.

It was something Sharon had, in recent months, become quite adept at. During the preparation for Steven's trial, she had worked closely with a private investigator who gathered information for her son's defense. Lanky, slow-talking P. G. Walls had been an officer with the Houston Police Department for twenty years before becoming a private detective. He had been so impressed with Sharon's willingness and ability to do record searches and locate phone numbers and addresses that saved him precious time and lent clear direction to his pursuit that he'd offered her a job as an investigator following Steven's conviction. Sharon had accepted and, with Walls acting as her sponsor, soon had become a licensed private investigator.

What had impressed Walls even more than Sharon's eagerness and thoroughness was the remarkable strength she'd displayed during her son's ordeal. Not once had she ever mentioned the possibility of finding some legal loophole by which Steven might avoid punishment. All she asked was for the judicial system treat him fairly.

Sharon was as levelheaded and fair-minded as any person Walls had ever encountered in his law enforcement career, and for that, he genuinely admired her.

While the assignments Walls gave her had generally been limited to such mundane tasks as courthouse visits in pursuit of paper trails left by clients, she had learned a great deal simply by watching how Walls conducted investigations. Never, however, had she imagined she would use her newfound expertise to look again into a family matter.

Gathering times, dates, and names of potential witnesses in Steven's case had been trying. The decision to do whatever she could to determine the truth about her granddaughter's death would, she realized, be even more demanding.

She began visiting the library to read medical papers written by doctors who specialized in the field of infant deaths, compiling a list of experts whom she methodically began contacting. Each time she found a receptive ear she would carefully describe the circumstances of Renee's death and pass along the limited autopsy information she had been able to gather from her repeated calls to pathologists assigned to the case. Several of those she contacted had been sympathetic, even expressing puzzlement. She learned a great deal about SIDS, the Sudden Infant Death Syndrome that seemed to be the medical catch-all diagnosis when no clear explanation could be found. No one, it seemed, was able to offer more than what she already knew: It was rare, indeed, for an apparently healthy child of two to die while sleeping.

Sharon also began listening more carefully to her daughter. If, in fact, Annette's angry accusations were groundless, it was important that she somehow find out. In the meantime, however, she would adhere to her mentor's golden rule: She would remain open-minded, setting aside her own emotional involvement as much as possible.

"When you think of something—anything—that could be important," Sharon told her daughter, "write it down and give it to me." She also suggested that it was time Annette spoke with her ex-husband about what had happened the night Renee died.

It was the second week of a colder than usual February before Annette could summon the strength to do so, using her concern over his payment of her student loan as her excuse for the call.

"How are you doing?" Shane had asked, after assuring her that he'd mailed a check only days earlier. Annette fought the urge to scream her reply. *How am I doing? My baby's dead, you asshole. How do you think I'm doing?* Instead, she remained composed, easing the conversation to Renee's death. On the table in front of her, a tape recorder slowly spun, waiting to capture . . . what? A sudden outcry of guilt? Some plaintive plea for forgiveness?

No, he said, he'd not heard any recent news from the medical examiners. "I can't believe it's taking them so long."

"Shane, did Renee act different or anything that night?"

"She was fine, running around, playing; didn't even fuss much about going to bed. I just can't figure it out. One of those guys who called said they thought it might have been some kind of severe bronchial infection or something like that. I don't know if they're guessing or what. I just don't know."

"You didn't hear her coughing or anything during the night?"

"I was in my bedroom, but the kids were in there with her. Somebody would have heard."

"I just can't make myself understand it," Annette said before moving to another subject. "Did you have any insurance on her? You know, Mother took care of all the funeral arrangements and I think the bill's going to be pretty high. Like maybe five thousand dollars."

"Yeah, I've been thinking about that," he acknowledged. "I need to get hold of your mom. I have this policy at work. I think it's two thousand or something like that."

His voice softened. "You know, I can't imagine going through all that, getting things ready like she did. I had a hard enough time just walking into the funeral home, ordering flowers, stuff like that." He would, he said, phone her mother to thank her and discuss payment for the funeral expenses.

There was a brief silence before he continued. "I can imagine how you must feel," he continued. "I think about her all the time, and I wasn't around her half as much as you were."

Annette fought back her tears. "I can tell you, there's nothing worse."

"I know," he replied.

"Do you still have her car seat?"

"Yeah, it's in my room."

"And Michelle wants to know if you have her sleeping bag. . . ."

"I'll get that stuff together and bring it over pretty soon."

She was relieved when Shane directed the conversation back to the night of Renee's death. "The last time they called," he said, "they were still planning to run some more tests. Some results from ones they've already done haven't come back yet."

"Are they checking to see if maybe she ate something by accident?"

"That's what worried me at first," he responded. "There's a lot of medicine and stuff in the kitchen. I wondered if maybe she got into something she wasn't supposed to. But its all up way out of her reach. I just don't see any way . . ."

Annette's patience was wearing thin. The casual manner in which he spoke—as if discussing the death of a stranger instead of their own flesh and blood—caused her stomach to knot. "She usually didn't wake up once she went to sleep," she noted. "Did you have any trouble getting her to go to bed?"

"No, not really. I laid down with them all until she went to sleep."

"Was she the last to go to sleep or . . ."

"I think she was the first," he said. "The others watched the rest of some movie on TV."

"And no one heard her coughing? Or saw her tangled up in her covers or anything?"

"Nothing. Everything was fine. But the doctors just keep saying it had to be some kind of respiratory infection."

"I just don't understand it," she said, her composure almost at its end. She listened as Shane urged her to let him know when the loan payment arrived. "And," he added, "say hello to Michelle for me."

"Good-bye, Shane," she said before forcing herself to gently replace the receiver. Only then did she let out an explosive scream. She had hoped for some hint of genuine remorse, a sign, however small, that he was feeling pain or guilt. And she had heard none of that in his voice.

It was only after replaying the tape of their conversation several times that something finally caught her attention. While listening for what he *had* said, she had overlooked what he *hadn't*.

"Shane gave me a pretty detailed rundown of everything that went on that evening," Annette would later tell her mother, "and said there had been nothing that could have led to what happened. He was certain.

"But, remember the police saying that he told them Renee had hit her head while jumping on his bed? He didn't mention anything about it to me."

The reason, she was sure, was because it had never happened.

///

Sharon needed a break. Consumed by her children's troubles she had, for months, felt as if her own life was slipping away. Steven's trial and conviction for murder had so emotionally drained her that she had even given brief and frightening thought to suicide. She had seen the fear and despair in her son's eyes when the judge had sentenced him to serve ten years in prison, and her heart had ached with a pain she'd never thought possible.

Until Renee had died.

Now that renewed pain was compounded by the uncertainties surrounding her granddaughter's death. The medical examiner's preliminary conclusions, she felt, were absurd, little more than a bureaucratic attempt to sweep yet another case into the records and move ahead to the next. At the same time, however, she simply could not bring herself to embrace Annette's unbending conviction that Shane was somehow responsible for the child's death. Such evil was light-years beyond her comprehension. Annette, she feared, was teetering on the verge of a nervous breakdown, her mental frailty giving life to an out-of-control paranoia.

In recent weeks Annette had begun to dredge up new horror stories from her marriage to Shane.

She told of the time they had gone into a pet store and seen two kittens to which she'd been immediately attracted. Shane, she said, had bought them for her as an early birthday present and she'd named them Crystal and Sugar. As they grew, Sugar had begun to display an unexplainable dislike for him, hissing if he attempted to pick her up, scratching him on several occasions. Though Sugar was Annette's favorite, Shane quickly developed an undisguised hatred for the cat.

"I came home from work one day," Annette told her mother, "and Sugar was gone. I looked for her everywhere, driving through the neighborhood, calling her name. Finally, Shane came in and I asked if he'd seen her. He just looked at me with a smirk on his face and shrugged. All he would say was, 'You're not going to find her.'

"I knew that minute that he'd killed my cat. Sugar was in a Dumpster somewhere. Just because he didn't like her."

She was also firmly convinced that Shane continued to stalk her, occasionally parking his pickup in a lot near the condo, watching her comings and goings. She admitted that she'd never actually seen him, but was certain it was his pickup. When Sharon tried to suggest that she might be mistaken, Annette stood firm. It was pretty difficult not to recognize, she argued. She'd seen the black vehicle hundreds of times. She recognized the National Guard license plate, the paratrooper insignia on the back window. It was Shane's pickup, all right, even if she hadn't seen him seated behind the wheel. For whatever reason, the man who she was convinced had killed her baby continued to watch her.

It was all becoming too much for Sharon. In hopes of a brief respite from all the questions and allegations, she planned a trip to the family farm in Hallettsville. She had not visited Renee's grave since the funeral and wanted to do so. A friend, Kathy McCall, who she'd worked with at a Houston bank years earlier, accepted her invitation to join her for a weekend in the country.

Though the clean, almost sweet Gulf Coast air was invigorating and the rural quiet a welcome escape from the city's round-the-clock outcries, Sharon was still unable to distance herself from her worries. They had followed her on the two-and-a-half-hour drive, then weighed on her with their full strength as she stood alone in the City Cemetery, shading her eyes against a midday sun to look down on the grave of her granddaughter.

Later in the day, as she witnessed the overwhelming sadness her friend was attempting to hide, Kathy smiled and placed a hand on Sharon's shoulder. "It might help to talk about it," she suggested.

Sharon needed no more invitation than that. For hours they sat on the porch, watching as squirrels played along the tree limbs and soft coastal breezes caused wildflowers to nod in silent approval. Sharon confided her concerns regarding Annette's insistence that some premeditated harm had come to her child, of the seemingly lackadaisical attitude of the police, and the snail's pace with which the medical examiner's office seemed to be moving.

"You know," she said, "it's crazy how you fixate on some little thing, unable to get it out of your mind until it's grown into something that you're convinced might be really important."

"Like what?" Kathy wanted to know.

"They said when the girls tried to wake Renee she was lying on her stomach, her head resting on a pillow. It just doesn't sound right. She never slept that way. From the time she was a tiny baby it was impossible to get her to sleep on her stomach. She always slept on her back."

Then, as if mentally switching gears, she began to smile. "I brought her down here with me just before Christmas. That night she was all over the bed, turning, kicking, rolling over on me. Several times I'd wake and have to move her back over onto her side of the bed. So, I finally got up and did what I'd always done before. I made us a pallet on the floor, piling pillows all around it so she couldn't roll off of it in her sleep. There was this big, comfortable bed and there we were, sleeping on the floor in our little pillow fort."

Sharon was nodding as she spoke, the faint smile still visible. "We had some wonderful times."

It was almost dark before she had purged her sadness and completed what amounted to the first requiem for Renee she had spoken.

Afterward, the two women sat for some time, neither saying

anything as they watched dusk approach. The evening brought with it a welcome coolness and the rhythmic chorus of the countryside's invisible night creatures.

"There's somebody I think you should talk to," Kathy finally said. During the years of their friendship she had never mentioned that her brother was a highly decorated deputy with the sheriff's department in Orlando, Florida. Trained at the FBI Academy in Quantico, he had earned a reputation as an expert on serial killers and was called on to consult with law-enforcement agencies throughout the nation. "Maybe," she offered, "he might have some suggestions."

Sharon could not help but wonder how someone thousands of miles away might offer any insight. How could he be expected to answer a total stranger's questions when they had already twisted into senseless riddles?

"Just talk to him," Kathy urged.

Sharon finally nodded. Why not? She was willing to give anything a try.

///

Riggs Gay was surprised and pleased to hear his sister Kathy's voice when he answered the phone. After a few minutes of family catch-up conversation, Kathy briefly outlined the purpose of her call and put Sharon on the phone.

Gay repeatedly assured her she was not imposing on his evening at home as she detailed the case. Quite the contrary, he insisted. What she was telling him was quite interesting.

Only after she had provided him with what she knew of the investigation and the early findings of the medical examiner did he begin to question her.

"What I'm asking," he prefaced, "are things you need to find out if you haven't already; things that might be an indication of foul play—if, in fact, there was any."

Sharon liked him. His voice, businesslike but gentle, was that of someone whose attention seemed genuine. "I understand," she answered.

Under the circumstances she'd described, he said, if her granddaughter had been a victim of a homicide, chances were statistically good that she had died of some form of poisoning or from asphyxia— suffocation. "That's where you start," he explained, then began to tick off questions for which he did not expect her to have answers:

Did the coroner find any indication of petechiae—small pinpoints of hemorrhaging that generally accompanied suffocation—in Renee's eyes?

Was the sleeping bag the child had been lying on taken as evidence and were samples of any fluid on it tested?

Were the mattress and bedcovers in Shane's room taken and tested?

Had toxicology tests been done? What about vaginal and anal swabs?

Were photographs of the child as she was found by investigating police available?

Riggs Gay was talking not as a doctor might, but rather as a trained homicide investigator. Though far from jaded, it had always been his nature to eliminate the worst-case scenarios first, to initially view any death through eyes looking for evidence of criminal behavior. With modern forensic technology, it was generally quite easy to dispose of such suspicions, thus setting minds at ease and saving doctors and investigators a great deal of wasted time.

"I'm going to ask these questions," Sharon promised.

"When you've got the answers," Gay replied, "I'd like to hear back from you."

///

A few days later, Shane Goode drove from work to the Alvin Police Department for a meeting with Detective Duckworth, expecting finally to be briefed on the findings of the medical examiner.

Instead, he found himself answering the same questions he'd been asked immediately after Renee's death. Duckworth explained that they were necessary only so he might be sure he hadn't missed anything that would need to be included in his final report. Nothing more than a paperwork thing, he said.

In truth, he simply wanted another look at Shane Goode—to take measure of his demeanor, his body language—and hoped to somehow determine for himself if he was speaking with a man who might possibly be hiding a secret.

They talked for half an hour, Goode rotely responding to questions that retraced the final hours of his daughter's life. Seldom did his eyes stray from the floor in front of him.

Finally, Duckworth reached across his desk for a porcelain cup. "Want some coffee?" he asked.

"No, thanks."

Assuring his visitor that they were about through, the detective excused himself and walked into the hallway. He stood there for several seconds, his empty cup dangling from one finger, and looked back at the slumped figure seated at his desk. Shane was still staring at the floor.

Something, the detective thought to himself, isn't right about this guy.

Ten

Across the front of the redbrick building located in the 1800 block of Houston's Old Spanish Trail is a boldly lettered sign that renders the site unique among the nation's coroner's offices. It is known as the Joseph A. Jachimczyk Forensic Center of Harris County, one of the few governmental monuments to bear the name of the person still overseeing the work being done inside. It is a building filled with the dark history of the city, much of it recorded during Jachimczyk's lengthy tenure. Just to the south is Ben Taub Hospital, whose mazelike, unair-conditioned basement once served as the county morgue where the bodies of the famous and infamous were delivered.

From his 1957 arrival onward, the Harvard-educated Jachimczyk supervised autopsies of many of the city's luminaries. After reclusive billionaire Howard Hughes died during a plane trip back to the United States, it was Jachimczyk who provided proof to the skeptics that the body he'd examined was, in fact, that of the legendary Hughes. When socialite Joan Hill, a world-class horsewoman and wife of successful plastic surgeon Dr. John Hill, died mysteriously, it was Jachimczyk's autopsy, following an exhumation of the body, that had finally pointed investigators to Mrs. Hill's husband. Jachimczyk had also guided the forensic investigation of the gruesome serial murders committed by Dean Corll and Elmer Wayne Henley. And with each headline-grabbing pronouncement, each television appearance or interview with a true-crime writer, his image grew.

So did stories of the independent manner in which he ran his office. County commissioners—whose responsibility it was to oversee procedures and expenditures of the medical examiner's office—were rarely consulted. Seldom, however, did they complain. As one of the most visible and highly paid employees on the county payroll (earning $150,000 annually), the man they were chartered to oversee had evolved into a larger-than-life character despite his diminutive physical stature. Dressed in his trademark seersucker suits and always wearing a colorful bow tie, he could be charming or chilling, depending on the requirements of the situation. Oft-described as "intellectually intimidating," he commanded the respect of those who worked for him, the undivided attention of jurors in front of whom he testified, and inspired palm-sweating fear in his enemies. He routinely brushed aside any criticism or second-guessing about his office and its procedures with a huffy arrogance that generated genuine awe in those brazen enough to speak out.

His office, he would quickly remind anyone who questioned his budget or the effectiveness of his six-member staff of pathologists, performed between 2,500 and 3,000 autopsies annually.

"Dr. Joe," as he was known within the corridors of the Spanish Trail building, ran his office with a military-like command, assisted by his chief investigator, Cecil Wingo. Though not a doctor, Wingo was a man who could be counted on to arrive at crime scenes dressed in his white lab coat and whose hair-trigger temper was well known to fellow workers and local law enforcement. Cecil Wingo was, in the minds of most, clearly the second-in-command at the Harris County M.E.'s office.

Such was the case in 1994 when the autopsy of Katherine Renee Goode was one of the 863 which Harris County pathologists performed on bodies delivered from 14 surrounding counties that year.

Brazoria County, with no medical examiner of its own, had contracted the Harris County M.E.'s office for years to conduct all postmortem examinations of its residents at a cost of $900 per exam.

The responsibility for performing Private Autopsy #94-058—that of Renee Goode—was assigned to Dr. Eduardo Bellas, a Cuban national who, twenty years earlier, had come to the United States to join Jachimczyk's staff. In recent years, as Jachimczyk neared his seventieth birthday and had begun to hint at retirement, Dr. Bellas quietly hoped he would one day ascend to the position of chief medical examiner.

On the afternoon of January 23, however, his attention was focused on the tiny form that lay before him in one of the facility's four autopsy rooms. Speaking into the microphone located above the stainless-steel examining table, he began describing the body: ". . . that of a well-nourished, well-developed Caucasian female child appearing older than the stated age of two years . . . measuring thirty-five and one-half inches in length . . . weighing twenty-six pounds . . . scalp covered with blond hair measuring eight inches in length . . . hazel eyes . . . teeth in good condition. . . ."

Nowhere did he see evidence of injury.

Proceeding, he carefully made a Y-shaped incision into the child's chest and began a methodical examination of the vital organs, viewing, then weighing the heart, the brain, kidneys, liver, and pancreas. The lungs, he noted, were congested.

Only when he examined the trachea and bronchial tubes, did he find anything that he judged at all out of the ordinary. There, he found an abundance of bloody froth. And there was rupturing evident in the cerebellar tonsils. Combined with the presence of the bloody froth and the congestion in the lungs, it suggested the possibility that some manner of asphyxiation had caused the child's death.

Nothing, however, triggered suspicion of foul play. Thus, in his report, Dr. Bellas wrote, "It is my opinion that the cause and manner of death of the decedent, Katherine Renee Goode, are undetermined."

///

It was a finding that dumbfounded Sharon Couch, at first draining her of even the energy necessary for immediate anger. The anxious waiting, the pleading, the determined attempt to remain patient, had resulted in nothing. She would never understand why the results were not available until *after* her granddaughter had been buried. The trained medical minds of an office that operated on an annual budget of well over three million dollars had employed their knowledge, technology, and state-of-the-art testing procedures and found . . . nothing.

Dr. Bellas's report had answered not one of the questions that had begun to haunt even her restless sleep. And now, there were even more questions:

What resolution was there to be found in his statement? How could the word "undetermined" be allowed to dismiss the death of a human being with even the slightest measure of satisfaction?

Slowly, her anger returned, quickly spreading to include the bureaucracy of the judicial system. On the repeated occasions when she had phoned the M.E.'s office in hopes of learning the cause of her granddaughter's death, her calls had been routinely routed not to Dr. Bellas but to Cecil Wingo. He had always assured her that the findings would soon be forthcoming and politely urged her patience. It was important, he explained, that all test results be completed in an orderly fashion before an official determination was made. Dr. Bellas, Wingo would tell her in a reassuring manner, was a very thorough pathologist. Though frustrated by the delays, Sharon had been able to find some degree of comfort in the measured-out bits of information Wingo would share with her and the promise that her questions would soon be answered.

It is doubtful that she would have been comforted if she had been aware of the manner in which the medical examiner's office had handled a series of autopsies performed on the children of Claudette Kibble, a young Houston mother.

In August of 1986 an ambulance was dispatched to Kibble's northeast Houston home, where her seventeen-month-old son was found unconscious. The mother explained that he had suffered a seizure while she had been bathing him. Pronounced dead upon arrival at the hospital, the infant's body was delivered to the M.E.'s office where an examination revealed that he had, indeed, died of an epileptic seizure.

The autopsy was performed by Dr. Bellas.

Over the next four years, two other Kibble children arrived at the morgue following seizures that only their mother had witnessed. One autopsy report again listed the cause of death as "epilepsy," the other "undetermined," effectively announcing that no further investigation would be necessary.

Angry Child Protective Services officials passed along information that each of the three dead children had a different father, thus drastically reducing the possibility of some genetic nightmare. Still, the medical examiners' office remained steadfast in its findings. When the Harris County District Attorney's office, highly suspicious of the deaths, launched an investigation, it met with the same stubborn response. An assistant district attorney forwarded the medical examiner's paperwork on one of the Kibble children to the San Antonio Medical Examiner's Office and was told that the office there would have ruled the death a homicide.

It was only after a tearful Claudette Kibble confessed to her mother that she had murdered the children—she had suffocated one and drowned the others—and charges were filed that the Harris County Medical Examiner's Office finally amended its rulings, concluding that each death was a homicide.

///

Sharon made no attempt to disguise her desperation when she placed a long-distance call to Orlando, fulfilling her promise to Riggs Gay that she would pass along the medical examiner's findings. She described to him a telephone conversation she had finally had with Dr. Bellas.

Assuring Riggs that she had carefully asked each of the questions he had raised, she admitted they had not seemed to create any real interest.

"He said the autopsy had been completely negative," she recounted. "There was no evidence of any physical damage, no petechiae in her eyes."

"If suffocation occurs slowly enough," Gay responded, "there would be none." He was wary of offering her false hope that some more definitive answer remained possible. However, the background on the child's death, which she'd earlier provided him, had been more than simply intriguing—it was troubling.

He asked if she could get a copy of the autopsy report and prints of any photographs taken of the body by investigators on the morning they had arrived at the Goode house.

The thought of viewing pictures of Renee as she lay dead on the den floor sent a sudden chill through her. "I think I can," she said.

"I'd like for you to send them to me," he said. "There's someone here in Orlando who I'd like to have a look at them." Then adding a word of caution: "I may be just wasting your time, you know."

Sharon cut him off. No one expressing interest in her quest for the truth was wasting her time. "I'll send them to you as soon as I can get them," she said as she began writing the address he was giving her.

Her concern over her granddaughter's death had now evolved into a full-blown obsession.

///

In the days to come, Sharon's thoughts rarely strayed from her task. She contacted the Alvin police regularly, determined to prod the investigation along. With her sister helping her research medical journals, she located and read a paper written by a Canadian pathologist on the unexplained deaths of children and contacted her. After listening to the story which Sharon had become so adept at telling, the doctor volunteered to look at the tissue slides taken during the autopsy if they were sent to her. Sharon phoned Detective Duckworth to share the news, providing him the doctor's number and urging that he contact her.

Several weeks passed before Sharon, her thin patience exhausted, again placed a long-distance call to Canada, learning that the slides had never been sent.

It was only then that she began to accept the fact that the police were no longer actively investigating the case. The medical examiner's ruling had, in effect, been the closure they needed.

Detective Duckworth, weary of confrontations and convinced no avenue of investigation remained, turned his attention back to narcotics and quit returning her calls. Those in the M.E.'s office who spoke with her insisted there was nothing more that could be done.

During one of her final conversations with Cecil Wingo, he tried once more to explain to her that "negative autopsies" were not that uncommon. Death, he said, sometimes comes in the most unbelievable ways. With that he had put forth a couple of theories that might have sounded comical had they not so infuriated her.

There was a possibility, he offered, that dust mites from the sleeping bag she'd slept in might have somehow invaded Renee's respiratory system and caused her death. Or, he continued, there had been a rare case reported in the Philippines where a child, in the throes of a horrifying dream, had been literally frightened to death in her sleep.

Absurdity aside, the message he was delivering was clear: It was time to let go, to accept the unacceptable.

It was a message Sharon chose to ignore. If neither law enforcement nor forensic experts would help, she would take her cause to the public. She would have to go all the way to Dallas before finding a sympathetic ear. There, officers of a nonprofit organization known as the Texas Association of Missing and Exploited Children, listened to her story and agreed to lend modest financial support to her latest idea.

Soon she and Annette were posting flyers in the windows of businesses throughout Alvin, Houston, and other surrounding suburbs. Daily they would walk among shopping centers, talking with store managers, pleading their case. In time, the photograph of a smiling Renee greeted patrons entering fast-food restaurants, grocery stores, Laundromats, and video arcades. The message on the flyer was simple: Anyone with any information concerning the death of Renee Goode was urged to call Sharon's number.

Soon, the same plea appeared on two billboards located in Alvin. One was placed on the highway leading from Houston, the other at the corner of Gordon—the city's main thoroughfare—and Meadowview, just a few blocks from the Goode house.

Though she would admit it to no one, Sharon knew there was little chance that some stranger might actually have information about Renee's death. On the other hand, the flyers and billboards would serve as constant reminders to Shane Goode and his family that the matter was not closed.

. . .

It was in late March that Donald Goode arrived at the police station, angrily looking for Detective Duckworth. His family, he said, was being harassed. There were hang-up phone calls at all hours. Rarely did a morning pass that he didn't find copies of the flyer bearing Renee's picture scattered in his yard. And there was that damned billboard which he and his wife had to drive past daily.

Goode was convinced the cruel mind games being played on his family were instigated by the police and insisted on filing a formal complaint. His wife, he said, suffered from chronic high blood pressure and the stress was making the problem worse.

"Sir," Duckworth replied, "I assure you the police have nothing to do with any phone calls or flyers. Or the billboard."

"The number for the police department's on it," Goode argued.

"That's right," the detective said, "but we had nothing to do with putting it up."

"Then it's got to be Annette," he said. "And probably her crazy mother."

Duckworth did not confide the fact he shared Goode's suspicions. Instead, he sought to calm him, reviewing the investigation that had been ongoing since they first met. He told him of the coroner's difficulties in determining the cause of death, of the frustration such a troubling case breeds.

"You're aware, I'm sure," he finally said, "that there are those who continue to believe your son is somehow responsible for the little girl's death."

"Yeah, I know." The anger had disappeared from Goode's once-booming voice. He made no mention of Shane's recent behavior, which had begun to trouble him and his wife. On the rare occasions when Carolyn had mentioned Renee's death to her stepson, his face would quickly turn red with anger, then he would storm from the room.

Donald Goode stared across the desk at the detective for several silent seconds. "I have some concerns about that myself," he finally said.

He was not alone.

. . .

Sunny Bradley, a thirty-year-old divorcée who worked as a window clerk at the post office with Shane, had been so troubled by Renee's death that she had attended her funeral, knowing all the while that she would not be welcomed either by Shane or Annette.

For eight months she and Shane had lived together—before one of his customary holiday-season "jokes" had brought an abrupt end to their relationship. In the months prior to their breakup, they had even begun to talk of marriage and he had broadly hinted that she could expect an engagement ring as a Christmas present. Too excited to keep it secret, Sunny had shared the news with a few close friends at work. In time, however, she would have to admit to those who asked that there had been no ring under the tree and that any discussion of marriage had come to an abrupt end.

Embarrassed and weary of Shane's behavior, she had finally asked him to move his things from her apartment. In retrospect, she would wonder why she had not done so sooner. Though she considered herself a strong woman, she had allowed herself to be manipulated. She routinely overlooked his lies, and turned her head to Goode's often strange behavior. Only after dismissing him from her life had she taken a hard look at the man she had considered marrying and seen his dark side: the Shane Goode who often retreated into a fantasy world, yet always became angry when she suggested that he did so; who constantly worried about money, even when his phone bill once reflected three hundred dollars in charges to sex-talk numbers in a single month. Finally, there had been his reaction to the death of Renee. When she had brought the subject up, he dismissed it quickly, as if talking about someone to whom he had no blood ties at all.

Shortly after Renee's funeral, Joanne Chadderdon had contacted Annette to tell her that "a woman named Sunny Bradley" had called to say she wanted to talk with her. "She said it was important," the lawyer said. "Do you know her?"

"No," Annette replied, "but I know who she is."

What she didn't say was that she had not the slightest interest in talking with any of Shane's old girlfriends.

Eleven

Sunny's urge to contact Annette grew even stronger in the weeks following the funeral. Resigned to the fact that Annette was not going to return her call, she wrote a letter and included with it a small gift that she felt the bereaved mother might like.

Unaware that Annette had moved into her own apartment, Sunny mailed it to Sharon Couch's home.

For several days after the package arrived, Sharon debated over whether to pass it along to her daughter. Concerned about Annette's still ragged emotional state and aware that Sunny had been involved in a relationship with Shane, she worried that whatever the parcel contained might be upsetting.

Finally, she opened it herself.

What she read was a moving, compassionate note written from one mother to another. Sunny described her feelings for her own son and daughter and the impossibility of even imagining the loss of one of them. She wrote that she had met Renee on one occasion when Shane had brought her and Tiffany by the apartment for a brief visit.

"I am enclosing a pair of earrings that Renee played with when she was here," she wrote. They had been lying on her dining room table and as soon as Renee had seen them she began trying to put them on. Sunny had helped her, held her to a mirror so that she might see herself, then watched as she danced around the room, smiling, shaking her head as she modeled the oversized silver drops. "Renee had wanted to take them home with her," Sunny's letter continued, "but I didn't let her. Now I wish I had. I just thought you might like to have them."

She concluded with a repeated request that Annette call her and a final observation that jumped from the page at Sharon.

Sunny, like Annette, feared that Shane might have had something to do with the death of his daughter.

For some time Sharon sat holding the earrings, letting her mind form a picture of a vibrant, happy Renee wearing them, doing her child's dance. In time, however, her thoughts returned to the letter. It was heartfelt, a gesture of genuine kindness that Annette should be aware of. But what of the suggestion that Sunny viewed Shane in much the same light as did Annette? Was it possible they were simply two women who shared a mutual anger over similar failed relationships? Were their respective feelings for Shane so shaded by hatred that their suspicions were only imagined?

Despite her efforts to support Annette, Sharon had repeatedly reminded herself that the only way a search for the truth could be properly conducted was by avoiding hasty conclusions. For that reason, she had continued to give Shane Goode the benefit of doubt. On those occasions when she felt her resolve slipping, she would ask herself the question that her mentor, P. G. Walls, had explained was the most important in any investigation: Where is the motive?

It was a question for which she had no satisfactory answer.

///

The three women were seated in the living room of Sharon's home, each at first visibly uncomfortable. After reading the letter, Annette had phoned Sunny and during a brief but pleasant conversation suggested they meet. Shane had been living with Sunny during the time he and Annette were at odds over the paternity testing and Annette hoped she might have some answers to questions she had regarding his attitude toward Renee.

Hesitantly at first, Sunny recounted conversations between her and Shane, repeatedly assuring Annette that nothing she was saying was meant as a cruelty directed at her. "There are just some things that I think you should know," she explained.

Annette liked her instantly. She liked the straightforward manner in which Sunny responded to her questions. There was a no-punches-pulled honesty about the woman seated across the room from her that quickly established an atmosphere of trust.

During the time she and Shane had lived together, Sunny said, he had told her about Renee's birth. At the time, however, he did not even know the child's name or whether it was a boy or a girl. "He only referred to her as 'Annette's child,' " she said.

Annette only shook her head, saying nothing in response.

"He was very upset about it," Sunny continued. "He told me that he'd tried to get you to have an abortion." The baby, she surmised, would have already been several months old at the time, yet Shane made it clear that he wanted nothing to do with it.

"When the court ordered him to take the paternity test," she said, "he was really angry. He said he didn't feel he should have to pay child support.

"I remember asking him several times if he had picked up the results of the test and he always had some excuse. One afternoon, after I'd been on him about it for some time, he finally said he would go by his lawyer's office and pick them up. But when I got home he said it had been raining too hard and he'd decided not to make the drive. When I asked why he didn't just pick up the phone and find out, he just stormed out."

The results from the tests and the court-ordered support payments, she recalled, had made him furious. "He said that if he was going to have to pay child support, he was going to ask for weekend visitation rights—just to make you mad."

The thing that seemed to concern Shane most, she said, was that he might be forced to sell his pickup to come up with the money. Finally, though, he'd gone to his father, who agreed to loan him five thousand dollars.

During the time they had lived together, Sunny remembered, he was always complaining of financial hardships. She'd done what she could, even putting him in touch with her insurance carrier who saved him five hundred dollars on car insurance.

He had not, she volunteered, been an easy person to live with.

For the first time Annette smiled, as a question she herself had been asked so often ran through her mind: Why had this woman stayed so long with him?

It was the same question Sharon Couch, a silent observer of the conversation, privately wondered about both of the women seated in her living room.

For days after their meeting, her conversation with Annette troubled Sunny. She found herself replaying Annette's questions and her responses in hopes there was something left unsaid that might lend some degree of comfort.

She had tried to be as honest as possible. When Annette had asked how she perceived the relationship between Shane and Renee on the one time she saw them together, Sunny had returned to the anecdote about the earrings. "While she was dancing around, showing them off," she said, "she went over and gave Tiffany a kiss. Then she came over to me and kissed me. But when Shane asked for one, she ignored him."

Had she been aware of any insurance Shane might have taken out on Renee?

It seemed, she'd said, that he'd checked on the possibility of taking out health insurance, but she wasn't certain.

Several days after her meeting with Annette, Sunny recalled a message that had been left for Shane on the apartment answering machine months earlier. The caller had identified herself as an agent for State Farm Insurance and said she was "getting back to him on the policy he'd asked about and needed the spelling of his daughter's name."

When she had relayed the message to him, Shane had quickly dismissed it with an explanation that he was thinking about taking out medical insurance on Renee, a child he'd repeatedly insisted he wanted nothing to do with.

Now, as she thought back on the conversation, Sunny recalled Annette saying that she had personally called the insurance company and had Renee added to Shane's company policy shortly after she was born. "Shane and I were still married at the time," Annette had explained, "so I did it without even bothering to tell him."

Finally, Sunny dialed the number of State Farm.

"Hi," she said to the agent taking her call. "This is Sunny Bradley. I'm going to be married soon to Shane Goode—he's one of your policy holders—and I'd like some information about additional coverage." As she spoke, she struggled to maintain a casual tone. "We'll be combining our families," she explained, "so what I'd like to do is take out the same coverage on my children that he has on his. Could you please tell me what that is?"

The agent said it would take only a minute to call the information up on the computer.

"Yes," she said just minutes later, "here it is. Your fiancé has life insurance policies on Tiffany Goode and Renee Goode."

"For how much?"

"Fifty thousand dollars on each," the agent replied.

Sunny's next call was to Annette.

///

Later that evening, Annette telephoned her mother to relay the information. There was no hint of surprise in her voice. "Mother," she defiantly asked, "who takes out a fifty-thousand-dollar life insurance policy on an eighteen-month-old child he's never even seen?"

Sharon Couch was momentarily speechless.

The elusive motive, she knew, had been discovered.

Twelve

For Detective Bodie Duckworth, the case—he wondered, at times, if it could really even be called that—had no handle onto which he could get a grasp, no real direction signals for him to follow. Since that January morning when he'd walked into the Goode house, there had been nothing to indicate that Renee Goode's death should be viewed as a possible homicide. And hadn't the medical examiner's findings ultimately confirmed his decision not to consider the Goode home as a crime scene?

He had to admit that the steadily increasing hostility displayed by Sharon Couch and her daughter disturbed him, but he'd heard such accusations and anger before. He had seen similar obsessions, with unrealistic expectations voiced by a victim's loved ones, demanding some magical solution that might end their pain. Duckworth felt sympathy for their loss but saw nothing in their claims offering any kind of substantial clue.

Sure, Shane Goode troubled him, but strange behavior was no probable cause for arrest. Who, for God's sake, plots and carries out a murder when there are no less than six potential witnesses in the house? It made no sense. Still, his talk with Shane had been unsettling to the point that he'd phoned Jeri Yenne, a Brazoria County assistant district attorney, for any advice she might have to offer. Her interest had seemed casual at best. Was there any indication of a motive? she had asked. Maybe a large insurance policy on the child? Duckworth told her he'd found nothing.

Perhaps, she had finally suggested, the matter could be set to rest by persuading Goode to submit to a polygraph test.

When Duckworth asked, Shane had immediately agreed, then failed to appear, phoning later to say he'd had car trouble. Twice more Duckworth had scheduled the test but Goode didn't show. He had, he finally told the detective, grown tired of answering the same questions over and over. "There's no way I would ever do anything to hurt my child," he insisted, dismissing the idea of being polygraphed.

And with that the detective had, for all practical purposes, put the matter to rest. Even if Shane Goode were to take the polygraph test and come across as an off-the-charts liar, what good would the knowledge be? There was no evidence, no history that marked him as capable of such an unthinkable deed. What existed was a medical examiner's report that said there was no way to definitively say how the victim had died. To prove that someone is guilty of a crime, it is necessary first to establish that a crime has been committed. The M.E.'s ruling had effectively blocked that first important step.

Translation: case closed, before ever opened.

Still, Duckworth had spoken with several doctors Sharon had asked him to contact and had looked into the possibility of having a second set of tissue-sample slides from the autopsy made and sent to them. That idea had been dismissed when he'd learned that the cost would be $637 for each set of slides and that there was no money in the department's budget for such expenditures. And, in truth, what could someone thousands of miles away see that the doctor who actually conducted the autopsy hadn't?

The entire matter was little more than a growing list of questions without answers, innuendo and accusation without a hint of fact to serve as foundation. Duckworth felt as if he was trying to hold quicksilver in his hand.

Now, there was this new suggestion that Goode might have murdered his daughter to collect on an insurance policy, which had spawned another round of angry accusations and grasping questions.

Detective Duckworth was therefore relieved when word reached him that his chief was loaning him to a newly formed narcotics task force in Galveston County. He eagerly accepted the new assignment, confident that he'd taken the investigation of Renee Goode's unexplained death as far as he possibly could.

///

Needless to say, it was not an attitude Sharon Couch shared.

Unaware that Duckworth was no longer pursuing the case, she contacted him to inquire about the testing procedures that were being done on the sleeping bag in which Renee had lain on the night of her death. It had, she understood, been sent to the Department of Public Safety forensic lab where it would be tested for any sign of body fluids.

Duckworth had seemed evasive as he told her that he had not yet received any results. Sharon had sensed a dismissive tone in his voice and quickly ended the conversation.

Then, as had become her pattern after contact with anyone at the Alvin Police Department, she spent the remainder of her day fuming. Desperate, she finally telephoned P. G. Walls. If anyone could give her direction, it would be the man who had helped her become a private investigator.

"They're not going to do a damned thing," she told the private investigator. "I've begged, I've gotten angry, I've tried giving them information, and nothing works," she said. "They just don't care."

As he listened, Walls already had a good idea of what was taking place. "It sounds like they're getting ready to cold file it," he said.

Sharon's brief silence communicated her puzzlement. "What do you mean, cold file?" she asked.

"It means they put the case file into the back end of some filing cabinet and everybody forgets it's even there," Walls explained. Throughout the nation, he knew, there were literally thousands of such cases, ranging from serial murders to petty theft, which were routinely marked "inactive" and stored away while detectives went in pursuit of new, more solvable crimes. The only way a "cold file" case was ever reactivated was if the perpetrator walked into the station and was successful in finding someone with time enough to listen to his confession.

Sharon was far from ready to let that happen. "Can we get someone else involved? What about the Texas Rangers? Would it help to contact the attorney general's office?"

"Let me call down to Alvin first," Walls urged, "and see what's going on."

/ / /

If, in fact, Sharon had an ally in her frustrating quest, it was in the form of a man whom she had never met—the forensic pathologist in Florida with whom Riggs Gay had put her in touch. During her telephone conversations with Dr. William Anderson in Orlando, the pathologist had confided his doubts that Renee had died of natural causes. His opinion, he cautioned, was little more than professional guesswork, however, and he would need to see autopsy photographs and view the tissue slides under his own microscope. He warned that medical examiners routinely discarded tissue slides after a certain length of time—generally six months following an autopsy—so time was of the essence.

"I'll get them for you," Sharon declared, giving no consideration to the fact she did not even know the process by which such things were handled.

"It could be expensive," Dr. Anderson warned, "and still might not reveal anything new."

"I'll get them for you," Sharon repeated.

She spent the next several days on the phone, first to the Harris County Medical Examiner's office—where she was told that a court order would be necessary before they could legally release the requested material—and then to the Brazoria County D.A.'s office. Sharon found herself talking with Assistant District Attorney Jeri Yenne, explaining her need and pleading for quick service of the necessary court order. "I'll have to speak with the doctor who is requesting the photographs and slides first," Yenne explained. "I'd like to know more about what is actually going on here. Have him call me before five o'clock."

Sharon detected a cold, businesslike tone in Yenne's voice that had become all too familiar to her in days past. Once again it had taken great restraint on her part to refrain from unleashing a blistering tirade against the insensitive, bureaucratic maze of the legal system.

"I'll contact him right now," she said

Moments later, she found herself in the position of refereeing a battle of egos. Catching Dr. Anderson in his office just before he was to leave for the weekend, Sharon explained her difficulties in obtaining the court order. "Well," the doctor replied, "just have the district attorney call me Monday."

Nervous and frustrated, Sharon explained that Yenne had specifically requested that he telephone her. "Before five o'clock," she hesitantly added.

The sarcasm in Dr. Anderson's laugh was easily detectable. "Well, bless her little heart," he said. "I guess she's the only person who is busy, huh?"

Sharon's patience was paper-thin. "*Please,* Dr. Anderson. . . ."

"I'll phone her immediately," he said. "Give me the number."

Breathing a sigh of relief, Sharon had but one more obstacle to overcome. The cost of recutting the tissue samples to provide a new set of slides, she had been told, would be $637, far more than she had in her checking account.

She would have to borrow the cash to pay for the money order she planned to hand-deliver to the M.E.'s office.

///

A couple of days later, P. G. Walls phoned Sharon to tell her he'd had a conversation with Sergeant Todd Arendell, the supervisor in charge of the Alvin P.D.'s investigative unit. "I've got good news and bad news."

"Give me the bad news first," Sharon moaned. "Let's get it over with."

"The sleeping bag," he said, "the one that the DPS is supposed to be testing—the police never even took it out of the Goode's house. They've never even had it, much less sent it off for any tests."

The sudden anger Sharon felt was paralyzing. Why would they let her think someone, somewhere, was doing something when in truth no one was even trying? She cursed under her breath.

Her voice was without the slightest hint of energy or anticipation as she asked for Walls's good news.

"The case," he said, "has been reassigned to a female detective named Sue Dietrich. She'd like to meet with you and Annette as soon as possible."

Sharon could muster no enthusiasm. Given a choice, she would like nothing better than never to see another member of the Alvin Police Department for the rest of her life.

Thirteen

Sue Dietrich's ascent to the rank of Detective Corporal in the Alvin Police Department had been a long and not always pleasant climb.

A resident of the community since she was six years old, she graduated from the local high school and community college, married, raised a family, and had never seriously entertained thoughts of moving from the comfortable place she called home.

It was in the early eighties, newly divorced and working as a civilian dispatcher for the department, that she began to consider police work as a career. When three patrol officer positions came open, she studied for and took the required test, only to be told later that her score ranked fourth on the list of applicants for the three available jobs. Disappointed, she returned to her dispatching duties with plans to reapply the next time a position came open.

A couple of weeks later, however, a resigning officer shared a secret that sent her in quick search of an attorney. The officer, leaving for a job in another city, confided to her that he had been instructed by the chief to alter the test scores to make certain that the Alvin Police Department remained all-male. Her score, he said, had actually been the best of all the applicants tested.

The police chief was fired following an investigation into the sexual discrimination suit Dietrich filed against the City of Alvin. When the city attorney contacted her with what he hoped was an amicable resolution to the matter—he offered her a job on the police force, beginning immediately—Dietrich quickly turned it down. She had no interest in getting the job that way, she explained, but was satisfied that the man who ordered her test scores altered had been dismissed. With that she dropped her lawsuit and took a dispatching job with the nearby League City Police Department. She also enrolled at the police academy at Houston Community College, more determined than ever to become a full-time officer.

Two years would pass before she reapplied to the Alvin Police Department. In July of 1983, she was hired as a patrol officer, effectively bringing to an end the "good-ol'-boy" era of Alvin law enforcement.

It took little time for the mother of two to prove herself and gain the respect of her fellow officers. If there was concern that a woman could not efficiently deal with the city's weary routine of domestic disturbances, break-ins, burglaries and the occasional Saturday-night drunk and disorderly, it quickly disappeared. In short order, Officer Dietrich advanced from patrol to a special county-wide investigative unit and was soon responsible for the headline-making arrest of a high-profile Angleton businessman. Soon thereafter came word from an informant that a group of Brazoria County underworld figures had taken out a contract on her life. Sue greeted the news with the observation that she must be doing something right if the local criminal element was that concerned over her investigative abilities.

For three years she worked as a narcotics investigator, and, once promoted to the rank of detective, took on the added responsibility of training newly hired officers. By 1994, Detective Dietrich was not only one of the most experienced officers on the force but one of its most respected.

She had followed the Goode case from a careful distance, mindful of the departmental rule that prohibited any officer from interfering in the case of another. It did not, however, prevent her from hearing things: that the Harris County Medical Examiner's office had, in effect, blunted any investigative progress with its "undetermined death" ruling; that the child's father was, at least unofficially, suspected of some manner of foul play; and that the family of Renee Goode was decidedly upset over what it perceived to be a lack of genuine interest on the part of the detective who had been assigned the case.

Sue Dietrich said nothing of her interest or the quiet empathy she was feeling for Sharon and Annette, two women she'd seen only from a distance when they'd come to the station to speak with Duckworth. She reminded none of her coworkers that she, too, had once lost a child.

Sue understood all too well the grief and frustration such a tragedy could cause.

His name was Tommy and he had been just seventeen months old when a rare virus that attacks the organs of only the very young and very old claimed his life. It had come suddenly, settling in his lungs and making breathing difficult. Sue Dietrich had immediately taken him to the pediatrician, describing her child's irritablity, his refusal to eat, and the fact that she could not even touch him without him crying in pain. The doctor's first reaction was that the child was suffering from a severe attack of asthma but suggested blood tests before making a diagnosis. Just two hours later, after reviewing the tests, she telephoned Sue and urged her to get her son to a hospital as quickly as possible. The doctor admitted she wasn't certain what might be wrong, but did feel it was serious.

At Children's Hospital in Houston. Tommy was treated as an asthma patient, placed beneath an oxygen tent in an effort to relieve the labored breathing which seemed to be worsening by the minute.

Sue Dietrich had been in the hospital room when, just a day later, her child slipped into a coma. A renowned specialist from Chicago was flown in to consult but soon admitted that there was nothing he could do to prevent the inevitable. Another week passed before an attending doctor finally approached Sue and her husband to explain that all signs of brain activity had disappeared and to ask if they wished to have their son taken off the respirator. It was a decision she could not summon the courage to make.

Later that day, the distraught couple made a brief trip back to Alvin so Sue might shower and pack clean clothing before returning to keep vigil over her child. They were met at the door by her mother. She was in tears as she told her daughter of the phone call she'd just received from the hospital. "Tommy's heart stopped beating," she said.

. . .

It was on a gloomy July Saturday afternoon, twenty years later, that Sue Dietrich sat alone in her home, thinking back on those traumatic days. At least, she found herself thinking, the cause of her child's death had ultimately been explained to her. Still, it had never really occurred to her what comfort such knowledge could provide, until she had contemplated the anguish of those who loved Renee Goode and who were now endlessly haunted by unanswered questions.

Finally, she reached for the phone and dialed the number of her sergeant. The family, she decided, deserved an answer.

Todd Arendell was surprised to hear from his detective on her day off. He was not surprised by her request. Yes, he told her, the Goode case had been placed in the inactive file after Detective Duckworth was assigned to the narcotics task force.

"Would you mind if I picked it up and worked on it?" she asked.

"Not at all," Arendell replied.

///

The following Monday morning she retrieved Duckworth's case file from the records division, made a copy for herself, and for the next several evenings sat at her kitchen table, reading and rereading officers' reports, witness statements, and, finally, the autopsy findings. It was the latter that most troubled her, not so much because of what it said but rather its lack of uniqueness. She compared it to numerous routine autopsy reports filed on adults and saw much the same jargon, the same basic fill-in-the-blank style. For an innocent child, a baby, she thought, there should be something different: perhaps something that demonstrated more concern, more compassion. Instead, the death of Renee Goode appeared to have been evaluated with nothing more than the clinical dispatch required by law. And it angered her.

For some time she stared at the cover sheet of the medical examiner's report, setting to memory the brief, dismissive statement: "It is my opinion that the cause and manner of death of the decedent,

Katherine Renee Goode, are undetermined." Below it was the signature of Dr. Eduardo Bellas, forensic pathologist.

She had no idea what more might have been done, yet there had to have been something that would advance the findings out of the troubling gray area of "undetermined," someone willing to look closer and question harder until a definitive answer was finally reached.

She contacted P. G. Walls, the private investigator she had been told was working for the victim's family, and again heard of the bitter feelings the mother and grandmother had for the Alvin Police. "I know," she told Walls, "that they are going to think it is nothing more than a continuation of the runaround, but I'd like to talk with them."

///

"The first thing I want you to understand," the detective said, "is that I wasn't assigned to this case. I asked for it. And I wouldn't have done so if I didn't think there was something more that could be done with it." Sue Dietrich was again at her dining room table as she spoke, this time with Sharon and Annette seated across from her. Having them come to her home instead of the police station, she felt, might offer a more comfortable climate in which to get acquainted. It would, she knew, also remove her visitors from the familiar sights and sounds that were sure to rekindle their negative feelings about the handling of the investigation.

She would, Sue explained, like to go back to square one. Though she had read the reports, she wanted to hear everything again. In front of her was a yellow legal pad on which she'd written several pages of questions she planned to ask.

For the next two hours she listened as Annette described the events leading up to Renee's final visit with her father, of the phone call alerting her that something horrible had happened, and the scene at the Goode house when she arrived. Annette detailed her stormy relationship with Shane and played the tape she'd made of the telephone conversation she'd had with her ex-husband in which he denied having any insurance on Renee other than the small policy he had taken out at his work. And she told of the information Sunny Bradley had shared with her.

Annette was certain that Shane Goode had murdered her daughter.

Sue studied her visitor as she spoke, watching as her emotions hopscotched from calm control to anger and tears. What she saw was a fragile young woman harboring enormous guilt for having allowed her daughter to make the fatal overnight visit—a woman still wrestling with her feelings about the man to whom she'd been married. At times, it seemed to the detective, it was an effort for Annette to muster the anger she displayed. Sue had seen it before: abused wives who hated their husbands for the physical and mental damage they routinely delivered, yet who, for reasons they could not begin to explain, still held deep-seated positive feelings about them.

Sharon Couch, on the other hand, was the controlled one. She wanted answers as desperately as did her daughter, yet was willing to let all pieces of the puzzle be assembled before allowing her suspicions to evolve into hard truth. Sue was impressed by the meticulous manner in which she had prepared her own case file, bound in a notebook and brought to the meeting. Using the techniques Walls had taught her, Sharon had assembled a variety of documents, from Renee's medical records to a detailed time-flow chart that recounted the final months of her daughter's marriage to Shane Goode. She had written records of every phone conversation she had made to the police, the medical examiner's office, and doctors whom she had contacted throughout the country. She had a file of neatly photocopied articles from medical journals, each dealing with symptoms similar to those which led to her grandchild's death.

Sharon Couch had clearly been doing her homework.

She told the detective about her conversations with the Orlando pathologist, Dr. Anderson, and of the fact that he was reviewing the autopsy photos and tissue slides which had finally been sent to him. Dietrich wrote down his number with a promise that she, too, would be calling him.

For the moment, however, it was most important that she get a feel for the characters in the tragic drama that was being outlined to her. Each question she asked, Sue quickly realized, bred a half dozen more.

"After you contacted Shane to tell him that you were pregnant and he suggested you have an abortion," she asked, "what was your reaction?"

Annette was silent for a moment before lifting her head and staring squarely across at the detective. "I told him I wouldn't do it for him again."

"Again?"

Annette nodded. "I'd gotten pregnant not long after we were married and he'd convinced me that the time wasn't right for us to have a baby. We argued about it some, but finally I agreed to have the abortion."

The question Sue had for Sharon was answered before she even asked it. The look on Sharon's face made it clear that she had not known.

For so long Sharon had blamed Shane's allowing her daughter to over-exert herself during that long ago move for the "miscarrage" Annette had described to her. Now she had a new reason for her anger. And a sudden new sense of sadness that her daughter had not given her the opportunity to offer comfort for the pain she had no doubt carried in the aftermath of the abortion.

There was, Sue Dietrich realized, clearly a history of tension and lack of communication between the two women seated at her kitchen table. And she pondered the irony that it had taken an unspeakable tragedy that would forever scar both their lives to finally unite them.

///

In Orlando, Dr. William Anderson had eagerly looked forward to the arrival of the tissue slides. Though his knowledge of the details was still sketchy, the case had intrigued him from the first telephone conversation with Sharon Couch. As the deputy chief medical examiner for Orange County, he had conducted over 3,000 autopsies. And while he had long since given up any attempt to explain his fascination for his work to those who viewed it as ghoulish and distasteful, Dr. Anderson took great pride in his profession. Life, he had decided back in his medical school days at the University of Miami and Duke, offered no greater challenge than the search for hidden truth.

It was this fascination that had led him to join a team of forensic experts on an expedition to Colorado in 1989 for the exhumation of the long-buried bodies of members of a mining party led by a man named Alfred Packer. Over a hundred years earlier, Packer and his followers had gone in search of gold in the mountains of San Juan. In time, after battling a brutal winter, only Packer returned to civilization. Five others who had been with him, he explained, had gone mad and one by one killed each other. Over the years, rumors grew that Packer had, in fact, murdered his followers and then cannibalized their bodies. The story, however, had remained nothing more than an oft-repeated folktale until Dr. Anderson and his associates examined the remains and added scientific fact to the rumors about Packer's horrendous deeds.

It was not, however, such forensic adventures upon which Dr. Anderson's growing reputation was based. For almost a decade he had found himself moving toward a field of pathology that had few specialists. That he had conducted hundreds of autopsies on infants and young children had earned him a media-born nickname for which he had little use. The Florida press had begun referring to him as "The Dead Baby Doctor."

When Sue Dietrich telephoned him to introduce herself as the newly assigned investigator on the Goode case, he had been careful not to lend false hope. "All I can say at this point," he explained, "is that what I've seen has indicated to me that there was nothing physically wrong with the child before her death."

It was Dietrich who first mentioned the possibility of a second autopsy.

"That," the doctor replied, "is the only way you're going to find the cause of death." He then issued a caution: "If the body is to be exhumed and another autopsy performed, it must be done as quickly as possible." The body of Renee Goode, he knew, had been buried for eight months, and the natural process of tissue deterioration would soon make a thorough pathological study impossible.

"I'll get back to you as soon as I can get a court order for the exhumation," the detective replied.

Dr. Anderson wondered if she had any idea how difficult that might be.

. . .

There is, within the mazelike workings of the American judical system, a political pecking order that exists in jurisdictions both rural and urban. Rank within an agency, be it police, sheriff's department, or the district attorney's office, is jealously guarded, often to the point of childishness. The same applies to territorial rights. Rarely—often only when forced—does one agency reach out the hand of cooperation to another. There is a protective, wary boundary of distrust that is seldom admitted but is a hard fact of law-enforcement life nonetheless. And there are sacred toes upon which no treading is condoned.

Among the most sacred is the medical examiner's office. It is there that doctors make all-important rulings which give direction to investigations and develop expert testimony that can sway the decision of jurors. Medical examiners often operate above and beyond political restraint without hint of governmental sanction. There is a powerful, godlike authority dealt many medical examiner's offices and those forced to rely on their cooperation are generally quick to bow to it.

Assistant District Attorney Jeri Yenne was shaking her head as she looked across the desk at her friend Sue Dietrich. "Do you realize what you're asking? Sue, this is Brazoria County. It's not going to happen."

"It has to," the detective argued. "There are a lot of things that point to the fact that this guy killed his own child—and he's going to get away with it if we don't find out how the little girl died."

Yenne leaned back in her chair, surrounded by the clutter of her small corner office, and locked the fingers of her hands together. "Then your gut feeling is that he did it?"

"Absolutely."

Sighing deeply, the prosecutor was silent for several seconds before she finally began to nod her head. "Okay, let me think about it and see what I can do."

Jeri Yenne understood well the passion that quickly develops during the investigation of a child's death. Assigned to child-welfare cases during the early days of her tenure with the D.A.'s office, she had often wrestled with the sense of sadness and outrage that grew from knowledge that an adult would intentionally harm an innocent and helpless child.

She also knew the hesitancy that district attorneys felt about challenging the ruling of a medical examiner, regardless of how questionable it might appear.

She had been a prosecutor for just over a year when the case of a seventeen-month-old girl had crossed her desk. The child had been rushed to a Lake Jackson hospital, suffering seizures, and had died in the emergency room. Later, when serious questions arose about the drug-related activities of the child's parents, Yenne had gone to District Attorney Jim Mapel to suggest that the body be exhumed and another autopsy performed. Despite what she considered to be compelling evidence that justified such drastic measures, he had refused her flatly. He did not, he told her, want to deal with the "heat" that was sure to be generated by an exhumation.

It was not until weeks after the funeral that the results of belated toxicology tests prompted the parents to confess to giving their child an overdose of cocaine on the night she had died. While her superiors cheered the ultimate conviction of the killers, Yenne found herself brooding over the fact that, had the parents not admitted their guilt, the lab findings alone might not have been enough to make certain they were punished for their crime.

She had never again asked for an exhumation or second autopsy.

Now, however, a phrase that Sue Dietrich had used in her argument hummed through her mind. Dr. Anderson had made it clear that there was "a small window of opportunity" in the matter.

Perhaps, Yenne decided, there might be more than one such window.

For the first time in her nine-year tenure in the district attorney's office, the political guard was down. Her boss had already announced that once his current term was completed he would not be running for reelection.

Maybe, she thought, the "heat" would no longer be so strong a consideration.

As she reviewed the case that Sue Dietrich had presented her, Yenne pondered myriad problems which she was sure the detective had not weighed. While the reports she read certainly gave rise to a certain degree of suspicion, there was not the slightest hint of the kind of evidence that breeds confidence in a prosecutor. Dietrich had promised that she would soon have documentation of the life insurance policy purchased by Shane Goode. And while it might serve well as a logical motive for murder, it would do little to advance the case legally. There had to be some proof that the father had committed murder—and, aside from the accusations of a grieving family and an angered ex-girlfriend, there was nothing in the file Dietrich had shown her that connected Goode to a crime. Nothing, in fact, to show that a crime had even occurred.

Yet there was that "gut feeling," an emotion she had relied on throughout her legal career, first during her three and one-half years as a defense attorney, then in her role as a prosecutor. She had heard the criticisms of her fellow attorneys who had warned against her tendency to "overreact," and knew that there were those who had viewed the intensity she brought to her prosecution of child cases as a show of what they referred to as her "mama instinct."

For several days she pondered the long-shot possibilities of the case, forcing herself to measure the overwhelming negatives that literally jumped from Dietrich's file. Yenne was trying vainly to hold to her new-sworn credo that she would not allow her emotions to drive her professional actions.

Still, she contacted Dr. Anderson and listened as he recounted his concerns, finding his arguments persuasive. Careful to emphasize the "if," she questioned him about the cost to the county of a possible second autopsy, asking about the chances of finding something that would justify her seeking a murder indictment. His answers did not lift her spirits. The exhumation, he estimated, would cost in the neighborhood of $3,000. His fee for performing the autopsy would be $250 per hour plus travel expenses. And, no, he could not give her any assurance that he would find anything that the Harris County Medical Examiner's office had not discovered.

If Dr. Anderson ever had "gut feelings" in advance of his scientific evaluations, he did not share them with the district attorney. The decision, he said, was hers to make.

Yenne was still pondering the pluses (of which she found very few) and the minuses (which now included finances) when she answered her phone to hear Sue Dietrich's voice.

Despite the fact that they had developed a kinship over the years—both had begun their professional careers as police dispatchers and had shared war stories of their work in a predominately male profession—Yenne detected little warmth in Dietrich's voice. The call, clearly, was professional.

"What's it going to take, Jeri?" the detective asked.

Yenne studied the ceiling of her office for several seconds, the phone cradled against her shoulder. Finally, she answered: "It's going to take my calling in every damn chit I've collected since I came to work here. I'll talk to Jim today."

///

Brazoria County District Attorney Jim Mapel was, in truth, far less a politician than many who hold public office. Over the years he had carefully assembled a staff of prosecutors whose abilities and instincts he trusted, then allowed them to proceed without undue second-guessing. He had but one credo which he attached to his elected position: Do the right thing. A Vietnam veteran, his lone vices were his smoking, which had prompted him to place a plaque on the edge of his desk that read "Thanks for not breathing while I'm smoking," and an occasional gambling trip to Las Vegas.

It was Mapel's gambling instinct that Yenne hoped to play on as she sat in his office, outlining the case.

"You really think he did it?" Mapel said.

"Yes, I do," she said, "but the only way we're going to be able to prove it—it's going to cost a lot of money—if we could just—"

Mapel smiled as he listened to Yenne's run-on sentences. He'd seen her like this before—her mind working faster than her speech, energy and emotions flowing full out. More than once he had cautioned her to slow down and take an occasional deep breath during her arguments to a judge or jury. At the same time, he admired the passion she brought to each case she undertook.

"Even if you come up with something from a second autopsy it isn't going to be easy," he warned. "This isn't going to make you very popular with—"

"I know. I know. But, Jim, there is something really wrong here, something that has to . . ."

Raising his palms in a gesture of mock surrender, he said, "I think we can come up with the money. And, what the hell? I'm not running again. Do it."

Yenne telephoned Sue Dietrich with the good news.

In time, the prosecutor knew, they would have to discuss a matter she was certain would not be greeted with nearly the same degree of enthusiasm.

"Can you come down early next week?" Jeri asked. "We need to talk."

"Sure." Sue Dietrich had not felt such a sense of euphoria in some time. Her life, which had been without real focus in recent months, suddenly had new direction and purpose.

///

Within the close-knit Brazoria County legal community, Tom Selleck's name had long since ceased to cause double takes from those to whom he was introduced. The novelty of having the same name as a well-known television and motion-picture actor had eventually run its course, replaced by the enviable reputation he'd earned as the chief felony prosecutor in the D.A.'s office.

Handsome, outgoing, and respected for his crisp and often dramatic arguments to juries, Selleck had, during his tenure, never lost a murder case.

Over the years he had developed a close kinship with most police officers in the county, often riding with them on patrol and encouraging them to contact him in the event they needed procedural advice or legal counsel. That he had suffered a minor gunshot wound years earlier while accompanying a police officer on an impromptu drug raid had greatly displeased his boss, who angrily insisted he had no business being involved in that phase of the judicial process. At the same time, the event had further solidified his standing among police officers, who viewed him not only as a trusted ally, but a stand-up guy not afraid to venture into the trenches.

He and Sue Dietrich had met five years earlier and a mutual admiration had gradually developed into a more personal relationship. Long divorced from her first husband, Sue had been surprised at her quick willingness to accept Selleck's marriage proposal.

Friends and coworkers had viewed them as the ideal couple, giving the union good odds against the traditional work-related pitfalls of "cop marriages." Both had a thorough understanding of their spouse's work and each had an intense dedication to the respective law-enforcement roles they were assigned. Routinely they sought each other's counsel on cases, Sue on some investigation she was conducting, Tom on the best way to approach a particular prosecution.

The seemingly idyllic union had lasted just over a year before Sue received a phone call from the irate husband of a woman who worked with Selleck at the Brazoria County Courthouse. His wife of fourteen years, he said, had admitted to an ongoing affair with "that sonuva-bitch lawyer" to whom she was married. In short order, Sue learned that the accusation was not only true but had, for some time, been common knowledge around the courthouse.

Angered and humiliated, she quickly filed for divorce and changed her name back to Dietrich.

Only once had she even considered the possibility of a reconciliation—during a fleeting but fragile moment when her emotional strengths were suddenly and completely drained. Several months after their separation, she had discovered a lump in her breast. Numbed by fear, she had telephoned Selleck one evening to ask that he return home, if only long enough to help her through whatever she might be facing. He had refused. Immediately, Sue Dietrich regretted her action and cursed the moment of weakness that had led her to make the call.

On that evening she had vowed that Tom Selleck would forever be nothing more than a bitter memory.

By the time she became involved in the Goode case, she had pushed the lump and its ominous warnings into the back of her mind. Whatever courage women summon to seek the truth about such things evaded her. For one of the few times in her life, she opted to deal with a troubling situation simply by doing nothing. And so she told no one else about the lump—not even her mother, who at the time was slowly dying of cancer.

///

Jeri Yenne had never spoken with Sue about her marital problems but, like everyone else in the D.A.'s office, she had heard the gossip about Selleck's affair long before the divorce proceedings were initiated. It had concerned her when she realized that Sue, once smiling and energetic, had begun to avoid visiting the D.A.'s office except on occasions when her job demanded it, and then only for the brief time such appearances required. It was grossly unfair, Yenne knew, that her friend had been forced into such an uncomfortable position. She worried that the matter which she needed to discuss with Sue was hardly going to make things more comfortable for anyone.

She was at her desk, staring into a computer screen, when Sue knocked against her open door. Motioning for the detective to take a seat, Yenne continued to focus on the monitor, avoiding for another few seconds the speech she was prepared to make.

It was then that Tom Selleck leaned his head in from the hallway. "Hello Sue," he said.

Ignoring the fact that she had not returned his greeting, he continued. "It sounds to me as if you have done some very good work on this Goode case," he said. "Congratulations."

Finally, Sue turned her head to face him squarely and speak to him for the first time in months. In truth, she had very little to say. "Fuck you," she replied.

Selleck forced a grin, nodded, and continued down the hall, unaware of the faint smile that had erased Jeri Yenne's previously sober expression. "Well," she deadpanned, "that gets things off to a good start."

Sue Dietrich frowned. "What do you mean?"

"How would you feel about . . ."

The prosecutor had not even completed her sentence before Sue rolled her eyes in realization of what was coming.

". . . Tom coming on board and being involved in the case?"

The D.A., Yenne explained, had made it clear to her in a series of discussions that if they were to seek an indictment in a case as difficult as this one, he wanted his most experienced prosecutor involved, particularly if it reached the trial stage.

"Look, I'm no dummy," Yenne pointed out, "but the truth of the matter is I've tried one stinking murder case in the seven years I've worked here. That hardly qualifies me as an expert. So, frankly, I would welcome the help. But for it to work—"

Sue interrupted her. "Look," she said, "I know this is awkward. Personally, I've got no use for the bastard. But, the fact is, he's the best prosecutor I've ever known. And if that's what it takes to get this job done, it's fine with me. I can deal with it."

"I'm not sure I could," Yenne replied.

Sue smiled. "You could if it was the only way you could be sure that Shane Goode is punished for what he did to that little girl."

It was at that moment that Yenne began to realize just how important the case had become to her friend. And that Sue Dietrich's dedication to the case was fast becoming contagious.

Soon, others would also feel the detective's single-minded determination.

///

As is the case with all governmental agencies, the appropriation of funding for any project is routinely slowed by the bureaucratic red tape in which it is certain to be wrapped. While the D.A. had approved funding for the second autopsy, it had hardly been an open invitation to visit petty cash and get whatever amount needed. What Jim Mapel had actually okayed was only the partial funding his office would be authorized to provide.

The first order of business for Yenne, in fact, had been to contact Sharon Couch and explain that if the procedure was to move forward, the cost of the exhumation of Renee's body would have to be funded by the family.

And, while the District Attorney's Office was prepared to pay the bulk of the expense related to the autopsy, it took an additional two thousand dollars provided by the county's Child Protective Services to get the dollar amount near the bottom line budget Yenne had worked out.

Still, she was one thousand dollars short and phoned Sue to request that she ask if the City of Alvin would contribute. Dietrich went immediately to her boss.

Alvin Police Chief Mike Merkel was less than encouraging. Only a week earlier a memo from the city manager had crossed his desk, announcing an immediate spending freeze. "The way I read it," he told his detective, "we can't even ask to buy a box of paper clips right now, much less help fund a private autopsy. I'm sorry." He did not have to verbalize the argument that was sure to accompany any such request, even in the best of financial times: Why bring in a pathologist from Florida to do work that Harris County's M.E.'s office is being paid handsomely to do?

"Do you have any objection to my speaking with the city manager?" Chief Merkel wished her well.

/ / /

At her desk, Sue Dietrich carefully assembled the presentation she planned to make. The city manager's secretary had told her that he would be free briefly at four in the afternoon and she sat, watching the clock, anxious to make the brief walk across the street to Alvin's City Hall.

In a folder she had placed a copy of the flyer that Sharon had distributed in hopes of getting additional information about Renee's death, a page from a legal pad on which she had written the brief summary of the case, and a color photograph of Renee, dressed in pajamas and a baseball cap worn backward, smiling angelically into the camera.

City Manager Marvin Norwood, Dietrich knew, had a granddaughter approximately the same age Renee had been when the photograph was taken.

West Point–educated, Norwood brought to his role of overseer of community finances a no-nonsense, all-business manner. He made no apologies for his military demeanor and his closely cropped crew cut, and if critics wished to label him a tight-fisted bean-counter, so be it. It was the job he was hired to do.

He judged small talk, particularly during business hours, an unpardonable waste of time. "What can I do for you, Detective?" he asked as Sue Dietrich sat across from his desk.

"I'm here to ask you for money," she replied. "I've been—"

Norwood was shaking his head before she could complete the sentence. "No salary raises will be considered," Norwood said, "until the spending freeze has been lifted."

"I'm not here to ask for a raise," the detective quickly responded. "I'm conducting a homicide investigation and if it is to be done properly, I need a thousand dollars from the city." She passed the folder she had prepared across the desk.

The city manager read her synopsis of the case and stared for some time at the photograph of the smiling child. Leaning back in his chair, he looked silently at his visitor. "Tell me a little more about the case," he said.

Nervously, Sue tried to recap the sequence of events that had led her to his office. She completed her narrative by saying, "We believe that the father murdered her for insurance money."

Leaning forward, the city manager placed his elbows on his desk. "How good a case do you have?"

"Sir, I believe with all my heart that this little girl was murdered."

"And you're absolutely convinced that the father is the guilty party?"

"Mr. Norwood," she replied, "I would bet my badge on it."

"And what if I tell you that the city doesn't have the money you need?"

Sue's quick response surprised her. It was not something carefully thought out, not a part of the presentation she had so carefully planned. Rather, it came spontaneously. "Then I go to the Credit Union and take out a personal loan," she said.

"I'll have you an answer before the end of the business day," Norwood said, glancing down at his watch. It was 4:20.

Sue made the walk back to the police station slowly, replaying the meeting in her mind, wondering if she had left something unsaid that might have been more persuasive, might have better signaled the urgency of her request. She had been in the city manager's office only twenty minutes, but it had seemed like an eternity.

Entering the station, she saw Chief Merkel walking down the hall toward her. The broad smile on his face tipped his proud announcement before he could make it.

"The city manager just called," he said. "He said you've got your thousand dollars."

Fourteen

To many of his coworkers, Shane Goode was a changed man in the aftermath of his daughter's death. Quiet and reserved—almost secretive—before, he had become far more social and outgoing in the months following the tragedy. Not only had he begun to occasionally accompany them for an after-work beer or two, but he had enthusiastically joined in the practice of buying a round for the table.

There had been some whispered surprise when he returned to work only days after the funeral, but it was soon forgotten. It was reasoned that for some, work is judged the best antidote for grief. Shane, they assumed, was one of those who could best deal with sorrow by staying busy.

Not only did he bring a new attitude to his job but seemed more wrapped up than ever in his National Guard activities. Recently, he had sought time off to attend a series of training schools at military bases like Fort Bliss, in Texas, Georgia's Fort Benning, and Eglin Air Force Base in Florida, where he added parachuting and new survival skills to his expanding resume.

Rumors of the accusations his ex-wife had made their way through the postal staff and were generally dismissed. Shane Goode might have his shortcomings, might even be a bit strange, but there was no way he could be a cold-blooded killer.

There was, however, one troubling question that continued to circulate when the tragedy was discussed. Shane had talked constantly about his daughter Tiffany, always quick to show her picture or introduce her to fellow workers when he brought her to the post office. But except for Sunny Bradley—who made it a point to avoid all conversation about Shane—other employees could not remember his ever mentioning that he had another child.

///

With the financing finally arranged and a date set for Dr. Anderson's visit to perform the autopsy, only one obstacle remained. It was imperative, Yenne and Dietrich agreed, that Shane not be alerted to their plan. No doubt comfortable that the investigation was ended, he had returned to a normal routine and had begun seeing a married woman who worked at the post office. Sharon Couch could vouch for that, having taken it upon herself to discreetly track his movements, often with the help of Sunny. Should Shane learn of the planned exhumation and second autopsy, however, he might well leave for one of his Guard training adventures and simply disappear.

"We want him believing all's right with the world," Yenne had said.

For Sue Dietrich, the course the investigation was taking was unlike any she had ever experienced. Never before had she made such a conscious effort to completely avoid a suspect. As eager as she was to confront Shane Goode, to get her first up-close look at him and hear his answers to her questions, she willed all the patience she could summon to stay away.

When, in fact, she had called a State Farm representative to alert the insurance company of her investigation and urge that payment of Goode's policy be postponed, she had spent an undue amount of time emphasizing the importance of secrecy. "I'm sure," Sue had suggested, "that there are any number of explanations you could give for a delay."

The agent laughed and agreed. The fact of the matter was, she noted, Shane had not yet contacted them regarding payment on the policy. After a check of her computer, in fact, she found that he had made an additional payment on the policy even after Renee's death.

That Shane had made no effort to cash in on the policy was, at first, troubling to the detective. If money had been the motive for Renee's death, then why wasn't he eager to get it? Why continue to make payments?

The agent's explanation quickly calmed her concerns. Only after the policy holder is provided a copy of the death certificate can he apply for payment. Obviously, she added, the coroner's office had not yet completed its paperwork. Sometimes, she said, it took months.

The longer the better, the detective thought to herself.

Sue Dietrich was not the only one whose paranoia was working overtime.

A petition for the exhumation of a body, Jeri Yenne knew, could be done only with the written approval of a spouse or parent. And while Annette, awarded managing conservatorship of Renee during the divorce proceedings, had been quick to volunteer her signature, Yenne could not free herself of the concern that Shane might somehow find out and seek to scuttle the plan—or, even worse, run.

Not even Sue Dietrich's fellow officers knew when she quietly visited the office of Justice of the Peace Jerome Jozwiak to finally get the order signed.

To accommodate Dr. Anderson's schedule, the exhumation was scheduled to take place on the seventh of October, 1994.

For all concerned, the next three weeks would seem endless. With the forward movement of the investigation hinging on the outcome of the autopsy, there was very little Yenne or Dietrich could do but turn their attention back to other duties. Sharon Couch passed her days by building a storage shed in her backyard, a long-delayed project. Annette did her best to hide her growing anxieties from her husband and daughter by immersing herself in work and school.

That apprehension would reach new heights on the morning of the autopsy.

. . .

Shane and Annette Goode on the day of their delayed wedding.

Annette and Renee.

<rotated>Brazosport Facts</rotated>

Wearing the sports coat that had been a Christmas gift from Annette, Shane Goode walks toward the courtroom for the beginning of his trial.

Shane Goode and his attorney
Skip Cornelius.

Brazoria County District Judge J. Ray Gayle.

Pat Stowers

sistant District Attorney Jeri Yenne.

Pat Stowers

Sharon Couch.

Alvin Police Department detective
Sue Dietrich.

Assistant District Attorney Tom Selleck

r. Linda Norton.

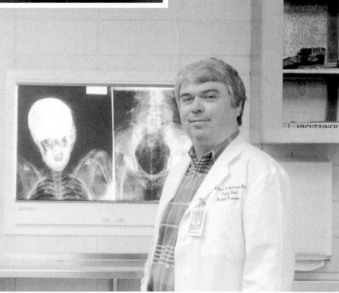

Dr. William Anderson.

Sharon Couch with her granddaughter Renee.

Carefully following Dr. Anderson's instructions, Sue Dietrich had contacted administrators at Alvin Community Hospital and reserved space where the autopsy could be conducted. The unopened casket had been delivered to one of the hospital's examining rooms the night before, guarded by Alvin police officers, to await the pathologist's arrival.

Upon inspecting the arrangement, however, the doctor was immediately troubled. The examining room lacked the running water he would require and the lighting was less than satisfactory. Additionally, it was located adjacent to the emergency room, which he knew could become a loud distraction at any moment.

It was Dr. Anderson who suggested an alternate plan.

After a lengthy phone conversation with the director of the nearby Oak Park Funeral Home, it was decided that the examination would be moved to the funeral home's preparation room, which was equipped with basically the same facilities found in a morgue.

When Sharon and Annette arrived at the hospital and were unable to find either the doctor or detective, they nervously approached a nurse's station for directions.

Sharon began explaining her purpose in being there. "We're members of the family—"

The elderly nurse cut her short. "I'm sorry," she said. "but I'm not at liberty to give out any information."

"You don't understand, we're supposed to—"

"I'm sorry," the nurse firmly repeated.

Frantic and angry, Sharon began searching for a phone, rummaging through her purse for Sue Dietrich's beeper number. As she hurried along the hall, another nurse moved to her side and without even looking in her direction, whispered. "Nobody's telling us anything," she said, "but they left through the back door about thirty minutes ago . . . with something covered by a sheet."

///

Horrified by her oversight the moment her beeper sounded, Sue immediately called the hospital pay phone number left by Sharon and began to apologize, explaining that the unnerving change of plans had come about swiftly. She gave the distraught grandmother directions to the funeral home.

Sharon Couch relayed the detective's explanation to her daughter as they rushed toward the hospital parking lot. Any anger she had felt was quickly replaced by her apprehension of the events that lay ahead. As she drove toward the funeral home, she found her jumbled thoughts beginning to focus on Sue Dietrich.

Dietrich had sounded as if already at wit's end during their brief phone conversation, and Sharon wondered if the detective would be able to get through the unpleasant hours that lay ahead. As they had become better acquainted, Sue had confided the loss of her own child and Sharon wondered if she would be able to muster the strength to stand watch over an examination that was certain to unlock old memories.

It was something that also concerned Sergeant Arendell. Since assigning her the case and watching the intensity with which she had pursued it, he had begun to feel concern when he learned that the exhumation order had been granted. He, too, knew the tragic history of Sue's son.

It had been with that in mind that he had, as subtly as possible, volunteered to travel to the Hallettsville cemetery and oversee the exhumation and return of the casket to Alvin. He had told his detective that he would stand in at the autopsy if she preferred. Sue had had no argument about his being there, she had said, but felt it was her responsibility to attend as well. It was, she said, part of the job.

Still, she harbored secret doubts, dreading what she would see when the casket was opened, and was glad that Arendell would be standing beside her.

///

The early stages of the examination were, in fact, more difficult than she had anticipated. Sue had stepped toward the gurney when the casket was opened and her eyes had fallen on the still-bright ribbons in Renee's hair. Silently she looked down on the tiny lifeless form surrounded by stuffed animals and favorite toys. Tears welled in her eyes as she backed away and began moving toward the door. She wasn't going to be able to handle it.

She had been sitting alone in an adjacent room for several minutes when Sergeant Arendell approached and pulled a chair up beside her. Placing a hand on her shoulder, he delivered a message from Dr. Anderson. "He hasn't done anything yet," Arendell said. "He's waiting for you. He asked me to tell you that this is Renee's only way of telling you what happened to her."

Sue stood, breathed deeply, and followed her sergeant back into the prep room. Except for occasional trips outside to briefly reassure Sharon and Annette that the examination was progressing, she gamely stood sentry over the now unclothed body, listening as the doctor carefully explained each procedure, dictating his observations into a recorder.

"The body is that of a normally developed white female child appearing the stated age of two years . . . measuring thirty-five inches in length and consistent with a weight of twenty-six pounds," the doctor said in a soft, measured voice. "The body shows evidence of interment, with a black mold present on the skin of the face, chest, abdomen, and extremities . . ."

Sue Dietrich watched as he gently bathed the mold away and begin his meticulous search for the cause of death.

It was early in the afternoon before he moved toward the final phase of the examination. Cutting through the body's tiny muscles, he removed the diaphragm so that he might view the back of the chest wall. The procedure, not done in the original autopsy, revealed telling dark signs of hemorrhage in muscle tissue near the ninth and tenth ribs.

It was then that he walked to the wall phone and placed a long-distance call to a colleague in Dallas. He had known Dr. Linda Norton since college days and considered her one of the most skilled pathologists he had ever met. Even before leaving Florida he had contacted her to discuss the planned autopsy and to ask that she stand by for any consultation that might be necessary. It was agreed that they would discuss his finding by phone as the autopsy was being done. Later he would send her tissue slides to examine.

For quite some time he methodically retraced his examination, concluding with a detailed description of what he'd found on the interior chest wall.

Such hemorrhaging, both doctors agreed, could only have been caused by extreme compressive force to the child's abdomen over an extended period of time. In all probability, it had taken Renee Goode five to seven minutes to die.

Dr. Anderson knew already what he would write in his postmortem Diagnostic Report upon his return to Florida: The cause of Renee Goode's death was compressive asphyxia resulting from sustained blunt force applied to the abdomen and lower thoracic area.

In layman's terms, someone had literally squeezed the life's breath from her.

///

In the hallway of the funeral home, Sharon and Annette rose to meet the detective as she hurried toward them. This time there was an urgency in her step, a look of calm on her face that had not been visible earlier.

Sue did not wait for them to ask. "Dr. Anderson," she announced, "says that Renee's death was a homicide."

Annette began to cry as her mother embraced her. Then Sharon reached out her hands to Sue. "You've done so much," she said.

"There's still a great deal that has to be done," the detective replied.

"I understand," Sharon replied. "But it has taken so much just to get to this point." That said, she motioned Sue to a spot out of Annette's earshot. "Can I ask one more favor?"

Sue nodded.

"Would you dress her before they put her back into the casket?"

Though she knew it would be one of the most difficult assignments of her law-enforcement career, Detective Dietrich promised she would.

. . .

Jeri Yenne had considered making the short drive to Alvin to attend the autopsy but had decided against it. The final weeks of a pregnancy had begun taking a toll, and her ankles were swelling badly as her body retained fluid. Her planned cesarean section, which was just ten days away, could not come soon enough.

Nor, for that matter, could word of Dr. Anderson's findings.

Throughout the day she had repeatedly whispered a prayer: *Lord, I don't want to falsely accuse someone of a horrible crime. I've got to know something for sure. I have to have some evidence. . . .*

She was on her screened-in back porch, mixing a sauce for the steaks her husband was preparing to grill, when the cellular phone she had been keeping at arm's reach rang. She answered to hear Dietrich's voice.

In a dry, breathless tone, the detective described the doctor's findings. "There was hemorrhaging, Jeri. He found it . . . the answer."

Yenne closed her eyes and her head began to nod slowly.

"You hear me?" Sue continued. "He says Renee's death was a homicide."

"I hear you," the prosecutor finally replied. Then she made the suggestion that Dietrich had been waiting for weeks to hear. "I guess," she said, "it's time that you got acquainted with Shane Goode."

Sue's first inclination was to drive immediately to Goode's apartment and begin the questioning she had so long been rehearsing. The rush of adrenaline she was feeling, however, served as a warning signal. From this stage on, she knew, the investigation would have to be conducted with the utmost care as it was readied for delivery to a grand jury.

As Dr. Anderson returned to Florida to prepare his written report, Sue Dietrich spent Sunday at home, again reviewing the case, this time paying particular attention to the initial statement Goode had given in the aftermath of his daughter's death.

"The less threatened he feels at this point, the better," Yenne warned when she called late in the day. "Give him the ditzy blond routine. Tell him they've dumped the case on you and that you're there just to wrap up the loose ends. If my guess is right, he's going to be very pleased to know that the whole thing has diminished to the point that it is being handled by a female."

For the first time in days, Sue Dietrich laughed, then affected a breathless, sing-song voice. "Well," she said, "I just hope that I don't mess everything up and make Mister Goode mad at me."

Yenne was also laughing as she hung up the phone. But in the days to come, she knew, there would be little room for frivolity. Even with the findings from the second autopsy, the case was circumstantial at best. No physical evidence connecting the suspect to the crime existed. The idea, in fact, that a murder could have taken place at a time when there were no fewer than six potential witnesses present would no doubt strain the imagination of the most inventive mystery writers.

And, if medical examiners' tradition continued, she held little hope that the Harris County pathologists would soon be willing to admit their mistake and suddenly embrace the findings of Dr. Anderson.

"A lot of ego-bruising is going to take place before this is over," she said to her husband that evening as they prepared for bed.

Bill Yenne gently embraced his wife. It concerned him that she had become involved in such a difficult case during the most trying time of her pregnancy. At the same time, he was keenly aware of the passion she felt for the dual role she had chosen for herself. He had every confidence in her as a mother, and as a prosecutor. Reaching to turn out the light, he smiled at her.

"You'll do what you have to do," he said.

///

Sue Dietrich had decided not to alert Shane to her visit. She knew of his failure to keep appointments with Bodie Duckworth and the polygraph examiner and feared that if she phoned ahead he might conviently find someplace else to be.

It was 7:30 in the evening when Shane, dressed only in a pair of gym shorts, opened his door to find the detective smiling at him.

Introducing herself, Sue quickly explained that she had been recently assigned to the case. When Goode made no move to invite her inside, she continued. "Look, I'd like to get this wrapped up and put away," she said. "My captain's on my ass, so is my sergeant. So, if I could just take a few minutes of your time . . ."

Shane finally nodded, smiled pleasantly, and invited her into the apartment. Motioning for her to sit in one of the two matching blue recliners which were separated by a small coffee table, he excused himself to the bedroom to put on a shirt and shoes. While he did so, Sue surveyed the sparsely furnished but neatly kept quarters. In addition to the two chairs, the table, and a lamp, the only furniture in the carpeted living room was a television set located in one corner. The walls were bare except for a recently applied coat of new paint. The only visible photograph was one of a young girl whom the detective assumed was Goode's daughter, Tiffany, in a frame positioned atop the TV set.

"I've been away at Jump Master school," he explained as he reappeared, pointing to the National Guard T-shirt he had put on, "and I've just moved in. Most of my stuff's still in storage."

Making a concerted effort to lend a casual air to her visit, the detective drew him into a brief conversation about the training he'd received. The animated response to her curiosity about the dangers of jumping from a plane disappeared when she changed the subject to the investigation she'd been assigned.

As if on cue, Shane struck the same pose she'd briefly seen when he'd come to the police station to speak with Detective Duckworth. Moving to the edge of the recliner, he placed his elbows on his knees and locked his eyes on the floor in front of him.

Sue found herself silently staring at the young man seated across from her. Shane Goode, she thought, looked like the guy every mother hoped her daughter might marry: clean-cut, well mannered, and obviously in good physical shape. He seemed shy, was soft-spoken, and looked several years younger than the thirty-four she knew him to be. The detective had always found it difficult to define the word "handsome," but had to admit that by most measures, Goode qualified.

For a half hour he answered her questions as if by rote, offering brief responses that were almost verbatim to those in the statement he'd given months earlier. It occured to Dietrich that there were other attributes that she should add to her mental list: Shane Goode had a remarkable memory and, if he harbored genuine emotion, he masked it better than anyone she'd ever encountered.

"I know," she said, "that you've done this before, but if you don't mind, I'd like to get a written statement while I'm here." Not allowing him time to argue that he'd already done so, she shrugged as if to apologize for the inconvenience. "It's routine when a case is transferred from one investigator to another."

As she spoke she handed him a blank statement form, explaining that he was not under arrest and that whatever he wrote would have to be voluntary.

"My handwriting is pretty hard to read," he said, still avoiding eye contact. "Why don't I just tell it to you and you write it out for me?"

Dietrich braced the blank form on a legal pad and placed it against her knees. "Okay," she said, "but after we're done you'll need to read this very carefully to be sure the wording is accurate, then sign it."

His statement, brief and clearly rehearsed, did not take long.

THE NIGHT I PICKED RENEE AND MICHELLE UP AND TOOK THEM TO MY PARENTS' HOUSE IN ALVIN, RENEE WAS FEELING OK. SHE DID NOT SEEM TO BE SICK AND SHE AND TIFFANY, MICHELLE, AND CHRISTY PLAYED UNTIL IT WAS TIME TO GO TO SLEEP. MY FATHER WAS AT WORK AND HE USUALLY GETS HOME ABOUT 2:30 A.M. AND MY STEPMOTHER HAD GONE TO BED BY THE TIME I PUT THE KIDS TO BED. AROUND MIDNIGHT I STARTED GETTING RENEE READY FOR BED. EVERYONE ELSE WAS ASLEEP.

SHE WANTED A SLEEPING BAG LIKE TIFFANY AND MICHELLE SO I GOT ONE OF MINE AND PUT IT ON THE FLOOR. RENEE WAS A LITTLE FUSSY SO I LAID ON THE FLOOR WITH HER. SHE CRAWLED ON MY CHEST FOR A LITTLE WHILE THEN SHE CRAWLED OFF ONTO THE FLOOR. A LITTLE WHILE LATER SHE WENT TO SLEEP. I THINK MICHELLE WAS STILL NOT ASLEEP. I GOT UP AND WENT TO MY BEDROOM AND WENT TO SLEEP. THAT NEXT MORNING TIFFANY CAME TO MY ROOM AND TOLD ME RENEE HAD SOMETHING COMING OUT OF HER MOUTH. I GOT UP AND WENT TO THE LIVING ROOM AND FOUND RENEE. I KNEW ONCE I PICKED RENEE UP THAT SHE WAS DEAD. SHE WAS LYING ON HER STOMACH. I DO NOT KNOW WHAT HAPPENED TO RENEE. I WAS THE LAST PERSON TO SEE HER

ALIVE AND SHE SEEMED OK TO ME. I DID NOT HEAR ANYTHING DURING THE NIGHT. RENEE IS A VERY HEALTHY CHILD.

DETECTIVE DIETRICH HAS HAND-WRITTEN THIS STATEMENT AND IT IS TRUE AND CORRECT.

RENEE WAS SICK AROUND NEW YEAR'S BUT SHE DID NOT SEEM SICK TO ME ON JANUARY 23, 1994.

It was, the detective thought, as if he were discussing the death of someone he'd never known. There had been no tears, no pauses for composure, not the slightest hint that grief for the loss of his own child remained. Sue felt a sudden chill as she read to him what she had written.

"That's what I remember," he acknowledged.

"I would like for you to read it over yourself—very carefully—before you sign it," she said, holding the statement out to him. "Just to be sure . . ."

///

Assuring Goode that she had everything she needed, Sue Dietrich was walking toward the door when he asked a question: "Do you have any idea whether the medical examiner's office is planning to do any more tests?"

"Not that I know of."

Shane nodded. "Then when do you think I'll be hearing from State Farm?"

The question surprised the detective. At no point in the interview had she brought up the subject of insurance. Standing in the doorway, she measured her answer carefully before replying. "Mr. Goode," she said. "I feel certain you'll be hearing from someone soon."

///

In the apartment-complex parking lot, Sue sat in her car for some time, replaying the encounter, wondering if she had accomplished everything she had hoped. In truth, her expectations had been guarded: The primary purpose of her unannounced visit had been to finally get an up-close look at her suspect. The new statement shed no additional light on the investigation except for the fact that Shane had again admitted that he was the last person to see Renee alive.

It was the two questions he had asked that most excited her. The man who had insisted to Annette that he had no insurance on Renee except for the small policy he'd taken out at work, was now very interested in when State Farm would be paying him fifty-thousand dollars.

Sitting in the darkness, she mentally inventoried her case—the statements Goode had made immediately following his daughter's death, the answers he'd given her, the reports, Dr. Anderson's findings—and a theory of how the murder was committed began to form.

Short of Shane confessing, it would be impossible to prove, but the detective suspected that:

At some point after all the children had settled in for the night, after he'd gotten a sleeping bag for Renee and lain with her, after all the other children were sleeping, he'd taken the baby into his bedroom and killed her there. He had then returned her to the darkened living room, placed her on the sleeping bag, and taken a shower, probably to wash away the droplets of bloody froth that had been left on his chest after he had pressed her against him until she had gone limp and stopped breathing.

And then he had gone to bed to wait for someone else to make the gruesome discovery.

As she gunned the motor and drove from the parking lot, Sue Dietrich felt the chill return. How could anyone do something so terrible, so inhumane? So absolutely evil?

Driving toward home, she found herself wondering if Shane Goode had slept on the night he committed the murder.

///

The following afternoon Annette once again stood beside her mother as a Gulf Coast breeze whispered a faint hint of fall across the Hallettsville City Cemetery. Joining them were Annette's husband and daughter.

They listened in silence as a minister read a passage of scripture, then offered a prayer as Renee's casket was returned to its grave.

Fifteen

Jeri Yenne's energy and attention to detail greatly impressed Sue Dietrich. From the moment the assistant district attorney agreed to take the case she had immersed herself in it, reviewing case law for any guidance it might provide, making voluminous notes to remind her of things that would need to be done months down the line, insisting on constant updates of even the most trivial events relevant to the investigation.

Her meticulous planning for the second autopsy was a case in point. Not only had she been careful to ascertain that all legal paperwork was in order, she had dispatched a cameraman to videotape the exhumation, then collected signed affidavits from everyone involved—cemetery officials to the police guards she appointed to stand sentry at the hospital—to show that the casket had not been opened until Dr. Anderson had done so. Yenne had spared no effort to assure the chain of custody of Renee's body and avert any allegation of tampering.

Now, with the pathologist's ruling that the child's death was, in all likelihood, the result of a homicide, Yenne had moved into a higher gear. Subpoenas were drawn up for everything from Shane Goode's financial and military records to Renee's medical history. Yenne wanted to know everything she possibly could about everyone involved before presenting the case to a grand jury.

Even that had become an exercise in preplanning, which again forced her to take the political climate of her office into consideration. Once again the "window of opportunity" was critical. That she had been able to get the second autopsy was, she knew, the direct result of her boss's decision not to run for reelection. Now, with campaigning at full bore and a new district attorney scheduled to take office in a matter of months, it was essential that Shane Goode be indicted before the outgoing Jim Mapel's successor took office and had the opportunity to review the case, deem it too much of a long shot, and rule against prosecuting.

The latter, she was convinced, was a real possibility if the attitude of her fellow workers was any indication. Several prosecutors with whom she had tried to discuss the case had simply shaken their heads and warned her that it appeared she had an uphill battle on her hands.

Over coffee one morning, she idly mentioned to Ron Helson, an assistant D.A. whose office was adjacent to hers, that she was having some problems with the case. Helson's response had been far from encouraging. "*Some* problems?" he said. "Jeri, your case is anorexic."

On the evening before she was to report to the hospital for her scheduled cesarean section, Yenne sat at her kitchen table until almost midnight, compiling a list of potential witnesses which she planned to interview personally in the days to come.

The case, she had promised Sharon and Annette, would go to the grand jury before 1994 ended.

///

Dietrich, meanwhile, had been delegated the unenviable task of alerting the Harris County Medical Examiner's Office to Dr. Anderson's findings.

Phoning Dr. Bellas, she quickly explained that she had been assigned the Goode case and had, during the course of her investigation, become convinced that the child's death had been caused by her father. She related the recent discovery of the insurance policy, of Shane Goode's financial difficulties, and his previous boasts to people that he had been trained to kill without leaving any sign.

"That's all very interesting, Detective," the pathologist replied, "but I don't see that it concerns me or this office."

"What I was hoping," Sue said, willing herself to maintain a pleasant voice, "is that you might consider looking at your autopsy report again."

There was no hesitation in Dr. Bellas's response, his voice instantly signaling his displeasure at her suggestion. "My decision," he said, "is final."

"I see."

"Is there anything else, Detective?"

Dietrich composed herself, containing the anger that she felt building. "Yes, sir," she replied. "We've had a second autopsy performed—"

"*What?*" Dr. Bellas's voice jumped several octaves.

"—and I was hoping you might look at the report prepared by the pathologist who—"

"No," the doctor said. "Absolutely not." He assured her again that he was quite comfortable with his own findings, explained that he was very busy, and abruptly ended the conversation.

Within the hour, the M.E.'s office's chief investigator Cecil Wingo was on the phone to Yenne, angrily demanding an explanation of what he called the "secret autopsy."

The conversation quickly eroded into a shouting match—Yenne futilely attempting to explain Dr. Anderson's findings and Wingo responding with outrage over the second-guessing of his office—before it, too, abruptly ended.

The prosecutor leaned back in her chair, fully aware that the confrontation she had predicted had now become a full-blown reality.

In a bassinet near Yenne's desk, her four-week-old daughter Samantha slept peacefully, a tiny smile lighting her face. Jeri looked down on her for some time, feeling of sense of calm beginning to slowly return.

"Well, young lady," she said as she bent to kiss her baby, "the missles are in the air."

• • •

It was essential, Sue Dietrich knew, that some manner of peace be struck with the medical examiner's office. While Dr. Anderson's findings had given forward motion to her case, providing necessary cause for arrest and now making an indictment likely, Dr. Bellas's refusal to reconsider could be a major obstacle when the matter went to trial. Unless Bellas agreed to reevaluate his own autopsy and acknowledge that he had failed to perform the crucial procedure that had led to Dr. Anderson's discovery, the jury would be subjected to little more than a verbal sparring match between dissenting pathologists.

In all likelihood, Yenne had warned her, the result would be a wash.

Sue determined that she had to persuade Dr. Bellas to review the results of the second autopsy. She contacted Cecil Wingo's office and set up an appointment in hopes that he might help pave the way.

Tom Selleck and the chief investigator were longtime friends, occasionally riding together with police officers or following along with Wingo's son, an investigator with the Brazoria County District Attorney's Office, as he worked cases. During her marriage to Selleck, Sue had become casually acquainted with Wingo and judged him an aloof but reasonable man.

Arriving at the M.E.'s office well ahead of the scheduled time of her appointment, she was informed by a receptionist that Wingo had been called out of the office because of family illness. Dietrich then asked if Dr. Bellas might be available and, after a considerable wait, was told that he wasn't. Promising to call and reschedule the appointment, the detective returned to Alvin, upset that her afternoon had been wasted.

She had just reached her desk the following morning when a furious Jeri Yenne phoned. "Why in the hell didn't you show up?" she demanded.

"What are you talking about?"

"I just got off the phone with Cecil Wingo and he said you didn't keep the appointment."

Dietrich responded to Yenne's anger with her own sharp tone. "I was there. I got there early, in fact." She explained what she had been told by the receptionist.

The detective could hear the frustration in Yenne's voice as she responded. "Make another appointment right away," she urged. "He said he'd allow you to come back one more time."

"He'll *allow* me?"

"Those were his words. Sue, dammit, do what you have to to make this work, okay? We've already got all the enemies we need."

"He's going to *allow* me to come see him?"

"Just do it," Yenne demanded.

Dietrich called and scheduled another visit to Wingo's office the following afternoon.

With Dr. Anderson's test results and photographs of the second examination in hand, she sat in the reception area, waiting to be called into the investigator's office. Finally, however, he emerged, immaculately dressed in suit and tie, not a strand of his thick white hair out of place. He closed the door behind him. "Whatever you have to say to me, Detective, you can say in the elevator. I have another appointment to keep."

Momentarily stunned by the sharpness in his voice, Sue battled to collect her thoughts. "What I was hoping," she said, "was to have some time to sit down and discuss this matter with you. I'd like for you to look at some of the material I've brought."

Even as she spoke they were entering the elevator and as the doors slid closed, Wingo fixed a stare at her. "You should know," he said, "that I do not appreciate being stood up when I've made an appointment."

He demonstrated no sign of interest in the folder she carried.

"I was here," Sue tried to argue. "Check with your receptionist . . ."

It was as if Wingo had not heard her; he focused his attention on the small wall lights that measured their descent. Stepping from the elevator into the lobby, he turned to her. "You should understand," he said, "that I am the busiest man in Harris County."

Dietrich stood in the open elevator, her body suddenly shaking with anger. The M.E. investigator had almost reached the front door before she was able to regain some degree of composure. "Mr. Wingo," she shouted, waiting for him to look back at her.

When he finally turned, she pointed a finger in his direction. "I want *you* to know that *I'm* the busiest woman in Brazoria County," she said.

As she drove southward toward Alvin, the scene still playing in her mind, a new uneasiness swept over her. Despite the subtle warnings she'd repeatedly heard from Jeri, Sue had not been willing to accept the fact that the Harris County Medical Examiner's office would react with such hostility to having its judgment called into question.

And she found herself wondering if the Brazoria County D.A.'s office and her own department would maintain the strength and commitment that would be demanded of the fight that lay ahead.

Later that evening, as she spoke with Yenne, the troubling doubts were erased. With or without the Harris County M.E.'s office, Jeri said, the case would move forward. "Beyond that," she added, "I can't guarantee you but one other thing."

"What's that?" Sue wanted to know.

"You'll not speak with anyone in the M.E.'s office again unless I'm there with you. Understand?"

Yenne said that she would call and set up another meeting.

"Would you do me one favor?" Sue responded. "Ask the asshole if it could be held somewhere other than in an elevator."

It was the sound of Yenne's booming laughter that finally lifted the detective's sagging spirits.

///

Few, in truth, knew how badly Sue Dietrich's spirits needed lifting. The investigation, even with its frustrations, provided her a badly needed respite from the ever-present awareness that her mother would soon die of the cancer that had spread throughout her body.

Though instinctively aware that their daughter carefully omitted any mention of the dangers related to her job, Marie and Dutch Coker enjoyed hearing Sue talk about her cases. Dutch made no secret of the pride he felt for her accomplishments, always quick to brag to cronies when she received a promotion or citation. Marie was less outspoken but no less pleased that her child had grown into a woman of great strength and purpose.

Now, however, that strength was being tested as Sue searched with little success for ways to comfort her ailing mother during her final days. By early November, doctors had told the detective that the end could come at any time.

At night, Sue would lie in bed beside her frail mother and they would talk—of past times remembered, of what Heaven might be like, and of the case she was involved in. Marie had been particularly interested in her daughter's investigation into Renee Goode's death.

"How could someone be so evil?" she asked one evening, as they lay together in the darkness of the bedroom. "I just can't understand things like that."

"Neither can I, Mama," Sue admitted.

"It must be so very hard for you." Marie gently moved her hand to her daughter's face, still the comforter despite her own pain.

They had also begun to speak openly about death. One evening Sue had asked what music her mother would like played at her funeral. "It probably isn't something that your daddy will approve of," Marie said, "but I've always been a fan of Elvis Presley. He had such a wonderful voice. Have them play 'Love Me Tender.' That was always my favorite."

In the darkness, Sue smiled. "Consider it done."

"And I want you to promise me something else," her mother said. "Don't give up on the case you're working on. It's important to a lot of people."

Sue lay quietly for several minutes, silent tears warming her cheeks. "Mama," she finally said, "when you get to Heaven, will you tell Renee that we're going to make things right?"

"I'll take care of Renee," she heard her mother whisper.

It was the last conversation Sue Dietrich had with her mother. The following day, Marie Coker lapsed into a coma.

///

Almost three weeks would pass before the detective found herself once again driving toward the Jachimczyk Forensic Center, this time with Jeri Yenne seated next to her.

At the D.A.'s request, Dr. Anderson had forwarded copies of the tissue slides from his autopsy to the Harris County officials and Yenne had resisted the urge to schedule another meeting until she felt they had had ample time to study the new findings.

Her patience accomplished nothing.

Seated in a large conference room, outlining the same evidence and suspicions that Sue had attempted to offer, Yenne realized in the first few minutes of the meeting that her arguments were falling on deaf ears. Wingo and Dr. Bellas made little effort to hide their impatience.

Sue remained silent until Wingo responded to one of Yenne's observations by again comparing Renee's death to that of a Filipino child who had died suddenly after exposure to dust mites. Dietrich laughed aloud and was still shaking her head in disgust when Yenne delivered a swift, under-the-table kick to her shin.

Wingo glared at the detective, then turned to Yenne. "We have looked at the tissue samples and do not agree with Dr. Anderson's diagnosis," he said. "That's our final word."

Dr. Bellas silently nodded his agreement.

Dietrich saw no reason to abide by Yenne's instructions that she keep her emotions in check and her mouth shut. "Gentlemen," she spat, "this sounds like nothing but damage control to me."

With that, the two men rose in unison and began to walk from the room.

As he reached the door, Wingo turned to the D.A. "Jeri," he said, "do you really need to bring in another doctor?"

"Yes, I do."

Wingo shook his head. "I really hate to see you embarrassed."

///

If their intent had been to discourage prosecution of the case, the effort had been of no avail. In time, Yenne knew, she would revisit the issue of the autopsy. For now, however, she would turn her efforts toward getting a grand jury indictment against Michael Shane Goode.

As they wound through the Houston traffic, Yenne asked Sue to pull into a shopping center parking lot. Hurrying into a Kmart, she purchased a large package of M&M's. The coated chocolates, she admitted, were her greatest weakness in times of stress.

"The ol' post-pregnancy diet will just have to wait a while," she said as she ripped the top from the bag.

///

An occasional M&M binge aside, Yenne seemed to be handling the building pressures well, focusing on such matters as piecing together a profile of the man she hoped to face in a courtroom one day soon. At times she felt she was reviewing the life of two people.

Shane's National Guard records, for instance, showed him to be a model soldier. On the other hand, his financial life was a disaster. Sharon's son, Steven, had written from prison to admit his role in the car-insurance scam and was willing to testify about the plot he claimed Shane had devised.

At the same time, word was getting back to the D.A. that Goode's fellow workers had quickly rallied around him, eager to list a variety of reasons why he could not possibly have had any involvement in the death of his daughter. There were even rumors of a defense fund being collected.

Then there was the growing office talk about the case. Fellow prosecutors, perplexed by Yenne's intensity, expressed doubts that it should even be presented to a grand jury. It was the still undecided grand jury date which was causing Jeri to feel the greatest amount of stress—and, ironically, the pressure was coming not from her detractors but from the few allies she had.

A year had passed since Renee's death, and Annette and Sharon were growing impatient. So, for that matter, was Detective Dietrich. Once Dr. Anderson had found evidence of homicide, Annette and Sharon assumed the indictment and arrest of Goode would quickly follow. They had been understanding of the delay caused by the recovery period Yenne needed following the birth of her child, and they knew that it took time for Dr. Anderson's written report to be completed. They were in agreement with the need to gather documentation from the insurance company which had issued the policy on Renee.

Still, Yenne had continued to delay, hoping that a less acrimonious relationship with the medical examiner's office might be established before she moved ahead. "That's not going to happen," Dietrich had repeatedly argued, "so let's get on with our business."

An attempt to assure Annette and Sharon that progress was being made turned into a disaster.

While Tom Selleck had not yet become actively involved in the case, Yenne urged that he meet with the victim's mother and grandmother. Seeing that the county's best prosecutor was assigned to try the case would, Yenne hoped, offer them some comfort, and perhaps reduce the constant stream of phone calls she was receiving from Sharon.

From the moment Sharon walked into the conference room with her now bulging file on the case, things had gone badly. Every mention of investigative work she had conducted drew Selleck's wrath. She should not, he said, be contacting the National Guard in an effort to track Shane Goode's whereabouts when he was off at training camp. It was not her job to talk with people like Sunny Bradley in an effort to gather background information on the suspect. Who had authorized her to visit the courthouse and seek out old records of Goode's divorce from his first wife? Or to make calls to the M.E.'s office?

"From now on," he said, "I don't want you contacting anyone regarding this case. It isn't your job, understand?"

Yenne, taken aback by the adversarial stance Selleck had taken, felt she should say something, should make him aware of the fact it had been Sharon who had provided virtually every worthwhile piece of information related to the case, but chose to wait until another time. For the victim's family to see that there was friction between the prosecutors handling their case would only worsen matters.

Stunned, Sharon held her anger in check as Selleck's tirade ended. "I understand," she said.

On that note the meeting had ended. It was time, Yenne decided, to check the calendar of the Brazoria County grand jury.

. . .

At five o'clock on the morning of December 7, a patrolman from the Alvin Police Department arrived at the Meadowview home of Donald and Carolyn Goode with subpoenas. The summons stated that they were to report to the Brazoria County courthouse in Angleton by 9:00 A.M.

There, the presentation Yenne had finally decided on would be a concise, streamlined review of the case.

Rather than have Dr. Anderson make another trip to Texas, she would offer a review of his findings of blunt force trauma and his opinion that Renee Goode's death was the result of a homicide. That done, she would put Shane's father and stepmother on the stand and ask them a series of questions that would provide jurors a picture of the events in their home before and after Renee's death. Finally, it would be Detective Dietrich's responsibility to explain the financial motive that had led to the murder.

The entire process took less than four hours. As Sue was leaving the grand-jury room, she was surprised when the foreman asked that she not immediately return to Alvin. "Detective," he asked, "would you mind waiting outside in the hall for just a few minutes?"

Normally, the grand jury hears a lengthy list of cases throughout the morning and into the afternoon before discussing their dispositions and announcing the panel's findings to the prosecutors. Thus neither Dietrich nor Yenne had expected a decision on the Goode case until late in the day.

Yenne, however, was smiling broadly as she joined the detective in the hallway. "They said they want to vote right away," she explained, relaying the message given her by the foreman. Then she offered her own observation: "They want you to leave the courthouse with the indictment in your hand." The prosecutor clinched her fist in a quick gesture of triumph. "Sue," she said, "this has never happened before."

Clearly, those seated on the grand jury were eager for the arrest of Michael Shane Goode to take place. In a matter of minutes they unanimously agreed that the evidence presented was sufficient to warrant an indictment.

Before noon, Detective Dietrich was en route back to the Alvin

Police Department as Jeri Yenne returned to her office where an anxious Sharon Couch awaited the news.

///

As she pulled into the parking lot behind the police station, Sue saw Bodie Duckworth walking toward his pickup. After rolling down her window and calling his name, she got out of her car and hurried in his direction. The two detectives had seen little of each other since his assignment to the narcotics task force and had not discussed the Goode case since Sue had taken it over. Still, she felt he should be among the first to know about the indictment.

"Let's go pick him up," she said. "We don't need a uniform. Just us. We'll flip to see who gets to put the handcuffs on him."

Duckworth's only response was to shake his head and say, "No thanks. It's your case."

"Dammit, Bodie, it's *our* case," she tried to argue, but he had already turned and was walking away.

Sue shrugged and went inside to pass the news of the grand jury's quick decision along to Chief Merkel and Sergeant Arendell. "Pick him up," the chief said. He suggested that she have Detective Carol Atkins, who had worked as her partner on previous cases, and Bobby Taylor, a uniformed officer, go with her.

The youthful Taylor was particularly pleased with the assignment. As they walked toward the squad car, he made no attempt to disguise his excitement. "You going to let me handcuff him?" he asked Dietrich.

Sue smiled. "Yes. I'll read him his rights and you cuff him."

The adrenaline rush that accompanies an arrest swept over the detective when she saw Shane's pickup in the parking lot. But it disappeared just as quickly when there was no response to a series of knocks at his apartment door. Suddenly she was struck by a cold jolt of concern that he might have fled. His parents had no doubt alerted him to their morning visit to the grand jury.

A phone call to the post office revealed that he had taken the day off to keep a doctor's appointment. He had, Sue was told, injured his back while lifting weights.

Locating a Houston police officer who worked security in the complex, the detective showed him the felony arrest warrant she was carrying and asked if he would use a passkey to open the door to Goode's apartment.

Inside, there was no sign of Shane or any indication that he had left in a hurry. It was only when Patrolman Taylor called her into the bedroom that Dietrich saw anything that looked out of place. As she walked through the door, Taylor was pointing down at a nine-millimeter handgun that lay in the middle of the neatly made bed. Dietrich silently picked it up, unloaded it, and returned it to its place. "Let's wait for him outside," she said as she lay the bullets on a nearby dresser.

The security officer joined them on the curb of the parking lot, curious about what Goode was being charged with. "Hey, I know the guy," he said. "We used to be in the same Guard battalion."

Now it was Dietrich's turn to become curious. "The word we hear," she offered, "is that he's had a lot of specialized training, guerrilla-action stuff, hand-to-hand combat . . . knows how to kill an enemy without leaving a mark."

The security officer was laughing before she could complete Goode's resume. "You're talking about this Shane Goode?" he said, pointing back in the direction of the apartment door. "No way. Hell, he's always been just a plain ol' radio man. Lugs the radio equipment around in a backpack on maneuvers."

Another two hours slowly passed before Sue recognized Donald Goode's car as it entered the gateway and wound toward the parking lot. In the passenger seat was Shane.

As Goode stepped from the car, dressed in jeans and a National Guard T-shirt, Officer Taylor quickly approached and ordered him to turn around and place his hands atop the hood. "You're under arrest for capital murder," he said. As he arranged Goode's arms behind his back and began snapping the handcuffs in place, Dietrich recited the Miranda warning.

Shane's father, who had accompanied him to the doctor, looked on in stunned silence. In time he turned to Detective Dietrich and, with fury in his voice, finally spoke: "You sorry motherfucker," he yelled.

"Sir," she replied, "we'll be taking your son to Pearland where he'll be arraigned by a Justice of the Peace, then he'll be transported to the Alvin Police Department. If you have any questions, you can call me there later this evening."

As they drove toward Pearland, a bedroom community on the northern edge of Brazoria County, Shane said nothing. It had, in fact, been his silence during the arrest in the apartment parking lot which Dietrich had found most interesting. When informed of the charges, he had shown no sign of surprise. Nor had there been the usual response of outrage and denial. If anything, the detective thought, Shane Goode had seemed to be strangely relieved.

By the time the arraignment was completed and the prisoner transported to Alvin, the media was out in full force. Camera crews from Houston television stations were set up in the parking lot adjacent to the police station. A group of newspaper reporters, armed with tape recorders and notebooks, talked among themselves. Several photographers pondered the best vantage points from which they might get a photo of the man being brought in.

Though not really surprised that the media had been alerted to Goode's arrest, Sue Dietrich rolled her eyes as they turned into the parking lot.

Her investigation, once conducted so quietly, almost in secret, was about to become what the reporters at the *Houston Chronicle* and anchors on the six-o'clock news liked to refer to as "high profile."

It was after the reporters had finally left to meet their deadlines that Detective Dietrich had Goode removed from his holding cell and escorted to an interview room. For several minutes she silently studied the figure seated across from her, his hands folded atop the table. She waited for him to make eye contact, then gave up and again read him his rights.

"Shane," she said, "do you want to talk about why you've been arrested?"

Goode slowly lifted his head and stared for a moment at the detective, his eyes giving no hint of the concern or fear common to most prisoners she'd interviewed during her career.

"No," he replied. "I think I need my lawyer."

Sixteen

Like many prosecutors of his status, Brazoria County assistant D.A. Tom Selleck viewed time management as one of the most vital aspects of his job. Juggling as many as a half dozen cases at one time, he saw his role as that of a delegator and advisor during their early stages. Investigators were assigned to gather evidence and subordinate A.D.A.s tended the task of filing routine motions and making pretrial court appearances.

Only when the trial date neared would he submerge himself in the case, locked away from the outside world in the weeks before he would be required to stand before a jury to deliver a sharp, well-defined opening argument. During those days of intense preparation Selleck would take no calls, sleep sparingly, and literally memorize even the most minute points of the case he was assigned to prosecute.

It was a style which earned him little favor from the office's investigators, who found themselves on-call around the clock as Selleck always discovered last-minute questions which demanded immediate answers. His method was much like that of a college student cramming for a critical exam—and he wanted everyone taking the course to help him prepare.

There was little room to argue his methods. Selleck went to trial prepared and polished. And he rarely lost.

Aside from occasional hallway briefings from Yenne on the progress of the investigation and the one less-than-pleasant meeting with the victim's family, Selleck had paid the case little mind until the indictment and arrest.

Now, two months into the new year, a trial was imminent and his interest had grown. Sitting in the office of newly elected District Attorney Jerome Aldrich with Yenne at his side, it was time to make a critical decision: Would they seek the death penalty for Shane Goode—which a capital murder charge entitled them to do—or request that a jury sentence him to life in prison if convicted?

If the prosecutors asked that Goode be executed by lethal injection for his crime, they would be obligated to not only convince a jury of his guilt but to prove beyond a reasonable doubt that he represented a continuing threat to society if allowed to live. With little proof of serious criminal behavior in Goode's background, no previous felonies committed or prison time served, it would be difficult.

On the other hand, even the most unsophisticated juror would know that a life sentence was, under Texas law, a misnomer, and that at some point in the future—twelve years on the average—Goode, if convicted, would likely be paroled. Historically, jurors were quick to criticize the legal system for allowing such a thing, yet were far more likely to vote for a conviction if spared the concern of blood on their own hands.

It was what most prosecuting attorneys would call a no-brainer. In the matter of the State of Texas vs. Michael Shane Goode, the maximum penalty they would seek was a life sentence.

In keeping with a long-standing tradition of the office, Aldrich instructed the prosecutors to make the family of the victim aware of the decision. Such a choice, he knew, was rarely popular with those who had suffered the loss of a loved one. Almost without exception, they were satisfied with nothing less than the Biblical eye-for-an-eye brand of justice. Even the most detailed explanation of the quirks and demands of the law would not convince them otherwise.

Still, Aldrich reasoned, the sooner they knew, the more quickly they could come to grips with what would transpire in the days to come.

Jeri Yenne dreaded the call she was assigned to make. Since the arrest, a steady stream of letters had been arriving at her office from members of organizations like Justice for All and Survivors of Homicide Victims, all urging the death penalty for Shane Goode. She was reasonably sure that the campaign had been set in motion by Sharon Couch.

///

Seated at the end of a long, polished table in the D.A.'s conference room, Selleck looked across at the two women who had arrived for the Friday morning meeting. He surpressed a frown at the everpresent bound file which Sharon Couch, seated next to Annette, had again brought with her.

He explained that they were hoping to go to trial sometime in April and that he would be the lead prosecutor with Jeri serving as his cocounsel.

"We've discussed the case at length," he said, "and have come to the conclusion that asking for the death penalty is not in the best interest—"

Sharon leaned forward. "But it's a capital murder case," she argued.

"One that has a lot of problems," Selleck replied. "We've got no witness, no physical evidence directly linking the accused to the crime, and conflicting autopsy reports. To seek the death penalty would be suicide in this case."

Sharon made no effort to hide her outrage. "If there had been blood spattered all over the walls . . . if you had some horrible crime scene photos you could flash around . . . you would damn sure be asking for the death penalty, right?" Before Selleck could respond, she added, ". . . but because it looks as if Renee just went peacefully to sleep, you won't do it. And that's not right. It's your job to do something about what was done to her."

Bristling, Selleck responded. "My job," he said, "is to get a conviction."

Sharon turned frantically to Yenne in hope of support. Jeri knew the horrid details of the case, she knew the dark evil that had caused Renee's death; as a mother, she could understand the suffering which Annette had endured.

Annette sat silently, observing the confrontation.

At first, Yenne had been somewhat surprised by what she perceived as a lack of interest in the case from Annette. Only as Jeri had gotten to know her and Sharon better did she understand. Still grieving and filled with anger, Annette was having great difficulty coping with Renee's death. Sharon Couch was the strength her daughter leaned on.

"We've all talked about this," Jeri finally said, "and have agreed it is the best thing to do. Sharon, I know that Shane Goode is guilty as hell and I want us to win this case. And the best chance we have of doing so is by not seeking the death penalty. I'm in full agreement with Tom."

Staring down at her silent daughter's trembling hands, Sharon inhaled deeply in an attempt to regain her composure. Placing a reassuring arm over Annette's shoulder, she looked across the table at Jeri. "You realize," she said, "this isn't going to be a popular decision."

"I know, Sharon, but it is the only way we're going to win this case."

Tom Selleck was already walking toward the door as she spoke.

///

It did not take long for the full force of Sharon's disapointment to become public. With the help of P. G. Walls, she had called a press conference just hours after leaving the D.A.'s office and had lashed out at the decision.

On Saturday morning, as Yenne sat on her back porch, holding her daughter and preparing to read the *Houston Chronicle,* her eyes were immediately drawn to a headline near the bottom of the front page. It read: "Kin angry death penalty not sought in tot's death."

"I feel we've let Renee down by not even trying to get the death penalty," Sharon had said. "I believe any person convicted of killing his child deserves the death penalty."

The reporter under whose byline the article appeared had also contacted Houston attorney Skip Cornelius, who had been retained to represent Shane Goode. "The case," he was quoted as saying, "is about as weak a murder allegation as I've seen in twenty-three years of practicing law."

For several minutes Jeri sat staring at the article, her attention moving from the text to the side-by-side photographs of Shane and his murdered daughter. For the first time she felt a rush of anger directed at Sharon. And a very real sense of betrayal. *Don't you know I'm the only person in the whole damn D.A.'s office who cares about your murdered granddaughter?* she thought. *Don't you know that it is going to be hard enough without you screwing things up and pissing everybody off?*

Picking up the portable phone that lay on a chair near her, Yenne dialed Selleck. "Have you read the paper yet?" she asked.

The stream of profanity he quickly unleashed was indication that indeed he had.

What troubled Yenne most on that disrupted Saturday morning, however, was not her own anger or even Selleck's vocal disapproval of Sharon Couch. Rather, it was the attitude she sensed Tom was developing toward the case itself. As much as she had hoped it might happen, none of her own passion had rubbed off on the man now assigned to serve as the lead prosecutor.

Already, in fact, he had drawn a hard line where the Harris County M.E.'s office was concerned. When Yenne had informed him that Dr. Bellas was unbending in his refusal to reconsider Renee's cause of death, she had mentioned the possibility that the case would be viewed by some as an attack on the M.E.'s office. "We're not taking them on," Tom had said. "I'm not putting Dr. Bellas or the M.E.'s office on trial. There's no way in hell that I'm going to jeopardize all the other murder cases we've got over this one.

"Shit, Jeri," he observed before ending their conversation, "we're going to have a hard time even proving there *was* a homicide, much less explaining who the hell did it."

He had, she thought, seemed more agitated than she could ever remember him being.

· · ·

Sharon did not help matters when, a few weeks later, she telephoned to tell Selleck that she had just spoken with Dr. Bellas. "There is no way he is going to agree with Dr. Anderson's findings," she said.

"Why the hell were you calling him?"

Immediately defensive, Sharon replied, "Because I want to know where we are on this thing. I want to know what you think about getting another pathologist to look at both Bellas's and Anderson's findings and see what he thinks. If he agrees with Dr. Anderson, you could use his testimony."

Selleck was livid. "And if he agrees with Dr. Bellas we just tell him to go quietly away and keep his mouth shut? Do you know what the penalty is for manipulating evidence?

"I thought you promised me you were going to stay out of this. Didn't we have an agreement?"

The silence on the other end of the line only seemed to irritate him more. "The fact of the matter is," he said, "you don't know everything."

"You're right," Sharon acidly replied. "And that's what scares the hell out of me. And it should concern you even more."

The conversation quickly degenerated into a shouting match—Selleck reminding Sharon that she had no law degree, Sharon responding by asking if all women angered him to this degree. "Maybe," Selleck said, "I should just withdraw from this case and let some other prosecutor try to keep you under control."

Perhaps, Sharon thought, that wasn't such a bad idea.

///

For Yenne, the role of referee was becoming unbearable. She could understand Sharon's fierce determination to see the case move forward, yet at the same time she shared some of Selleck's frustration at the hands-on involvement she constantly demanded.

Keeping the two from each other's throats was vital, Jeri felt, but she could see no way to accomplish such a feat. Talking with Sue Dietrich about the problem was little help.

Calling the detective to relate the latest verbal slugfest between Sharon and Tom, Yenne said, "Sharon's running amok again."

Sue had only laughed, leaving no doubt as to whose side she was on. "Sharon Amok," she said. "I like that."

The new nickname privately shared between the prosecutor and the detective would remain.

So would Sharon's determination. Little time passed before she was on the phone to Yenne, relating Selleck's threat to remove himself from the case. "I don't think he believes he can win this case," she said, "so I'm going to call Jerome Aldrich and ask him to assign a special prosecutor." She was talking rapidly, her voice high-pitched.

"Sharon, wait a minute."

"Jeri, it has nothing to do with you," she continued. "I want you involved. I appreciate everything you've done so far. But if Tom Selleck doesn't have the balls to stick with it, I damn sure don't need him."

"We *do* need him, Sharon. Believe me. Despite whatever differences you might have with Tom, it is important that you understand that he is very good at what he does. He's a great trial lawyer, I assure you. Don't do anything until you hear back from me, okay?"

The following Monday morning, Yenne phoned Sharon to tell her that Selleck had assured her he would not be excusing himself from the case.

What she did not mention were the steadily growing office rumors that the new district attorney and Selleck were at odds. Tension had arisen over Tom having made decisions related to the deposition of cases without first consulting Aldrich.

Sharon Couch, it appeared, was not the only one unhappy with the way things had been going lately.

Seventeen

Within Houston legal circles, Skip Cornelius is considered among the elite of criminal defense attorneys. Though he lacked the high-profile visibility of Racehorse Haynes or the DeGeurin brothers, Mike and Dick, his reputation as a gifted lawyer with a persuasive courtroom style was well earned. Like most, he had first made his mark as a hard-driving prosecutor in the Harris County District Attorney's office before the prospect of six-figure fees lured him into private practice.

In the days immediately following his son's indictment and arrest, Donald Goode had heard Cornelius's name often as he searched for a lawyer. Cornelius was expensive, he was told, but an excellent attorney: thus, Goode borrowed from his retirement fund and took out a second lien on his home in order to make the financial arrangements necessary to retain him.

In his twenty years of legal experience, Cornelius had never seen a case with less hard evidence taken to a grand jury. And, in the months preceding his client's scheduled April trial date, he would also come to admit that he'd encountered few prosecutors with more tenacity than the woman in the Brazoria County D.A.'s office who was preparing the case.

Jeri Yenne, he quickly found out, was not only a stickler for detail but held religiously to the rules of discovery. Routinely, Federal Express packages arrived at Cornelius's Houston office bearing copies of Shane Goode's bank records, canceled checks, and military records. There was documentation of every doctor's visit Renee Goode had made in her short life, paperwork detailing the court-ordered child support his client had been required to pay, and a witness list that constantly underwent revision and addition.

Finally, Skip had telephoned Yenne to good-naturedly suggest to her that he had only limited cabinet space in his office and her almost daily mailings were taking up much of it.

The conversation did little to slow the flow of paperwork. Clearly, the prosecutor attached significance to minute discoveries which Cornelius seriously doubted would advance her case at all. The fact, for instance, that Shane had failed to mention Renee on any of the family histories he'd filled out for his National Guard records interested Yenne far more than it did the defense attorney. Such oversight, Cornelius was convinced, hardly offered proof that Shane Goode was a murderer.

For Yenne, however, preparing a case for trial—particularly if it lacked the conveniences of a smoking gun or eye witness or signed confession—was like piecing together a box puzzle. One never knew until it was finally assembled what small portion might make the picture whole.

In addition to subpoenas for paperwork, she believed strongly in developing a firsthand relationship with those who might eventually take the stand as witnesses. "I've never felt comfortable," she explained to Sue Dietrich, "meeting someone I'm going to ask important questions just minutes before they take the stand."

Thus, as the time neared for Goode's trial, she took to the road, sometimes working late into the evening. At home, Bill Yenne would often answer a late-evening phone call with a response that became something of a running joke. "Where are you now?" he would ask, instead of answering with the standard "hello."

Such calls had come from Houston, where his wife waited patiently for Donald Goode to report for his night-shift duties at the post office, or from the living rooms of those named on her witness list. Aware of the dedication his wife attached to her job and comforted by the knowledge that John Blankenship, an investigator with the D.A.'s office, accompanied her, Bill Yenne summoned patience and only warned that she be careful. And with that, he would return to his responsibility of watching over the children until she arrived home.

There would be times when it was almost midnight before she would silently tiptoe into her children's rooms to kiss them goodnight and whisper an apology for not having been there to tuck them into bed.

"Just bear with me," she pleaded with her husband. "It will be over soon."

Even a broken toe, suffered when she tripped over her infant daughter's car seat in a darkened hallway, failed to slow her. While still on crutches, she and Tom Selleck traveled to Orlando to meet with Dr. Anderson and review his findings and the testimony he would offer.

Bill Yenne had never seen his wife so consumed by a single case. Weekends, generally reserved for backyard barbecues and leisure time with her family, had become long workdays.

///

Sitting on the patio, silently watching as his wife sipped from a cup of coffee cradled in her palms and enjoyed the warmth of an early morning sun, Bill Yenne made no mention of his concern for the weary look on Jeri's face.

Later in the day, Jeri Yenne and Skip Cornelius would be flying to Dallas where Cornelius was scheduled to meet with one of his expert witnesses, Dr. Charles Petty, former head of the Southwest Forensic Laboratory. Cornelius wanted Dr. Petty to review the forensic evidence in the case and had requested that the tissue slides from both autopsies be sent to his office.

Making no effort to disclose her knowledge of the hostility that Petty felt toward Linda Norton, Jeri had innocently explained her reluctance to turn over the slides as a fear they might somehow be lost. She suggested to Cornelius that his witness would be more than welcome to visit Dr. Norton's office, which was just a few miles away, and conduct his review there. Cornelius had been surprised when the elderly Petty flatly refused what had sounded like a convenient and logical accommodation.

Yenne, expressing mock surprise at Petty's stance, had then offered a solution: She would accompany Cornelius on the trip, they could go by Dr. Norton's office to pick up the material, then take it to Dr. Petty. Her presence, she said, would satisfy her concerns over custody of what she felt was the most important hard evidence she had to offer a jury. She made no mention of the fact that it would give her a rare opportunity to get a read on a key defense witness.

She had been pleasantly surprised when Cornelius quickly agreed to her suggestion. Still, she was not looking forward to spending so much time in the presence of the lawyer she would soon face in the courtroom.

"I'm getting really tired of him treating me like I'm some nice little lady who doesn't know her ass from third base," she told her husband as she rose to prepare for the trip. "I hate the way he talks to me like I'm some misguided little girl. Damn, I hate it."

Bill smiled at his wife's indignation—and the colorful language that rarely emerged except when she was in the midst of preparing a particularly difficult case.

/ / /

Before his retirement, Dr. Charles Petty had spent over two decades as the chief medical examiner of Dallas County, commanding a reputation as one of the premier pathologists in the nation. Born in Montana and educated at Harvard Medical School, he had overseen thirteen thousand autopsies during his lengthy career.

As important as his medical credentials were to any defense lawyer, it was Petty's courtly manner that had made him such a sought-after witness. No juror would ever see the ego that examining-room colleagues knew all too well. Rather, juries saw a gentle, gray-haired man who smiled often and spoke in a pleasant voice that conveyed reassurance and wisdom. Dr. Petty was, if nothing else, a real charmer when he wished to be.

Though she knew him only by reputation, Jeri Yenne had been

concerned about his appearance since receiving a phone call from Dr. Norton, alerting her that there were rumors afoot that he might testify for the defense. "If he does," Dr. Norton had warned, "don't try to go after him on cross-examination. The man knows more about pathology than the rest of us put together. He's brilliant—and terrific on the witness stand. He can eat you alive, smiling the whole time he's doing it."

Yenne saw little of Petty's charm as they met in his office. She and Cornelius had picked up the slides from Dr. Norton and made the twenty-minute drive to Petty's office. There, they had waited while Petty first read the autopsy reports, then viewed the slides under his microscope.

Finally, he lifted his head, removed his horn-rimmed glasses, and spoke. "This is nothing more than a bunch of folderol if you ask me." Looking at Cornelius, he said, "I have reviewed the three items you asked me to, and I am in complete agreement with Dr. Bellas. I see nothing here that can tell me how the little girl died."

With that, he turned to Yenne with a slight smile. "Ma'am, do you have any questions?"

Taken aback momentarily by the unexpected opportunity, the assistant district attorney waited several seconds before responding. "Just one," she finally said. "Have you had an opportunity to look at the exhumation photos taken by Dr. Anderson?"

"No," he replied, "they weren't among the items I was asked to review."

"Thank you, Dr. Petty," Yenne said, concluding with a businesslike handshake. Another question was racing through her mind as they prepared to leave but she dared not ask it. There would be time for that later, when a jury could hear his answer.

Why, she wondered, would a man with a reputation for great thoroughness and caution render an opinion after looking at only three of the fourteen pieces of forensic evidence that she planned to present during trial?

Her speculation was that Cornelius, confident that her case was without merit, had not felt it important to bother his witness with unnecessary clutter.

. . .

"You realize what he has to say is going to be quite damaging to your case," Cornelius said as their plane climbed above Dallas's Love Field and set its course for the forty-five minute flight back to Houston.

Yenne did not bother to look up from the in-flight magazine she'd been idly flipping through. "He said exactly what I'd expected him to say," she replied.

Cornelius could not help but admire her stubborn determination.

If nothing else, she had convinced him of something he'd have given odds against when he was first hired by Donald Goode. There remained absolutely no doubt that they would go to trial, regardless of the insurmountable weaknesses he perceived in her case.

"Look," he said, "we're both mature adults. We both know the law. The only difference is I've been doing this a lot longer than you have . . ."

"So?"

"So, I want you to keep one thing in mind. If you're going to be a trial lawyer, you have to be ready to accept the fact that someone wins and someone loses. No bargains. All deals go out the window. It's all or nothing once you take a case into the courtroom. If you can't accept that, you have no business being a trial lawyer."

He was, she felt, already consoling her. "I agree with you completely," she replied. There was a brief pause before she lifted her eyes from the magazine. "The reason this one is going to trial is because I have no doubts that your client is guilty."

Cornelius rolled his eyes. The woman seated next to him was perplexing. "Jeri," he argued, "you're going to have a big problem even proving that there was a homicide. And if you get over that hurdle, how are you going to prove it was my client who did it?" With that, he paused briefly, then added, "And I'm not saying my client did anything."

"I guess," Yenne responded, "that will be my problem to deal with. All I know for certain at this point is that your client is a stone-cold baby killer and that what I'm doing is right."

For the remainder of the trip they sat in silence, both aware that their relationship was doomed to fall far shy of any kind of friendship. It was not until they began their descent that Cornelius spoke again.

"You know," he said, "years ago, when I was still a prosecutor, I had this rape case that I got very emotionally involved in. The victim was a woman with a long history of mental instability. She'd had delusions of being raped on a number of occasions when, in fact, nothing of the sort had happened. But this time, it *had* happened. She had been raped. I knew it. And I knew that the man we were trying was guilty as hell. Everyone in my office told me that as soon as the woman's mental background came out my case was lost. And, you know, I figured they were right. But I put my case on anyway, hoping for a little divine intervention, all the while assuming that the jury would walk the guy.

"But you know what? The jury happened to believe my woman's story and came back with a guilty verdict."

Cornelius did not even look in Yenne's direction as he spoke. Now it was her watching him, keenly aware that his sudden reflection had not been the least boastful. Though not sure of his reason, she sensed that he had told it more for his own benefit than hers.

Cornelius's mood quickly lightened and the smile returned to his face. "So," he concluded, "if you're right—and I'm certainly not saying that you are—maybe God will do something like that for you."

It was an observation Jeri Yenne pondered for days afterward. Looking back on it, she found herself wishing that she'd confided to Cornelius something she'd told no one.

She had, since the day she took the case, been regularly seeking counsel of a higher power.

///

Among the most difficult jobs Yenne assigned herself was that of interviewing the other children who had been in the Goode home on the night of Renee's death. Her years of investigating child-abuse cases had provided her ample experience for such a task, but it had never gotten any easier. The idea that an innocent child had to be dragged into the legal process grated on the prosecutor.

Still, despite the fact that Detective Dietrich had already provided her with the children's statements, Jeri felt obligated to speak with them herself.

Sitting in Kaye Goode's home, talking with Tiffany, Yenne was quickly convinced that the young girl loved her father deeply. And that she had also loved Renee.

Tears brimmed in Tiffany's eyes when she mentioned that she was the only one of the older children who had really wanted to play with Renee that night. "I miss her a lot," she said.

It was she, not her father, who had taken Renee into the bedroom that evening and changed her diaper. Tiffany had no idea why he would lie about such a small thing.

Yenne sat across the room, listening to the pretty little girl, careful to hide her concerns about her. In the prosecutor's files were statements of certain friends and associates of Shane's that suggested that something was unusual about their father-daughter relationship. Tiffany herself had innocently admitted that Shane often took her dancing.

Despite her determination to seek out every blemish she could find on Shane Goode's character, Jeri found herself hoping that at least some of her suspicions were unfounded.

The visit with Michelle had been no less trying. Sitting between her mother and grandmother, having been assured that Yenne was a friend, she had once again detailed the events surrounding her sister's death. She, too, had begun to cry, but waited until Jeri left before confiding to her mother the reason she had become so upset.

"I feel so bad," the child explained. "Like it was my fault."

Annette had consoled her, assuming that Michelle's feelings of guilt sprang from the fact that she had been told to watch after Renee, that she had, in essence, been charged with her safety.

Michelle continued to cry, shaking her head. "Mommy," she finally asked, "have you ever wished somebody was dead?"

Annette hugged her distraught child to her chest.

"One time," Michelle sobbed, "I got real mad at Renee and I thought that. I wished that she was dead."

"Don't cry," Annette whispered as she stroked the little girl's hair. "Renee knows that you loved her."

"I really did," Michelle cried. "I loved her a lot."

///

Christine Goode—Shane's niece, who had been living with his parents at the time of Renee's death—had been placed in a girls' home in the Texas panhandle shortly after the tragedy. She had, according to reports Yenne heard from family friends, become increasingly defiant and unruly, at odds with the still-ailing Carolyn Goode and performing poorly in school. At the suggestion of a child psychologist, Christine had been sent off to the Cal Farley Girls' Ranch.

Located near the cotton-farming hamlet of Whiteface, the school was the offspring of an all-boys home that was founded by a benevolent professional wrestler who had modeled the facility after Father Flannigan's famous Boys' Town. The Ranch, as it was called by residents, offered a fully-accredited school, a regimented lifestyle, and a program of strict discipline designed to steer troubled children back toward acceptable behavior.

Christine had been at the Ranch for three months when Yenne and Detective Dietrich, accompanied by juvenile officer Valerie Wright, visited her.

On the short flight to Lubbock—from where they would rent a car and make the hour's drive across the dusty, windswept landscape of the panhandle—Yenne pulled a large manila envelope from her briefcase. In it was the complete set of autopsy photographs which she had requested from the Harris County M.E.'s office.

As she idly thumbed through the pictures, Jeri suddenly felt the sharp edge of Sue Dietrich's elbow against her rib cage. Turning to the detective, she saw her cutting her eyes toward the back of their seats.

Jeri turned to see the ashen face of a young fellow traveler, peering over her shoulder at the gruesome pictures spread before her. Embarrassed, Yenne hurriedly returned them to the envelope as Sue attempted to mask a bemused smile.

The visit with Christine would offer little in the way of new insight. The girl's recollection of what transpired at her grandparents' house was no different from what she'd given the police: She'd gone to her own bedroom. She recalled Shane peeking his head in her door to say goodnight. Later, she'd heard him taking a shower.

Only when Yenne asked her if she had received any letters from Shane or her grandparents since coming to the Ranch did she show any enthusiasm. Yes, she had, the youngster said, and hurried off to her room to retrieve them.

It saddened the women when she returned with a photo album in which she had carefully mounted the letters. In the months since her arrival, there had been two from her grandmother and one from Shane. Each was brief and chatty, obviously written in response to her own letters.

That evening as she wearily returned home, Jeri made no attempt at silence as she entered the room of her sleeping four year old. Rather, she woke him and pulled him into her lap.

"Logan," she said, "Mommy's home. I missed you."

Sleepy-eyed, the youngster returned his mother's embrace. Born just two weeks before Renee, he had struggled to understand why his mother had been spending so much time away.

"Why did you have to go someplace?" he asked.

Yenne pulled him tightly against her. "Because, honey," she said, "I had to go help a little girl."

///

As the date of Goode's trial neared, the ever-present anxiety Yenne had felt about the case had begun to subside. Confident in her checklist style of preparation, she had routinely kept Tom Selleck abreast of what she was doing. Soon, she promised, she would be ready to offer him the material he would need as lead prosecutor on the case.

The intoxicating sense of urgency she had begun to feel would, however, quickly vanish when a new problem developed.

Annette and her husband were expecting their first child in the spring and the pregnancy had, in recent months, become increasingly difficult. The doctor, Vince Campise explained to Yenne, had begun to express serious reservations about his wife's ability to deal with the physical and emotional stress of the upcoming trial.

He had, in fact, strongly advised against her serving as a witness.

Sue Dietrich only briefly considered her phone bill when she recieved a message to call Yenne—it had climbed to almost three hundred dollars monthly since she and Yenne had first begun their late night discussions of the investigation—then returned Jeri's call.

"We've got a problem," Yenne said, agitation clear in her voice.

"So what's new?" the detective replied in an attempt to lighten the mood.

"We're going to have to ask for a postponement."

Sue's mood immediately changed to match that of her friend. "Why?"

The prosecutor outlined the concerns of Annette's doctor.

"There's no way in hell we can risk starting the trial and finding out right in the middle of things that she's in the delivery room and can't testify. Or wonder what kind of mental frame of mind she'd be in even if she could testify. We've got to wait until she's had her baby," she said. "I spoke with Sharon and she says Annette's already one raw, exposed nerve end. There's nothing else we can do."

She didn't have to explain that without Annette's testimony there could be no case. Neither did she have to mention the new legal step Cornelius was certain to take. By asking for a postponement of the trial, the state would open the door for Goode and his attorney to immediately seek a bond-reduction hearing.

In all likelihood, the judge would drastically reduce the amount originally asked for.

"We're going to have to let the sonuvabitch out of jail," Sue said, as if reading Yenne's thoughts.

"It could happen," Yenne replied.

And it did.

On April 12, Shane Goode was released on $80,000 bond posted by his father, walking into the fresh air of Angleton after four months in the Brazoria County jail. His trial date was reset for August.

For Sue Dietrich, the new month—not even half over—had already been a disaster. Goode's release, while disturbing, had not been the worst news.

Her father, she learned, had also been diagnosed with cancer and the doctors estimated that he had less than a year to live. Mixed with the sorrowful prospect of losing her other parent was the renewal of silent concern she had about her own health. The lump in her breast had, she feared, grown larger, yet she still refused to do anything about it. For the time being, Sue decided, uncertainty was better than having to deal with yet another trauma in her life.

After confiding her father's condition to Yenne during one of their late-evening phone conversations, the detective explained that she could best deal with the news by staying busy.

"In that case," Yenne had said, "see if you can keep up with what our boy's doing now that he's back out in the free world. And see if there's anyone out there who knows something about him that we don't."

The likelihood that Detective Dietrich might happen onto some case-making revelation was, Yenne knew, remote. Sometimes, however, work offered remarkable cure for a variety of professional and personal ills.

Sue went about her new assignment with a vengeance, keeping track of Goode from a discreet distance. While most of Goode's co-workers were hesitant to speak with her, one had mentioned the name of another woman with whom Shane had become romantically involved shortly before his arrest. Several times the detective had attempted to contact the woman during working hours with no success. Each time Sue had left a number, requesting that the woman return the call at her earliest convenience.

Finally, resigned that she was not going to cooperate, Sue called her home. The woman's husband answered.

The detective introduced herself and quickly explained the purpose of her call. "I'm investigating the death of Renee Goode," she said, "and I'm sure you're aware that her father has been indicted and charged with the murder."

"I don't know anything about it," the man answered in a disinterested manner.

"Well, sir," Sue continued, "I have information that your wife and Shane Goode are, in fact, good friends, and I'd hoped to talk with her about him."

"My wife doesn't know any Shane Goode," the husband replied, his tone suddenly hostile.

"Apparently she does," Sue argued. "In fact, I'm told that she corresponded with him while he was being held in jail and that she visited him there on several occasions. I have information that she regularly deposited money into his commissary account. I have good reason to believe that your wife and Mr. Goode were quite good friends. So if you would please ask her to call me when—"

"I told you, goddammit, that my wife doesn't know anybody by that name." And with that, he slammed down the receiver.

It was early the following morning when a call to the office was routed to Dietrich's home as she dressed for work. The woman she'd unsuccessfully been attempting to reach for days was on the phone, in a rage as she cursed the detective. "Because of your call," she screamed, "my husband has left me. You've destroyed my marriage and I'm going to sue your ass off."

Sue Dietrich, a woman with neither patience nor pity left for cheating spouses, calmly suggested that her caller "take a number and get in line."

///

Aside from the fact the administrator of the post office had ruled that he could not return to work until the criminal charges were resolved, Shane Goode appeared to resume his life with little evidence that his incarceration had affected him in the least.

With no job and ample free time, he began a rigorous training routine at one of the Pasadena gyms, made occasional appearances at the local country-western dance clubs, and enthusiastically returned to his National Guard activities.

When flooding of the nearby San Jacinto River drove people from their homes, he was among the Guardsmen called into duty to build sandbag levies and help evacuate families from low-lying areas. When Texas governor George Bush gave a speech at Ellington Air Force

Base to announce the signing of a new Crime Victim's Law, Shane Goode was, ironically, among the uniformed officers standing at parade rest just feet away.

The following day a concerned investigator with the Travis County D.A's office who was also a member of the National Guard telephoned Yenne from Austin. He had, he explained, received an anonymous report that a Guard member charged with capital murder and out on bond had been allowed within a few feet of the state's highest-ranking official.

Yenne had laughed as she told him that he was obviously speaking of Shane Goode. "You can tell the governor," she said, "he has nothing to worry about. He's far too old to interest this guy."

As if on a mission, Goode sought out former coworkers to assure them that there was no truth to the charges against him and that he would soon be back on the job. And, while many were quick to voice their support, some even asking if they might contribute to some sort of defense fund, there were those who had doubts.

One morning, while driving through a residential area, Shane recognized the mail carrier, a coworker with whom he was only slightly acquainted. Pulling over, he started up a conversation which, as usual, quickly turned to his proclamation of innocence. The mail carrier, a deacon in his church, listened only briefly before cutting his visitor short. "Look," he said, "I've got mail to deliver. Whatever took place between you and that little girl is none of my business. That's between you and God."

And with that, he had walked away.

Such were the stories Sue Dietrich gathered as she marked the slow passage of time until August. As evidence, she knew, the stories she was hearing amounted to nil. Still, their gathering kept her busy. And, perhaps, sane.

Yenne, too, was in constant search of additional preparations she could attend to, checking for anything she might have overlooked, or a potential witness who had not been contacted. In truth, the delay had not only provided ample time to ready the case but left her with time on her hands.

One afternoon while seated at her desk, reading through files that she had all but set to memory, she picked up the phone and called volunteer investigator John Barnes. "There's something we need to do," she informed the investigator.

Within the hour they were in her car, driving south toward Hallettsville. The one thing Jeri Yenne had not done was visit Renee Goode.

Standing at the foot of the grave, she silently stared down at the marble headstone, realizing for the first time just how closely she had allowed herself to bond with a child she'd never known. Before moving away she snapped a picture of the gravesite, then turned to her investigator. "I think," she smiled, "we're now ready to go to trial."

Six weeks before jury selection was scheduled to begin, her pronouncement would be shrouded in doubt.

///

As is so often the case, the news wound its way through the office grapevine long before there was an official announcement. Tom Selleck, Jeri heard from a fellow prosecutor, had resigned.

Whether it had been his idea or an alternative offered by D.A. Aldrich was the topic of much debate—as was the reason for the dispute. There had been, some suggested, heated discussions behind the closed doors of Aldrich's office about Selleck's decision not to prosecute a D.W.I. offender.

In a matter of minutes Yenne was in Aldrich's office. "You can't do this," she pleaded. "You can't let him resign now. Dammit, Jerome, I need him. We're scheduled to go to trial in six weeks."

Aldrich only shrugged. "I'm not sure," he finally said, "that I understand what you're so upset about. From what I hear, you've been doing all the work and Tom hasn't done jack shit."

"But you know he was going to be the lead prosecutor."

"Not anymore," the D.A. replied. "It's your case."

Yenne slumped in a chair, inhaling a deep breath as she pondered the sudden turn of events.

"You'll do fine," her boss assured her.

"I'm going to need some help," she finally managed to say. Suddenly moved from second chair to first, she found the thought of trying the case paralyzing.

"We'll find you someone."

///

Those initially suggested to serve as Yenne's aide were attorneys involved in various cases of their own. They would do what they could to help, but other responsibilities would make it difficult for them to be present in the courtroom for the duration of the trial. "I don't want the jury to see one of the prosecutors ducking in and out," Jeri had argued. "If they are to realize the importance of this case, they have to see the lawyers sitting at the prosecutor's table all day, every day. Find me someone who can devote all of his energies to what we're trying to do."

She had not met Tony Latino, a barrel-chested, soft-spoken attorney who had joined the new D.A.'s staff just weeks earlier. His primary assignment was to be the hot check department, Aldrich explained, but he brought with him some experience in capital murder cases.

Latino had not yet even settled into his new office when Yenne entered and laid a stack of files on his desk. "Read these," she said, "and let me know what you think."

"When do you go to trial?" he asked as she was turning to leave.

"Two weeks."

The following morning he appeared in Yenne's office. Again there was no time wasted with get-acquainted chatter. Instead, he immediately launched into a discussion of the case, posing questions, making observations. He'd done his homework.

"Can we win it?" Yenne asked.

"I believe so," he quickly answered.

Jeri liked the man who was assigned to assist her but was concerned that the crash course he would need to get up to speed on the case would not be sufficient preparation. She had literally lived the case for months, immersing herself in it as she'd never done before. How, in just a couple of weeks, could he be expected to understand the importance she had long assigned the case?

"Maybe," he suggested, "having someone who can view things from a new perspective will be beneficial."

"Welcome aboard," Jeri said, smiling as she extended her hand to her new trial partner.

///

As the date for the trial neared, Yenne had begun sleeping fitfully, often waking to pace the house and look in on her children. One night her husband woke to find her sitting up in bed, her face buried in her hands.

"You okay?" he said.

"I was dreaming," she said. "I was at the medical examiner's office, trying to get them to explain about lividity and hemorrhaging and things like that. They took me into the examining room to show me Renee's body."

Bill Yenne moved across the bed to comfort his wife.

"Her little body was lying there on the table," she continued, "and I was looking down at it. And, all of a sudden, she opened her eyes and looked at me." Tears had begun to make their way down her cheeks.

"God, Bill," she said, "it was like she was telling me I had to do something to help her."

"You will," he said, reaching to wipe away his wife's tears. "Soon."

///

Sue Dietrich had made it a practice to drive, occasionally, past the home of Donald and Carolyn Goode, and had become increasingly concerned when she saw no indication of their presence. No car was ever in the driveway and the window shades of the modest brick home were always drawn. Only when the detective contacted a friend who lived in the neighborhood was she assured that the Goodes were still residing at the Meadowview address. However, the neighbor confided, there was some talk that they were planning a vacation that would put them out of town during their son's trial.

It was important, Sue realized, that they be served with subpoenas as quickly as possible. The neighbor agreed to phone her the next time he was certain the Goodes were at home.

The following Saturday morning Sue was washing her hair when her beeper sounded. Dialing the number that had been left, she heard the neighbor's voice. "This is your spy," he joked. "Mr. Goode is mowing his front yard as we speak."

Not even bothering to dry her hair or consider makeup, she quickly made the short drive to the Meadowview address. Donald Goode cut the engine of his mower as the woman in jeans, a sweatshirt, and dark glasses approached, but said nothing when she held out the subpoena. "Sir," she said, "I also have one for your wife."

"She's not here."

"In that case, I'll be back." Sue was speaking over the sound of the lawn mower which the elder Goode had already restarted.

Two days later Dietrich was making one of her routine drives through the neighborhood when she saw Carolyn Goode unloading groceries from the trunk of her car. As the Alvin police car pulled into the driveway behind her, Mrs. Goode dropped one of the bags she'd just lifted from the trunk and began walking hurriedly in the direction of the garage.

Quickly out of her car, Sue shouted, "Mrs. Goode, I know who you are and I have a subpoena. If you won't take it, I can just leave it here in the trunk of your car. Either way, you are officially served."

Carolyn Goode turned and walked slowly back to the officer, extending her hand to take the document that required her to join her husband as a witness at her stepson's trial.

Saying nothing, she hurried into the house. As the detective backed away, the bags of groceries remained in the trunk of the Goode car.

Eighteen

The Trial

And this is how it ended: on a gray morning with a steamy August rain dancing in the streets of Angleton as people hurried toward the welcome cover of the Brazoria County Courthouse. Some stopped briefly to shake water from their umbrellas and speak to the clerks and bailiffs who stood in the dry shelter of the overhang near the front doors, smoking final cigarettes before beginning their workday. Others made their way through the double doors quickly and in silence, clearly not pleased to have been summoned to the marbled building that sprawled over a two-block area.

Inside, the aroma of freshly brewed coffee scented the air near the small cafeteria located just off the lobby and the wooden benches were fast filling with the players who kept the county's hall of justice humming: grim-faced men hoping a judge had wakened in a good mood and would not look too unkindly on their varied transgressions; women eager for divorce decrees to finally be heard or custody issues settled; well-dressed attorneys peering into briefcases as they outlined last-minute tactics to anxious clients; uniformed police on hand to offer testimony who made no attempt to hide their impatience; and an assortment of family members, young and old, on hand to lend whatever moral support they could provide.

· · ·

On this Tuesday morning, there were clear signs that something out of the ordinary was in the offing. The presence of television trucks in the nearby parking lot and the small cluster of sleepy-eyed reporters seated at the table nearest the entrance to the cafeteria, passing time reading the morning paper or sipping coffee from styrofoam cups, was certain indication that this would be no routine day. So, too, was the fact that on the third floor, bailiffs were instructed that anyone wishing to enter District Judge J. Ray Gayle's court had first to be searched.

In a corner of the downstairs lobby, the young man who had caused this wave of late-summer excitement stood with his parents and an attractive woman whom he had recently begun dating. Dressed in a charcoal blazer, dark slacks, and a tie, his shoes spit-polished, Shane Goode looked more like an up-and-coming lawyer than a murder defendant.

Though Shane would probably not have been flattered by the comparison, several reporters had remarked that he and John Wayne Bobbitt—the infamous spouse who gained national notoriety after his angered wife severed his penis—looked remarkably alike.

If Shane was concerned about the opening of the long-delayed event, he hid his apprehension well. Donald and Carolyn Goode seemed more uneasy than their son. As Shane talked casually with his girlfriend, his parents sat side by side, saying nothing, their eyes focused on some distant point across the room.

Upstairs in the D.A.'s office, Jeri Yenne paced and looked at her watch. Five minutes had elapsed since she'd last checked the time. Neatly stacked on the edge of her desk were the files and reference books she would take into court with her. Her ammunition, she said.

The smile she summoned to acknowledge Sue Dietrich's arrival was brief. She knew there was no need to hide her nervousness from the one other person in the world who best understood the importance attached to what was about to happen.

"You're going to be great," the detective offered.

Yenne moved to the door and closed it before she spoke. Then, taking Dietrich's hand, she said, "I want you to do something for me."

"What's that?"

"Something I don't do often enough," Jeri replied. "I want you to pray with me."

In the cramped office, sealed from the noisy bustle of the new business day that was beginning down the hall in the D.A.'s office, Yenne sought divine guidance and justice.

With that, she reached into her pocket and handed Sue a strand of opaque beads. "You know," she explained, "that I'm not a particularly spiritual person. But a friend of mine brought these to me after a trip to the Holy Land. I want you to have them."

Sue clutched the beads. "Can't hurt," she said in an attempt to lighten the mood. Never in her law-enforcement career had she seen a prosecutor so determined, so focused on the task that awaited.

///

Four women and eight men had been seated on the jury during the previous day's voir dire. There, they had gotten their first glimpse of the contrasting styles of the two attorneys who would try the case: Cornelius had been smooth and polished, exuding the confidence that is a defense lawyer's most valued weapon. Yenne, on the other hand, had appeared nervous, constantly gesturing to accent her points. Several times throughout the day she had caught herself talking too rapidly, her sentences running together, and had offered a smiling apology to the jury panel. Still, she, too, had a weapon that was likely to serve her well during the course of the trial: The jurors quickly recognized that the prosecutor felt a great passion for her task.

That passion would carry over to her opening statement.

///

Standing in front of the jury box, Yenne methodically outlined the case: the tortured relationship between Shane and Annette, the bitter divorce, the financial problems, and, finally, Renee's death and the motive. "This man," she said, turning to face the defendant, "had not wanted his child, had told Annette to have an abortion. Even after Renee was born he referred to her only as 'Annette's baby.' And for almost a year and a half he showed no interest, didn't even see his daughter. But after he took out a fifty-thousand-dollar life insurance policy . . ."

At the defense table, Shane sat rigidly, hands folded in front of him, listening as if the prosecutor was speaking about someone else.

Yenne previewed the testimony they would hear, closing with the promise that "Dr. William Anderson, one of the nation's leading experts on child death, will be here to tell you the horrible story of how Renee died."

She was unaware that, during the final fifteen minutes of her summary, she had begun to pace back and forth in front of the jurors. Their eyes had followed her as if they were viewing a tennis match.

Cornelius's opening statement was more brief and, predictably, portrayed his client as the victim of an angry vendetta by a scorned ex-wife. It was Annette who had tried desperately to put the marriage back together; it was Annette who, so paranoid over the possibility that Shane might get back together with his first wife, had made enraged threats to kill Kaye Goode. He claimed that if anyone had murder in her heart, it was Annette, not his client.

He promised that there would be testimony that directly contradicted Dr. Anderson's findings that Renee had died of compressive asphyxia. The sad truth was that Renee had been another tragic victim of Sudden Infant Death Syndrome. It was also possible that the blow to the head she'd recieved after that December tricycle accident had played a part. "We'll never really know," he stated. What he did promise was forensic testimony that would convince them that what Dr. Anderson viewed as hemorrhaging was nothing more than the residue of the lividity, the gravity-induced pooling of blood in the child's back. It was something commonly found in all postmortem reviews.

And the fifty-thousand-dollar insurance policy? It was the kind that thousands of caring parents take out on their children. An investment. For Renee's college education.

It was a claim that neither Annette, nor her mother, nor Detective Dietrich would actually hear made. As sworn witnesses, they would not be allowed inside the courtroom until called to the stand. As the trial got underway, they kept vigil in a conference room adjacent to the D.A.'s office, passing time by taking turns playing hangman and tic-tac-toe with Michelle on a portable chalkboard that had been stored in the room.

The waiting wore most on Sue. Despite the judge's admonition to witnesses not to discuss the case, Annette tried repeatedly to ask her questions about what evidence was being presented, urging that she speak with Yenne during the breaks and solicit progress reports. Despite Sue's attempts to explain why, it was difficult for Annette, who had recently given birth to a son, to understand that their discussions over the long months that had finally led them to this tiny room were suddenly no longer allowed.

Sharon, meanwhile, paced nervously, constantly peeking from the door to see who might be standing in the hall waiting to be called to testify.

It was the first time Sue had experienced firsthand the agony families endure while awaiting a trial's outcome, barred by a law that refused them the right to witness events that would have a direct bearing on their lives. The detective found herself silently contemplating the unfairness of it and wishing that Yenne had not requested that she be on standby in the event some last-minute question arose.

"At least we're not the only ones in the dark," Sharon said, after making another check of the hallway. She had caught a glimpse of Shane's parents, standing near a window, holding hands and staring out at the rain.

///

Yenne wasted little time getting to the heart of her case. Following the testimony of Alvin PD patrolman Terry Earl—who recalled the scene he encountered in the Goode house the morning Renee's death was discovered—and that of Hallettsville funeral director Daniel Kubena—who discussed the exhumation that had taken place the previous October—the prosecutor called her star witness to the stand.

From the moment she had begun preparing her trial strategy, Jeri had planned to call Dr. Anderson to the stand as early as possible. The vast majority of the American public is eager to believe what a doctor says—particularly if he is one with a gift for connecting with the layperson. She was convinced that the Florida doctor would come across as highly qualified and authoritative without seeming patronizing. He would not be one of those expert witnesses who flaunts his education and vocabulary. Dr. Anderson won't talk down to the jury, she was certain.

She was confident that his testimony would accomplish the first big step the state needed to take: Dr. Anderson would convince the members of the jury that a murder had, in fact, taken place. After that, it would be up to Jeri to reveal Shane Goode's serpentine trail of lies to show that he was the one who had committed the crime.

Peering over reading glasses, which he used occasionally to consult his notes or view the photographs Yenne displayed, the doctor painstakingly detailed the autopsy he had performed, explaining how the hemorrhaging would not have been detected had he not first surgically removed the child's diaphragm to get an unobstructed view of the interior of the victim's back. Responding carefully to each of the prosecutor's questions, he assured the jurors that he was certain that he had not mistaken lividity for the localized hemorrhaging he had found. And the simple fact that he had found evidence of trauma ruled out the possibility Renee had been a SIDS victim. No, he said, there was absolutely nothing to suggest that it was a relatively mild blow to the head after falling against a coffee table that had caused the child's death.

"This child," he said, "died as the result of intentional force. I would consider her death a homicide."

With that, Yenne reached into a box located beneath the prosecution table and approached the witness stand with a stuffed doll that was approximately the same size Renee had been when she died. As she handed it to the doctor, the jurors leaned forward.

"Doctor," she said, "would you demonstrate for us how compressive force might have been applied in this instance?"

Standing in front of the jury box, he slowly drew the doll to his chest with his arms around its back. Then he began to squeeze.

For the first time since they had been seated, the jurors, turned their collective gaze upon the defense table and the man on trial.

Cornelius's response on cross-examination was to again revisit the lividity issue and to question how such internal damage could have been done without leaving the slightest bruise or abrasion on the outside of the body. He then began an accusing series of questions about the fee the doctor would receive from the state for performing the autopsy and offering expert testimony. His message was far from subtle: The man on the witness stand should be viewed as nothing more than a hired gun who had come to town to fight the state's battle.

His questioning completed, Cornelius took the chair next to Shane and leaned toward the defendant. "I think," he whispered, "we scored some points."

For Yenne, the trial's opening day had focused on the technical and clinical. On Wednesday, she would raise the emotional temperature of her case.

Dressed in a tailored, cream-colored suit, Annette Campise moved toward the witness stand with purpose, passing near the defendant without so much as a glance. In fact, she rarely looked in Shane's direction as she detailed their turbulent life together.

Her responses to Yenne's questions, at times so soft-spoken that jurors were forced to lean forward in their seats to hear her, painted a portrait of a mean-spirited husband who was abusive and a father who demonstrated no interest in their child for most of her short life. It was not until the prosecutor introduced into evidence a video that had been taken at the Waxahachie home of Annette's in-laws during Renee's last Christmas that Annette's emotions crumbled.

On a television monitor tiny Renee danced, pointed gleefully toward a brightly decorated Christmas tree, and mugged for the camera. Annette buried her face in her hands as she began to sob.

Yenne remained silent until her witness slowly regained her composure. "Now," the prosecutor continued, "let's talk about the events leading to the night of January twenty-two. . . ."

Before the day ended, the jury heard about the terrifying call Annette had received and her recollections of the scene that greeted her when she arrived at the Meadowview address that morning. Only when she described her ex-husband's behavior in the Goode den did she look in his direction.

What she saw was a blank stare on his face. It seemed to Annette as though he had willed himself to ignore everything she was saying.

Late the following day, Cornelius had his opportunity to cross examine. Before passing her witness on to him, Yenne asked Annette to recount the arguments and legal actions that had resulted from Goode's unwillingness to pay child support.

The jury also heard the replay of the Valentine's Day telephone conversation during which Goode had denied having any insurance on Renee other than the small policy he'd taken out at work.

In less than two days of testimony, Yenne had offered medical proof that Renee Goode had been murdered and provided the jury with a disturbing picture of the man on trial for that crime. With the evidence of the phone conversation, she began to reveal the tangle of lies that Shane Goode had told in an effort to prove himself blameless.

Cornelius, who believed in a firm but mannerly style of cross-examination, spoke pleasantly to Annette. He was genuinely sorry for her loss, he said, but had a few questions that he had to ask. Gradually, he focused on the allegations that his client had failed to make child support payments.

"At the time of Renee's death," he said, "isn't it true that Mr. Goode had made child-support payments totaling fifty-one hundred dollars?"

Annette stared angrily at the attorney. Clearly she viewed him as the enemy. "Yes," she said.

"And did he follow court orders to pay lawyers' fees related to the custody hearing?"

"Yes."

"And your school loan?"

"Yes."

Methodically, Cornelius attempted to alter the picture of Shane Goode as a financially desperate man who had turned his back on his child. While the payments had been sporadic and, in some cases, long overdue, his client had been making an honest effort to meet them, even borrowing money from his parents to pay what was owed. The fact that he had fought for visitation rights was a plus that the jury should not ignore.

Shane Goode might not be a viable candidate for Father of the Year, but Cornelius had succeeded in softening his image.

Yenne quickly responded with a series of witnesses who documented the fact that Shane had insured his daughter's life for $50,000. She then called Renee's pediatrician to the stand to testify that Renee had suffered only the normal childhood ailments before her death. In his opinion, Renee had been an exceptionally healthy child.

Donna Kinsel, a senior labor-relations official with the postal service, brought with her records that showed the value of Goode's company life insurance policy was $46,000, not $160,000 as he had indicated to State Farm officials. Another of Shane's lies exposed.

Watching the jurors carefully, Tony Latino struggled to determine the jury's reaction to each witness. If the series of important financial and medical records being introduced into evidence—vital building blocks in the foundation Yenne was carefully building—impressed them, it was difficult for him to tell.

It would be easier to gauge their reaction when thirteen-year-old Christine Goode, recently arrived from the girls' home, took the stand to recall the night of Renee's death. Speaking in a soft voice and glancing repeatedly at her uncle as she answered Yenne's questions, Christine recounted the earlier New Year's Eve gathering in the Goode home, explaining how Renee had become sick after Shane left.

"Uncle Shane," she said, "was dressed up real nice," she remembered. "He went out dancing."

In doing so, she revealed another of Shane's lies which, Yenne hoped, was not lost on the jury. Even the children knew that Shane had not abandoned them that evening to answer a distress call from a friend.

Christine spoke about the January night of Renee's death, of an evening of playing hide-and-seek, watching television, eating cookies and pizza, and of her uncle eventually telling them it was time to go to bed.

It had been sometime around 1:00 A.M., she testified, when Shane had looked into her bedroom and said goodnight. She could not remember another time when he'd ever done so. Then she had heard water running in the hallway bathroom. Sitting up in bed, she had seen Shane's reflection in the glass of a hallway picture frame as he took clothing from his dresser.

Little time was left in the day when Goode's former wife, Kaye, took the stand to detail the child-support arrangement the courts had demanded following their divorce. Initially, she said, Shane had been ordered to pay $161 every two weeks. Later, the amount was increased to $200 bimonthly and he was ordered to pay her attorney fees and the cost of the tutoring that Tiffany required.

She had only learned of the $50,000 life insurance policy that Shane had also taken out on her daughter when Detective Sue Dietrich had informed her. To Sue's surprise, Kaye had not appeared to be overly concerned for her child's safety.

Shane smiled at his ex-wife as she stepped from the witness box at the end of the day's testimony.

///

In the parking lot of the nearby Homeplace Inn, Skip Cornelius, relieved that the weather had cleared, had changed into running clothes and was doing a series of stretching exercises in preparation for a five-mile training run. When a reporter stopped by to ask his take on the prosecution's case, he shook his head and smiled. "This one's not going very far," he said.

At home with her husband, Jeri Yenne reviewed the day's proceedings as she began clearing the dinner table. She felt good about the way things were going. Her witnesses had come across as sincere and believable and the evidence she had introduced was difficult for the defense to refute.

"Then why aren't you smiling?" her husband asked. Bill Yenne knew there was something more on his wife's mind than the testimony of witnesses or the reaction of jurors.

She finally admitted that it was the cocksure attitude of Skip Cornelius that troubled her. His laid-back style of cross-examination, his body language at the defense table, the confident smile he seemed always to have for her when she looked his way, bothered her far more than she wanted to admit. "I'm just so damn tired of him talking to me like I'm a little girl," she said.

Bill Yenne could not hide his amusement at his wife's ire. If a personality conflict with the defense attorney was the most troublesome aspect of the battle she was fighting, there was little cause for concern. "Let him underestimate you," he suggested. "That will be his undoing before all this is over."

. . .

By nine the following morning, all signs of Yenne's frustration were gone as she escorted Tiffany Goode toward the witness stand to begin a new day of testimony. Her hair in a ponytail, Goode's twelve-year-old daughter did her best to project a mature, serious look as she waited for the prosecutor to adjust the microphone in front of her.

Her recollection of the "slumber party" was much the same as that of Christine and it helped refresh jurors' memories of the previous day's testimony. However, it was clear that she held far stronger feelings for the defendant toward whom she looked often as he smiled back at her. She said that her father had taken good care of everyone that night. "He was careful to cut the pizza into little bites for Renee so she wouldn't choke on them," she volunteered.

She also remembered seeing Shane cry bitterly the next morning when he realized that Renee was dead.

As she questioned the youngster, Yenne could not help but wonder if her responses had been rehearsed; if, perhaps, Goode had helped his daughter to remember things somewhat differently.

The prosecutor hoped that Tiffany's answers to subtle, seemingly unimportant questions would remain with the jury.

In describing the events that preceeded everyone going to bed, Tiffany had said that she, not her father, had taken Renee into the bedroom to change her diaper.

"Did your daddy ever change Renee's diapers?" Yenne asked.

"No, he never did that."

When Tiffany described the frantic conversation with the 911 operator who asked if Shane knew how to perform CPR, she included the fact that Shane had said that he didn't. Yenne hoped the jury would find it strange that someone with a military background, a man who zealously sought new avenues of survival training, would not know the simple fundamentals of CPR.

The prosecutor kept reminding herself that the lies would be Shane Goode's downfall.

"That morning in the den," Cornelius said during his brief cross-examination, "what did Annette say when she came in?"

"She went to my dad and said, 'What did you do to my baby?' "

"And what was your dad doing at the time?"

"He was crying and upset that Renee had died," Tiffany replied.

Cornelius then dismissed the young witness, satisfied that the reaction she described was hardly that of a cold-blooded murderer.

///

The building of a legal case frequently strains the patience of jurors who neither know nor care about the fundamentals of the law. Why certain people who are far removed from the central events of a crime are asked to take the stand, only to introduce a document or set the stage for a future witness, is often lost on the layperson. Even more frustrating is the endless repetition the lawyers solicit from witnesses.

The testimony of Shane Goode's stepmother shed little new light onto the events that had transpired in her home that January evening. Still in pain following her visit to the dentist, she had retired to her bedroom and was not seen again that night.

However, it was essential that Yenne put her on the stand. In order to convince the jury that Shane Goode had murdered Renee, it was necessary for the prosecutor to methodically eliminate all other possible suspects. She also wanted the jury to hear about a telephone conversation Carolyn Goode had had with Sunny Bradley.

"I talked with Sunny in the spring of 1994," Carolyn Goode said.

"And did she ask how Shane was dealing with Renee's death?"

The witness was aware that Sunny had provided the D.A.'s office with a tape she had made of the conversation. "I told Sunny that when we tried to talk with him about what happened to Renee he got mad. He would get red in the face and wouldn't talk about it."

///

Yenne thought that Sunny Bradley was one of the most courageous witnesses she planned to put on the stand. During the early days of the investigation when Shane's fellow postal workers so quickly rallied to his defense, Sunny had become something of a social outcast as soon as it became clear that she felt he was guilty.

Following Goode's arrest, several of her fellow workers had signed a petition which they presented to their supervisor. Goode, the man they once so vocally supported, now frightened them. They expressed fear that he might return to the post office and seek retribution against Sunny for her cooperation with the authorities. The petition suggested that, in the interest of everyone's safety, Sunny should be terminated.

To his credit, the supervisor had chosen to ignore the request.

Meanwhile, Sunny ignored the scorn of her coworkers and had willingly accepted the subpoena when it was delivered to her window at the post office. She was prepared to detail Goode's attitude toward "Annette's child."

Tony Latino's only concern was that Cornelius might attempt to persuade members of the jury that their witness had been motivated by something more than truth and justice when she agreed to testify. "He'll do his damnedest to make her into a rejected lover seeking revenge," Latino had warned Yenne.

"And when he does," Yenne observed, "she'll chew him up and spit him out."

Latino, offering no further argument, smiled broadly. He liked the growing confidence he was seeing in his fellow prosecutor.

///

"When Mr. Goode told you that Annette had given birth to a child," Yenne asked, "what was his attitude?"

"He wasn't happy about it at all."

"Had he even seen the child?"

"No," Sunny replied, "and he said he had no desire to do so."

The prosecutor led her through a series of questions about Goode's admission that he had urged his ex-wife to have an abortion and his growing frustration over being forced to make child-support payments.

"And what was his reaction when the court finally ruled that he must make those payments?"

"He said if he was going to have to pay child support, he was going to demand visitation rights."

"Even though he'd never even seen his daughter?"

"He said he would do it just to make Annette mad."

She had had serious concerns about the cause of Renee's death from the moment she had found a note Shane had taped to her apartment door, advising her that his daughter was dead. "I first thought it was Tiffany," she said, "but when I called him, he told me it was the baby. He told me he had no idea what had happened."

"Was there anything else about the conversation that stands out in your mind?"

"There was no emotion in his voice."

Finally, Yenne directed Sunny to the matter of the life insurance policy whose existence she had discovered. "I just knew he had to be benefiting from it in some way," the witness stated.

Throughout her testimony, Sunny had responded to Yenne's questions in a firm, businesslike manner, never raising her voice, providing little hint of her personal feelings toward the man on trial. By the time her testimony ended and Judge Gayle called for the noon recess, she had provided the jury with a dark and troubling portrait of Shane Goode.

In her office, Yenne sipped a soft drink and nibbled M&Ms during the lunch break, contemplating the questions that Cornelius would have for Sunny. Her only real worry was that he might succeed in provoking Sunny to reveal the anger she felt toward Shane. She knew that a few explosive responses could deal a serious blow to her witness's credibility. Sunny, a woman with strong opinions and a hair-trigger temper, wasn't likely to retreat from whatever verbal confrontation Cornelius might attempt to initiate.

As she sat passing the time, counting the minutes before court would reconvene, Jeri found herself pondering the striking differences in the women who had been attracted to Goode. Annette had been emotionally frail, the perfect target for someone who wanted to dominate a relationship. Sunny, on the other hand, seemed so self-assured, even headstrong—hardly the kind of woman Shane could control. Yet both had been drawn to him as if hypnotized—eager to please, hoping to spend their lives with him.

Therein, Yenne knew, lay the greatest problem the jury would have. Regardless of whatever testimony they heard, they were looking across the room at a defendant who was too handsome, too middle-class, to be a murderer. Shane Goode wasn't the Hillside Strangler or Charles Manson. He was the guy next door.

///

Sunny Bradley sat nervously in the witness box as the jury filed in for the afternoon session. When all were settled, Judge Gayle nodded toward the defense table. "Your witness, counselor."

Cornelius adjusted his jacket as he slowly got to his feet. "I have no questions for this witness," he said.

Any attempt to repair the damage Sunny had done, he must have reasoned, might very possibly make matters worse. He had read her statement to the police: a document filled with unconfirmed suspicions about his client, recollections of his appetite for kinky sex, and her firm belief that Shane had killed Renee with money as his motive. Yenne, he knew, had held back during direct examination, waiting for a second barrage when given the opportunity to re-examine the witness.

While there might be little evidence to back up Sunny's allegations, she was too effective a witness to risk trying to discredit her in front of the jury. Cornelius judged the gamble too risky.

Yenne's reaction was a mixture of surprise and sudden concern. Turning to Latino, she whispered, "Is our next witness here?"

///

The previous evening Yenne had spoken once more with Dr. Bellas. Despite a review of Dr. Anderson's slides, photographs, and written report from the second autopsy, his position on Renee's cause of death had not budged.

Still, she knew that whatever damage he might do her case was best done as a witness called by the prosecution. *We've nothing to hide, ladies and gentlemen of the jury. We're bringing you all the evidence, everyone's viewpoint. Then you decide.*

During their conversation she had been straightforward. "Is there *anything* you can honestly say that might benefit the prosecution?" she had asked. "Can you say that had you performed the same surgical procedure done in the second autopsy that you might have found signs of the blunt trauma?"

She knew the answers even before asking her questions.

"I'm sorry," the pathologist had said. "I can't."

Well-trained in giving testimony, the doctor looked toward the jury box as he replied to each of Yenne's questions. Speaking in a thick Spanish accent, he went through the mandatory review of his professional credentials and the function of the Harris County Medical Examiner's Office. Then, at Yenne's request, he began to describe the autopsy he had performed on the afternoon of January 23.

Every detail was given in careful response to a question posed by the prosecutor; every observation made only after it was requested.

"Dr. Bellas," Yenne finally asked, "were you able to determine what killed Renee Goode?"

"I was not able to determine the cause of death of the child," he answered.

As she passed the witness, Yenne was already replaying the doctor's testimony in her mind. She had been careful not to ask questions that would allow him the opportunity to launch into a tirade against Dr. Anderson's procedures. And she had avoided any accusations that might have triggered an angry reply. She had accomplished nothing, really, except to have him admit that he did not know what the cause of death might have been. Still, in light of the fact Dr. Bellas was, for all practical purposes, a key defense witness, it had seemed too easy. She had expected something more.

Even as these thoughts ran through Yenne's mind, Cornelius had begun posing his questions to the doctor. Wasn't it true, he asked, that there had been a great deal of pressure from members of the deceased's family and the authorities for him to revise his opinion?

"I spoke with the child's grandmother several times," Dr. Bellas answered. "And I met with Mrs. Yenne and a detective who was involved in the investigation."

"And what did they want?"

"They all wanted the same thing: to know if I could determine the cause of death. All I was able to tell them was that I didn't know. That's what I consistently told everyone: I don't know."

"And has anything caused your opinion to change?"

The doctor adjusted his glasses and looked again toward the jury box. "I prefer to continue to say, I don't know."

"Then you found nothing that would indicate to you that the child's death was a result of mechanical asphyxiation?"

"I can't say it was death by mechanical asphyxiation nor can I say that it was not. I just don't know."

During the afternoon break which immediately followed Dr. Bellas's testimony, there was, for the first time since the trial had begun, a look of concern on Cornelius's face. Moving near Yenne, he shook his head. "I have nine pages of interview notes I've taken from Dr. Bellas," he said, "and they literally gut your case. But he didn't say any of it on the stand."

Yenne did not reply. Was it possible, she wondered, that the doctor had finally begun to doubt his own conclusions, despite all the stubborn refusals and angry tirades that had marked their relationship over the past months? Could it have been that his repeated "I don't know" was his way of excusing himself while subtly signaling the jury to ponder another doctor's evaluation?

She would never know. In any case, Dr. Bellas's ego had not flared during his testimony. There had been no real indignation directed toward Dr. Anderson and his findings. Only "I don't know."

For weeks Yenne had agonized over Dr. Bellas's testimony, never completely comfortable with any line of questioning she considered, afraid that he might deal a mortal blow to her case. Suddenly it was over, and her case remained intact. As he took leave of the witness stand, a weight lifted from her shoulders. Feeling a new surge of energy, she was anxious to move ahead.

For the remainder of the day, Yenne worked to establish the fact that no one else in the Goode house could have caused Renee's death. A female juror dabbed her eyes as ten-year-old Michelle recalled the discovery of Renee's death.

"When I woke up," she said, "Tiffany was watching cartoons on TV. She said she was going to get some cereal and I tried to wake

Renee. Something was coming from her mouth. I shook her, but she wouldn't wake up. Tiffany went to tell Shane and I called my mother."

It was late in the day when Donald Goode was called to the stand. He answered Yenne's questions in a sharp, controlled tone, his only show of emotion coming when he was asked about his May 1994 visit to the Alvin Police Department. His anger was evident as he described going there to complain about the billboard that had been erected near his house and the flyers seeking information on Renee's death that were being tossed into his yard at night.

In short order, Yenne called Detective Bodie Duckworth to the stand to question him about the visit from the elder Goode.

Donald Goode had been convinced, the detective said, that the police department was somehow involved in an effort to harass the family.

"Did you have any other conversation with Mr. Goode?" Yenne asked.

"I told him that I had concerns that his son might be involved in the child's death."

"And what was his reply?"

"He said that he had the same concerns."

///

That evening Skip Cornelius extended his training run by several miles in an attempt to exercise away the sudden wave of frustration that had swept over him. He had been confident that the responses of Tiffany and Dr. Bellas on cross-examination would lend strength his client's position, yet he had been disappointed. Now, he would have to return Donald Goode to the stand to refute the conversation that Detective Duckworth had recalled. "The sonuvabitch is lying," Goode had assured him.

The prosecution had certainly won the day. On Friday, he hoped to slow the state's momentum.

. . .

For much of the morning Jeri Yenne carefully guided Detective Dietrich through a detailed account of her investigation, finally focusing on Sue's first encounter with Shane Goode. The statement she had taken from the defendant was read.

"How would you describe Mr. Goode's demeanor that evening?" Yenne asked.

Dietrich, who had been directing her answers to the jury, turned in her chair to look at Goode. "It was not that of a father whose daughter had died." She added that he had seemed far more interested in learning when he would be contacted by State Farm.

"Pass the witness," Yenne said, turning toward the prosecution table.

Sue's eyes followed Skip Cornelius as he walked silently toward a large poster board which leaned against the wall near the jury box. Unfolding a blowup of the statement Shane had given the detective the previous October, he attached it to the board and turned it so that it was in full view of the jurors.

"Detective Dietrich," he said, "do you recognize this as a reproduction of the statement you took from Shane Goode?"

"Yes."

"And is that his handwriting?"

"No, sir. It's mine."

In the gallery, a female spectator who had been following the trial intently leaned toward her husband and whispered, "Where's he going with this?" The man cupped his hand to her ear. "This," he predicted, "is where they put the cop on trial."

Indeed, Cornelius wasted little time in his effort to cast suspicion on Detective Dietrich. For the jury to believe that Shane Goode had committed the murder for which he was charged, Cornelius knew, it was imperative that they believe everyone else in the house was sleeping when the crime occurred.

He called Dietrich's attention to a line on the first page of the Voluntary Statement and asked that she read it aloud.

Sue did so in a firm voice. "Around midnight I started getting Renee ready for bed. Everyone else was asleep. . . ."

"Everyone else was asleep," Cornelius repeated, letting a finger trace the sentence. "And just below that is Shane Goode's signature, right?"

"Yes."

"And your initials. S.D."

"That's correct."

Cornelius pointed out that for someone to successfully commit the terrible crime of which his client stood accused, it would be essential that there be no witnesses. "You would want to be sure everyone was asleep," he stated.

Then he asked the witness when the final sentence on the page had been written.

"It was written as Mr. Goode was giving his statement to me."

"Not later? Sometime after you had had time to read it and realized that you needed him to say that everyone was sleeping?"

Sue maintained her composure. "It was written as Mr. Goode gave his statement."

Cornelius directed the jury's attention to Shane's tight, scratchy signature at the bottom of the page. The sentence in question, he pointed out, was written at an upward angle. "As if to avoid running on to a signature that was already in place," he observed.

He then turned his attention to the final page of the statement, pointing to a line that was not spaced as uniformly as the others. "This is also written in your hand?" Cornelius asked.

"That's correct."

"And would you read it, please."

Sue turned to the board. ". . . I did not hear anything during the night. Renee is a very healthy child."

"Renee is a very healthy child," the attorney repeated. "Why do you suppose he would say that?"

"I'm sure that I had questioned him about his general observations about her health."

"But it would certainly help your case if he acknowledged that she had appeared in good health before . . ."

"I wrote what he told me," Sue said firmly.

Arms folded, Cornelius silently studied her handwriting, a gesture that invited the jurors to follow suit. The brief sentence did seem to have been squeezed in.

But had it been added at a later date, sometime after Shane Goode had signed it? Had the detective later decided to enhance it? If so, why had she not fashioned an addendum that would have been even more incriminating?

Sue Dietrich waited until she was excused from the witness stand before venting her anger in the privacy of Jeri Yenne's office. "That's it?" she spat. "That's his fucking case?"

Yenne made no attempt to calm her.

"I'll tell you one thing," Sue continued. "The minute I get back to Alvin I'm telling the chief that he's going to buy me a tape recorder. I'll never take another statement again that isn't taped."

Sue had realized that, after nine years on the force, there were still lessons to be learned.

As the detective fumed, Yenne looked over a list of questions she planned to ask her final witness. Dr. Linda Norton, she had been informed, was en route to the courthouse.

///

In the earliest stages of his discussions about the death of Renee Goode, Dr. Anderson had consulted with the Dallas pathologist whom he'd known since medical-school days. The case, he had informed her, was not only fascinating but one on which he felt he might need a second opinion. Dr. Norton, who had worked several exhumation autopsies with him over the years, had been quick to warn her friend that the likelihood of finding any evidence that would contradict the ruling of the Harris County Medical Examiner's office was remote. Still, she had agreed to review his findings.

There had, in fact, been considerable discussion about asking her to be present during the second autopsy, but they had finally agreed that she could stand by her phone in Dallas to discuss any questions that might arise during Dr. Anderson's examination. Later, she would review the slides, photographs, and his written report and offer her independent opinion.

Dr. Anderson knew that she would not hesitate to disagree with his findings if she felt he might be wrong.

In fact, if there was a pathologist in the nation who had earned a more distinguished reputation than the Florida doctor, it was the fifty-year-old mother of two.

Ironically, her first taste of national fame was not the result of her years of work in child-related deaths—work which colleagues at the Dallas County M.E.'s office had been more than willing to assign her: rather, it was the exhumation and second autopsy of accused presidential assassin Lee Harvey Oswald which she performed in 1981. A British journalist, Michael Eddowes, had published a book in which he had alleged that a lookalike Soviet agent had defected to the United States and assumed Oswald's identity prior to the murder of President Kennedy. The writer had filed suit to force an exhumation which would determine the true identity of the body which had been buried in the accused assassin's grave. Following a lengthy legal battle, Oswald's widow had become weary of the constant speculation and finally gave her consent to the examination. Because the lawyers representing the writer had known Dr. Norton from her work on an earlier unrelated case, they urged that she be assigned to oversee the exhumation and perform the controversial autopsy.

In doing so, Dr. Norton suddenly became a public figure—one who dealt a crushing blow to conspiracy theorists worldwide when she announced that the body buried in Oswald's grave was that of Lee Harvey Oswald.

Norton was also involved in the high-profile case of an upstate New York mother named Waneta Hoyt. Over a six-and-one-half-year period, from 1965 to 1971, five of Mrs. Hoyt's children—ranging in age from 48 days to 28 months—had died, each of them a victim of what local doctors had classified as Sudden Infant Death Syndrome. Dr. Norton had first read about the case in a medical journal article authored by the children's pediatrician and soon became convinced that the deaths could be more easily explained. She insisted to the local authorities that a serial killer lived in the Hoyt home and that the killer was most likely the children's mother.

For several years she lobbied for an investigation, finally gaining the attention of a newly elected D.A. Eventually, a case was made against Waneta Hoyt and the woman confessed to the suffocation murders of her children.

Dr. Norton's role in exposing the horrendous crimes had elevated her to the stature of an internationally recognized expert in the death of children.

As she walked into Judge Gayle's courtroom to serve as the final witness in the state's case against Shane Goode, her erect carriage made her look taller than her five feet, six inches. Dressed in a business suit, her hair styled in a short, casual cut, the doctor smiled briefly as she settled behind the microphone.

For the next half hour she added firm emphasis to the testimony given by her colleague on the opening day of the trial. Poised and with a firm air of authority, she seemed a kindly professor lecturing to a group of attentive students: a woman certain of herself and her professional convictions.

Again the jurors were forced to view the disturbing series of photos that depicted the area of hemorrhaging in Renee's back. Dr. Norton had reviewed the initial autopsy performed by Harris County and reiterated that she felt it was incomplete. Had the surgical procedure Dr. Anderson performed been done originally, she said, the cause of death would never have been in question.

"And, after your review of all the evidence, Doctor, what is your diagnosis of the cause of death?" Yenne asked.

"In medical terminology, the cause of death was compressive asphyxiation. Extreme pressure was applied to the child's abdomen and the flow of air to the lungs was cut off." She did not wait for the prosecutor's next question. "Brain death would have occurred in five minutes or so, but it likely took ten to fifteen minutes to accomplish full heart arrest."

There was no mystery. This, she said, was no SIDS death. Pausing to let her eyes roam the jury box, she added, "This was a homicide."

As Yenne took her place back at the prosecution table, Tony Latino slid a yellow legal pad toward her. On it he had written his critique of the doctor's testimony: *She's the best expert witness I've ever heard,* he had written in large block letters.

The prosecutor nodded her agreement as Cornelius stood to begin his questioning. "Your *theory* is based on your experience with other cases," he suggested.

"No," she replied. "My testimony is based on the evidence I have reviewed."

"During the course of your review did you find any physical evidence that showed that the mouth or nasal passage might have been blocked . . . ?"

To his right, jurors were beginning to stir. One crossed his legs, another leaned back against her seat. Mesmerized by Dr. Norton's testimony during Yenne's direct questioning, they had clearly heard enough. Now, they were ready for their lunch break.

///

In the hallway, Sharon Couch stood waiting as Dr. Norton walked from the courtroom to catch a midafternoon plane back to Dallas. Extending her hand to the woman whom she'd never met, Sharon said, "Doctor, I want to thank you for everything you've done."

Dr. Norton recognized the voice she'd heard months earlier on the phone. "You're Sharon Couch." She smiled. "And I want to thank *you*. You're a very courageous lady. I'm sorry for what happened to your grandchild, but you should know that in all likelihood your efforts saved another little girl's life."

As she had reviewed the case prior to her testimony, Dr. Norton had taken particular interest in the fact that Shane Goode had also taken out a life insurance policy on his older daughter. The doctor was convinced that Tiffany Goode would have been the next to die.

///

Yenne had planned to end her case on the high point of Dr. Norton's testimony, but during the lunch hour she found herself agonizing over the the testimony jurors were certain to hear from Shane's father when the defense began putting on its case.

Sergeant Arendell had arrived from Alvin and was ready to take the stand when the afternoon session got underway. He had been present when Donald Goode came to the police station to complain about the harassment he felt was being directed at him and his family.

Did he remember, Yenne asked, what Mr. Goode's reaction had been after Detective Duckworth expressed concern that Shane might somehow be involved in his granddaughter's death?

"Mr. Goode dropped his head and conceded that he had the same concern," the sergeant answered.

With that, Jeri Yenne turned to the judge. "The state rests, your honor."

///

In the judge's chambers earlier in the day, Yenne had predicted that she would complete her case by early afternoon. Since the defense's forensic expert would not be available until Monday morning, it had been agreed that Cornelius would not call his first witness until Monday morning.

The plan was slightly altered after Donald Goode insisted that he be put on immediately.

Thus the first witness for the defense took the stand shortly after three on Friday afternoon.

Donald Goode glared in the direction of the prosecutors as he stated that he had not done or said anything to police to indicate that he believed his son was involved in Renee Goode's death.

Outside, a torrential rain had once again begun to fall, promising a wet weekend.

At the doorway of the courthouse, Skip Cornelius and his wife Laura looked out at the dark rolling clouds in disgust. If they were to maintain the training schedule they had set to prepare themselves for an October marathon they planned to run in Laura's home state of Pennsylvania, they needed to run at least ten miles on Saturday.

///

As reporters prepared their weekend wrap-ups and speculated about whether Shane Goode would soon take the stand in his own defense, they talked among themselves about an unusual aspect of the trial that would not be in their stories.

Traditionally, lawyers and their clients take advantage of court-room breaks and lunch hours to review testimony and talk strategy. The reporters knew that it was not uncommon for a defense attorney to adopt the calming role of baby-sitter during a trial.

For all practical purposes, it seemed, the relationship of Skip Cornelius and Shane Goode did not extend beyond the defense table. No one had seen the Houston attorney arrive early for any pretrial discussions with his client. During breaks, Goode sought the company of his girlfriend or his parents and brother, who had made frequent visits to the courthouse. On several occasions, he had sought out buddies from the National Guard who stopped in to listen to testimony and offer words of support. Cornelius, meanwhile, chatted with his wife and children who regularly drove down from Houston to attend.

When the day's proceedings ended, Goode went one way, Cornelius another. If the lawyer and the accused had bonded, it was not evident to the seasoned trial-watchers.

There was one thing the two men seemed to have in common: Each continued to exhibit a remarkable air of confidence.

///

On Monday morning, Dr. Charles Petty arrived at the courthouse early, and chatted amiably with bailiffs while waiting for Skip Cornelius to appear. The man who had, before his retirement, spent twenty-one years as chief medical examiner in Dallas would be the defense's second witness of the day.

Dr. Norton would not have been surprised. Long before the D.A.'s office was officially notified that Petty would serve as a defense witness, she had predicted he would testify.

Dr. Petty had been a close friend and mentor during the years she worked for him at the Dallas Institute of Forensic Science. A rift had developed in the aftermath of the Oswald autopsy, however, and soon Dr. Norton left for a better paying, less stressful job in Alabama. Longtime friends of both found Dr. Petty's sudden hostility to his colleague difficult to understand. Some suggested privately that it was nothing more complex than a case of bruised ego—that Petty harbored great resentment over the fact that Dr. Norton had been hand-picked to do the Oswald autopsy and, as a result, had garnered worldwide publicity. Others wondered if the disagreement was over office policy, particularly Dr. Petty's firm rule that no cooperation should be extended to defense attorneys. Dr. Norton admitted that the entire matter perplexed her, yet neither would discuss the cause of the strained relationship, even with their closest mutual friends.

Clearly, it was not a rift that time was likely to heal. Soon everyone in the legal community knew that if a lawyer needed expert testimony to refute Dr. Norton's, Charles Petty was the man to call. In recent years, then, their paths had crossed frequently.

Yenne recalled Dr. Norton's earlier warning as she drove toward the courthouse. She had spent a restless night attempting to determine the best way to conduct her cross-examination. She thought back to her trip to Dallas with Cornelius and asked herself the purpose of the visit to Dr. Petty's office. She had wanted to know specifically on what evidence he based the opinion he would give. She recalled that he had viewed only three of the fourteen autopsy-related exhibits she had introduced into evidence.

As she walked from the parking lot in the direction of the courthouse, she decided that her cross-examination would be short and as nonconfrontational as possible.

///

Dr. Petty, a charming and grandfatherly figure, was no stranger to this kind of proceeding. Smiling toward the jury box, he recalled a remarkable list of accomplishments. World War II gunnery officer, Harvard Medical School, a career during which he'd conducted over thirteen thousand autopsies.

He told Cornelius that he had reviewed the autopsies that had been performed by Dr. Bellas and Dr. Anderson.

And what had his reaction been to the autopsy done by the Harris County M.E.'s office?

"Dr. Bellas's autopsy," he said, "was well and appropriately conducted." Then, turning to the jury, he began to detail the difficulties that accompany the examination of small children. "You have a real problem right off the bat," he explained, "for the simple reason that people that age aren't supposed to die."

He had reviewed the slides prepared by Dr. Bellas. "My examination," he noted, "gave me no clue as to the cause of death."

Soon Cornelius asked his witness about the second autopsy, establishing that Dr. Petty had also reviewed slides prepared by Dr. Anderson.

"Did a review of those slides give you any clue as to the cause of death?"

"No, they did not," the doctor said.

And what of Dr. Anderson's suggestion that there was evidence of hemorrhaging in the child's lower back?

"What I noted in the photographs which I reviewed," he responded, "looked like a very small puddle of blood. I could not tell, even under a microscope, that there was any evidence of hemorrhaging."

"Not at all?"

Dr. Petty nodded. "Not at all."

"In your best medical opinion, Doctor, can you tell us how Renee Goode died?"

"I'm saying that I just don't know."

For emphasis, Cornelius repeated his question. "Can you determine the cause of death?"

"I'm sorry," the doctor said apologetically. "I cannot. I did note in Dr. Bellas's report that there was some indication of a slight hardening of the lining of the heart. That might or might not indicate some problems with the heart."

Cornelius then suggested the possibility that the child might have died as a result of a seizure during which she became entangled in her bedclothes and smothered.

Dr. Petty testified that he did not agree with the scenario.

Yenne responded with a methodical list of the forensic evidence the state had introduced—tissue slides, autopsy photographs, written reports—asking each time if the doctor had studied them before making his determination.

The doctor repeatedly smiled and answered, "No."

///

Judge Gayle had no sooner retreated to his chambers during the morning break when Detective Dietrich appeared at his doorway. He smiled as he waved her inside.

She wasted no time pleading her case. "You know, Judge," she said, "I've worked on this case a long time. And I know that the defense has invoked the rule. But I'd like very much to be in the courtroom when Shane Goode testifies."

Linking his fingers, the judge leaned forward at his desk as if lending consideration to the request. "I don't see why not," he said. With her testimony concluded, the possibility of Dietrich being influenced by anything heard from the witness stand no longer existed.

She was already seated when Yenne returned to the courtroom. Moving quickly to her, the attorney leaned over Sue's shoulder and whispered. "I'll bet you my next month's salary," she said, "that Skip doesn't ask him if he did it."

With that remark, Yenne walked toward the front of the courtroom before Sue could reply.

Only a few feet away, Shane Goode talked casually with a friend from his Guard unit who enthusiastically described a meeting that had been held the previous evening. Shane said he was glad the trial was coming to an end. He didn't want to miss any more meetings.

///

On the stand, Goode demonstrated no sign of apprehension, responding to his attorney's questions in an almost conversational tone. His marriage to Annette, he said, had "been pretty much rocky from the beginning." He could not remember a time when their relationship had really been in sync.

Annette's abortion during the early stages of their marriage had been something to which they had mutually agreed. "We had a lot of bills at the time," he explained. "We discussed it at length and came to the decision that it wasn't the right time to have a baby."

They had, he said, both tried to salvage their relationship even when things had become unbearable. In early 1989, he recalled, he had agreed to accompany Annette to marriage counseling meetings. Annette, however, had seemed constantly obsessed by a fear that he might one day return to his first wife.

"And was there some way she made you aware of that concern?" Cornelius asked.

Shane nodded. "She told me that if I ever went back with my first wife she would kill me. She would kill us all."

In the gallery, Sue Dietrich wondered why Goode had never mentioned such threats when she had interviewed him.

The jury looked toward the witness stand as he began to detail the futile attempt at reconcilation and how he had become aware that Annette was going to have a baby.

"I knew it was possible that it was my child," he admitted. "We were in my apartment when she told me about her falling in the shower and going to the emergency room and learning that she was pregnant. She said she wanted us to get back together and that there was no way she was going to consider having another abortion.

"She told me if I didn't want to have the baby I could just punch her in the stomach right there and get it over with. Then she stormed out."

There was no emotion in his voice as he related the anecdote.

Cornelius then questioned Goode about Sunny Bradley and the cause of their eventual breakup.

"I was living with her when I got the divorce papers from Annette," Shane recalled. "Once it was obvious that the divorce was going to go through, Sunny began asking me what I thought about where our relationship was headed."

"And what was your response?"

"I told her that I could see us getting married at some point in the future," Shane answered. "Then, the very next day at the post office, a friend came up, gave me a hug, and said she'd heard that Sunny and I were getting married."

The problems in their relationship escalated when, instead of giving her an engagement ring for Christmas, he had given her a sweater and earrings. "She told me that she felt there must still be something going on between Annette and me. That's when I first told her that Annette was pregnant."

A month later, he said, Sunny asked him to move out.

Although unspoken, the message to the jury was far from subtle.

Spurned and jealous, Sunny Bradley had sought her revenge against Shane Goode from the witness stand.

Finally, Cornelius turned his questioning to Renee.

In contrast to what his ex-wife had told the jury, Shane insisted that he had been looking forward to seeing Renee once a visitation schedule was agreed on.

Then why had he failed to keep his first scheduled visitation?

Goode smiled. "I went to Dallas to the Cotton Bowl game," he said. "I watched the Texas Aggies get whupped."

From her vantage point in the back of the courtroom, Sue Dietrich studied the behavior of the man on the witness stand, angered by his flippant answers to the questions, by his lies and half-truths. She could only hope the jury was as irritated by his arrogance as she was. *The same old Shane,* she thought to herself. *No emotion. Very matter of fact. Always in control. Jesus, hasn't anyone bothered to tell him that it would benefit him if he did show some feeling of remorse for his actions? Maybe even squeeze out a tear or two?*

As the thoughts ran through her mind, Shane began to explain his purchase of the life insurance policy.

A friend in the National Guard who was a former insurance salesman had told Shane that the policy would be a relatively economical way to insure his daughters' educational future. "I still maintain Tiffany's policy," he said, looking into the audience where his daughter sat in the front row, next to her mother.

His expression did not change as he recalled the morning that Renee's death was discovered. "When I picked her up," he recalled, "her body was already cold, her legs were stiff, and there was some discoloration on one side of her face." Even had he known how to perform CPR, it would have been to no avail.

He was sitting on the couch with Renee in his lap when Emergency Medical Service personnel arrived.

At the prosecutors' table, Tony Latino leaned toward Yenne. "He's not going to ask him," he said in a whispered announcement of what he was already judging to be the defining moment of the trial. Jeri nodded silently. It was at that moment she became certain that Skip Cornelius knew his client was guilty. But, she thought, he was not going to allow the little asshole to commit perjury.

As if on cue, the defense attorney quickly asked Shane to describe the discussions he had had with police that morning, his interview with Detective Duckworth at the police station, and, finally, his encounter with Detective Sue Dietrich.

Cornelius reminded him that the detective had said there was no momento of Renee in Goode's apartment on the night of Sue Dietrich's visit. Introducing a small Plexiglas frame with a snapshot of the child in it, the attorney asked his witness to identify it.

"That's a picture of Renee," Goode said. "It was sitting on the coffee table in my apartment the night Detective Dietrich came to take my statement."

Again there was a lengthy discussion of the statement he had given. Moving to the blowups which remained mounted on the board, Cornelius asked that Shane read it carefully.

"That line that says 'Everyone was asleep' wasn't on the statement when I signed it," he testified.

///

Jeri Yenne was not going to allow Shane the opportunity to shed tears during her questioning. It was time to bring the trial to a close.

She zeroed in on the motive she had set forth in her opening statement. Through a series of brief questions, she established that at the time of his daughter's death, Shane Goode had been drowning financially. She established his income, then matched it against outstanding debts he'd incurred—his truck payment, household bills, the loan he'd received from his father, attorneys' fees, and the child support payments he had been ordered to pay for Tiffany and Renee. The evidence made it difficult for him to deny.

There was only one question about which Yenne was certain he would lie. The Polaroid print she hid in the palm of her hand would provide her a dramatic close to her cross-examination. On her trip to Hallettsville's City Cemetery, which now seemed so long ago, she had snapped a picture of Renee's headstone.

She would ask Shane if he had ever visited his daughter's grave. If he answered that he had, she would ask him to describe the headstone, then put into evidence a photo that proved him a liar.

Yenne clutched the picture of the granite marker with the tiny angels engraved on each side of the words "Beloved Daughter" as she posed the question.

Goode's answer surprised her.

"No," he said, "I have never visited Renee's grave."

It was on that admission that she passed the witness.

///

For all practical purposes, the legal battle had ended. Cornelius quickly introduced a succession of minor witnesses who offered the jurors little in the way of vital information. The woman whom Shane had gone out to see on that New Year's Eve when Renee had become ill gave her explanation for Goode's departure that night. The boyfriend she'd been out with that evening had begun to flirt with another woman and she had phoned Shane to ask him to come get her and give her a ride home. Seeing how upset she was when he arrived, he had talked with her for some time before he returned home. Shane's brother, Dennis, recalled a conversation with an angry Annette during which she had threatened to kill both Shane and Kaye if Goode ever left her. Finally, a Guard platoon member took the stand to swear that there was nothing in their training routine that would have taught Shane Goode or anyone else how to kill without leaving a trace.

It was late in the afternoon when the defense rested and the judge informed members of the jury that they would hear closing arguments the following morning.

///

Wearing a light blue dress that Sue Dietrich had helped her select for the occasion, Jeri Yenne would be the first to address the jury. By law, the prosecution is allowed to present its closing argument in two segments. Yenne would speak first, yield the floor to the defense, then return for her final say.

The first segment of her argument was spent reviewing the evidence that had been presented and demonstrating that all the elements included in Goode's indictment had been proven.

The first display of passion came from Cornelius. "First," he said, "I want to tell you that I'm sorry that this child died. But I also have to say to you that this trial has been like a long scene from *Alice in Wonderland*."

As he refreshed the jury's memory of the medical findings of the Harris County M.E.'s office and pointed, once again, to the lack of physical evidence linking his client to the crime, his voice rose. "You haven't heard *any* real evidence," he insisted. "What you've heard is a lot of theories and opinions. I'm not quibbling over the *amount* of evidence. The simple fact of the matter is, there is none that indicates that the defendant ever harmed this child."

As he spoke he lifted his arms, extending his hands in a palms-up gesture. A plea for reason. "I've never seen a jury that would vote to convict anyone on the amount of evidence that has been presented in this case," he observed.

The baritone thunder of his voice had barely died when Yenne stood. Her voice was now soft, almost pleading, as she moved to the railing of the jury box. She reminded the jurors that there *was* evidence: the convincing testimony of Drs. Anderson and Norton. The insurance policy. Financial problems. The lies. And words from the defendant's own mouth that he was the last person to see the victim alive.

"There is evidence," she reiterated.

"We went into the ground for our facts," she continued. "We exhumed a two-and-one-half-year-old child's body. And what we found was a tragic story as old as mankind itself.

"You remember the story of Cain and Abel. You remember how the Lord went to Cain, a man who had slain his brother, and asked, 'Where is your brother?' And you remember Cain's reply? 'I am not my brother's keeper.' But he also says that his brother's body calls to him from the ground.

"Renee did the same.

"So, riddle me this: There's been a homicide and you were the last person with the victim. Who does that make you? I submit, ladies and gentlemen of the jury, that makes you the killer."

• • •

The wait for a jury to arrive at a verdict is, for everyone concerned, an agonizing exercise. Time's normal march is reduced to baby steps. Those who have participated in the trial process—be they the accused, families of the victim, lawyers, media, or simply courtroom visitors who enjoy real-life drama over afternoon soaps—struggle with the wait. They pace, read newspapers and paperback novels, drink coffee, smoke cigarettes, and gather into huddles to speculate on the outcome. Traditionally, reporters argue the pluses and minuses of the case and wager on how long it will take for a decision to be reached.

For Cornelius and Yenne, veterans of the game, there was a strong desire to get as far away from Judge Gayle's courtroom as possible, to seek fresh air and reason, to try to forget what was at stake. At the same time, both felt the need to stay close, as if their being nearby might somehow speed the process.

Jeri Yenne chose to keep vigil in her office. It was there that Sue Dietrich reported to her that the judge had called sheriff's deputies into his chambers to discuss a plan to escort the defendant to freedom should he be found not guilty. Due to the emotional nature of the case, he felt it would serve the court's best interest if Shane Goode did not have to parade past members of his deceased daughter's family or be swarmed by reporters.

Yenne understood that such a precaution was necessary but could not ignore the burning in her stomach caused by the idea of Goode going free.

"It's not going to happen," Sue insisted.

"It can't," Yenne responded. "It just can't."

Dietrich roamed the halls, stopping to speak briefly with Sharon and Annette, then moving on to strike up idle conversation with courthouse employees. She visited the cafeteria for coffee, then stepped outside for a cigarette. Keep moving, she told herself, and maybe time will do the same.

Finally, she wandered back into the courtroom. It was empty except for the bailiff who stood sentry outside the door of the deliberation room. Joe Lipscomb had worked in Judge Gayle's court for years; he had known Sue Dietrich for most of her professional career and considered her a friend.

That friendship, however, had developed not so much because of the judicial linking of their jobs but rather because of their shared interest in the local high school football team. During the time that Sue's son Adam played for Alvin High, it was Lipscomb who served as public address announcer at the stadium each Friday night.

Moving to sit next to the detective, he said nothing as she scanned the headlines of a discarded newspaper.

Sue finally broke the silence. "What do you think?"

Nodding in the direction of the jury room, he said, "This is the quietest jury I can ever remember." He noted that frequently deliberations become heated and voices are raised in angry arguments which easily filter beyond the protection of the closed door. "There hasn't been a peep from this group."

Translation: There was apparently little disagreement over what the verdict would be, but the silence provided no clue as to which way the jurors might be leaning.

Sue folded her newspaper and turned to face the bailiff. "Joe," she said, "this case means a great deal to me."

"I'm aware of that."

"So I need for you to do me a favor," she continued. "You'll know the verdict before you bring the jury back in, right?" Lipscomb nodded.

"Then, do this for me. If they've found him guilty, give me some sign. You don't have to look at me, just smile."

Making no promise, the bailiff rose to return to his post.

///

The jury had been out three hours when a buzzer sounded and a red light went on above the door of the deliberation room, signaling that a verdict had been reached.

Soon the once-muted third-floor hall erupted into a flurry of activity as lawyers hurried back to their posts and spectators formed impatient lines, eager to pass through security and into the courtroom. A hum of anticipation echoed through the gathering.

As if summoned for some bizarre curtain call, many of those

who had testified or heard their names mentioned from the witness stand entered and silently took their places. Shane stood near the defense table, quietly talking with Tiffany, who was seated in the front row next to her mother. Goode's parents smiled encouragingly in his direction, as did his brother. Sharon and Annette were seated directly behind the prosecutor's table, surrounded by friends and family. Reporters scrambled for locations that would provide them viewpoints from which to see the key players' reaction to the jurors' decision.

By the time the judge took the bench, a standing-room crowd had filled his courtroom. The judge motioned for the bailiff to bring in the jury.

For Sue Dietrich, who clutched Jeri's beads tightly in her hand, the long seconds after Joe Lipscomb disappeared into the jury room seemed endless. Finally, he reappeared, leading the jurors on their last trip toward the jury box.

There was a faint smile on his face.

As members of the jury settled into their places, Sharon turned and reached across the back of her bench, taking Sue's hand. Her face was suddenly ghostlike. She had waited so long for this moment, had tried to imagine how it might be, and finally she knew. She felt a kind of gripping fear she'd never before experienced. "What do you think?" she whispered to the detective.

Sue squeezed her hand and smiled. "I think," she replied, "that the jury's going to do the right thing."

Standing at the prosecution table, Jeri Yenne had no warning signal arranged and therefore no idea of what the verdict would be until she actually heard the word "guilty." When the word was spoken, her legs buckled slightly and Tony Latino gently placed his hand against her back to steady her.

Across the room, Shane Goode maintained the controlled demeanor he'd displayed throughout the trial, refusing to reveal how he felt.

For several seconds after those around her had begun sharing smiles and hugs and joyful tears, Sharon Couch sat as if frozen, staring toward the front of the courtroom. Eventually, she let her eyes trail across the railing to rest briefly upon the judge's bench, the jury box, the witness stand—as if to capture forever the memory of what had just transpired. Then she turned to her daughter and they tearfully embraced. Even as she cried, there was a look of peace on Annette's face that her mother had not seen in months.

"You've still got a job to do," Sharon said.

Annette had spent much of the previous evening preparing the victim's impact statement which she would be allowed to give in the event Shane was found guilty. Though she dreaded the idea of returning to the witness stand, she recognized the opportunity to finally publicly express feelings she had restrained for so long. It was her chance to speak out about her murdered daughter.

This time as she walked to the front of the courtroom, she made no attempt to look away from Shane. On this occasion, it was he who avoided eye contact.

"The defendant," she said, leaning toward the microphone positioned in front of her, "should now have to look into the eyes of the surviving victims, just as he looked into Renee's eyes as he was ending her life so cruelly.

"Renee's birthday is August twenty-seven. In just two weeks she would have been four years old, but the last birthday party she had was only her second one. Renee lost the opportunity for many firsts— the first day of school, her first dance, high school graduation, marriage, children, grandchildren.

"Renee lost the chance to be a big sister to her baby brother. And he has lost a wonderful sister. He will only know her through pictures and videos.

"Life has many joys to give but there is nothing that can replace the loss of Renee. Part of me died with her and nothing will ever change that or the pain that accompanies me every day."

She paused briefly and began to cry before continuing. "Her life was taken from her so early. She could have been anything: a teacher, doctor, lawyer, even an astronaut. But she will never be able to achieve any goals that she might have set for herself—which not only makes this a great loss for our family but society as well.

"Renee was a bright, cheerful, lovable child, full of energy and so very affectionate. But we will never feel her touch or hear her voice again. She is always in my thoughts but all I have left of her are memories.

"This case has touched the hearts of many people who I deeply thank.

"My life will never be the same without her. The pain is constant and nothing can reduce or relieve it. I have a great emptiness in my heart because part of me is gone, buried with Renee. I have a new son but he does not take the place of Renee. With him, I realize just how much is missing from my life with Renee gone."

For the first time since she had begun, anger then crept into her voice. Clearly, she was now speaking directly to the man convicted of her daughter's murder. "I hope that Renee can finally rest in peace, knowing that her killer is being punished as much as the law will allow. I hope that during his years in prison the defendant will meet people that treat him with the same love and compassion that he showed for Renee on January twenty-third, 1994."

She continued with a melancholy remembrance of her baby and an apology she'd been making privately for a long time. "I still look back for her some days, then suddenly realize she's not here and will never be. I'll never forget the look in her eyes as she left on January twenty-second. It was as if she knew she would never be coming back.

"I see her eyes all the time. I will never forget them. I just ask her forgiveness for letting her go with the defendant that last night of her life. I wish I could take her place and remove all the pain she had to endure.

"I want Renee never to be forgotten."

Tiffany Goode had sat quietly while the verdict was read and as Annette had spoken. In recent days, she had occasionally acknowledged a quick smile from Shane as he had turned toward her. Always smiling back, she clearly had no real understanding of the gravity of the events transpiring before her.

It was only when Judge Gayle ordered Shane Goode taken into custody and she watched as a sheriff's deputy placed handcuffs on her father that she began to cry and tried to reach across the railing toward him. Kaye Goode wrapped her arms around the distraught youngster and hurried her from the courtroom.

A few feet away, Yenne and Latino accepted the congratulations from colleagues who had abandoned their posts in the D.A.'s office to attend the reading of the verdict.

In time they would learn that the jury's first vote had been eleven to one in favor of guilt. On a second ballot the decision had been unanimous.

Leaning against the defense table, looking out on the celebration, Skip Cornelius loosened his tie and shook his head. "For the record," he said to a reporter who approached, "no comment. Off the record: We got good-ol'-boyed today." Clearly, he was eager to get away from Brazoria County and a brand of justice he found discomforting.

In the hallway, Donald Goode stood before a television camera, his face red with anger. "My son was framed," he insisted.

Sue Dietrich hurried past the cameras and tape recorders without comment, suddenly anxious to get out of the building. She would wait until later in the evening to call Jeri and congratulate her. And Sharon and Annette would want to be with their family. She could talk to them tomorrow. Or the next day. For a change, there was now plenty of time. The urgency which had for so long fueled her every waking hour was gone.

As she walked from the courthouse, stopping for a moment to light a cigarette, she felt a sudden urge to cry, to release all the pent-up emotion that had boiled inside her since that day she had called Sergeant Arendell and asked permission to investigate the case. Instead, she buried her hands in her jacket pockets and continued toward the parking lot. She'd taken only a few steps before she stopped again, pulling the strand of beads Jeri had given her from a pocket. Once more gripping them tightly, a smile began to spread across her face.

She would need to give them back. But there was plenty of time for that, too.

///

In the days following the verdict, a steady stream of floral arrangements arrived for Sue Dietrich at the Alvin Police Department. Some bore notes of congratulation from friends: Most, however, were from people she had never heard of, showing appreciation for the work she had done. In Angleton, Jeri Yenne's office had also begun to take on the look of a botanical garden.

There were cards, letters, balloons, and boxes of candy. An Alvin woman, perplexed as to how to show her appreciation, finally phoned to tell the chief that a three-hundred-dollar account had been established at a local doughnut shop in Detective Dietrich's honor for all members of the Alvin PD.

One afternoon Sue was called to the reception area where a woman who looked vaguely familiar waited. "I just wanted to come by and shake your hand," she said, "and tell you what a wonderful job we all felt you did," she said.

"I appreciate that very much," the detective responded, then, almost as an afterthought, asked, "who's 'we'?"

"I was one of the jurors," the visitor said.

Sue's mind flashed back to the day she had testified and she remembered seeing a faint smile she believed she'd glimpsed during a moment of eye contact with one of the women seated in the jury box. Nodding, the smiling detective shook her visitor's hand. "Yes," she said, "I remember you."

Sharon and Annette were not forgotten. Florists regularly visited their homes for days and their phones rang constantly. Only when they drove to Hallettsville to visit Renee's grave and spend the weekend in the country did they finally have an opportunity to relax and reflect on what had happened.

In time, though, the euphoria passes and life's regular routine returns. One evening, several weeks later, Sue Dietrich sat talking with her sister Kaye, describing the frustration she was feeling over an assault case on which she'd worked the previous night.

"These two old men," she said, "have been best friends since they were little boys. They loved each other. But they both got drunk, started arguing, and one stabbed the other four times, very nearly killing him.

"It really upset me—because, dammit, things like that just don't make any sense. Sometimes, in fact, I don't think anything I do makes sense. It never seems to end or get any better. I'm just so tired of it all."

Her sister smiled. "Yes," she said, "but it's what you do."

Afterword

There is no real ending to a story such as this. For all the talk of closure and justice being finally done, the pain lingers. Memories of such a nightmare do not simply go dormant; wounds never completely heal. It is as if the passions attached to the death of Renee Goode are seared into the hearts and souls of all those whose lives became entwined with hers.

Those involved have moved ahead but still find themselves occasionally looking back on a tragedy impossible to forget. Such will likely be the case forever.

Long after the trial, Assistant District Attorney Jeri Yenne still had a snapshot of Renee prominently displayed in her office alongside pictures of her own children. More than once her husband gently suggested that the case, the trial, and her response to Shane Goode's appeal were history. Perhaps, he said, it was time to put the photograph away. Yenne always agreed with him, yet it remained in her office until she resigned in late 1996 to enter private practice.

Sharon Couch has become a dedicated advocate for procedural change in the way medical examiners conduct autopsies on children. She lobbies, writes letters, and is an active member of the victim's rights group, Justice for All. Calls now routinely come to her from parents and relatives who once stood in her shoes, worried and suspicious that a tiny loved one's death might not have been accidental.

She pays regular visits to her son in prison, looking forward to the day he will gain his release and have an opportunity to restart his life. It pleases her that she has seen maturity in his attitude and that he views his scheduled parole hearing in 1998 as a chance to begin his life anew.

If there is good that blossoms from tragedy, it can be found in the new bond that developed between Sharon and Annette in the trying days that followed Renee's death.

Still, there are moments when Annette will grow suddenly quiet and sad, a signal for husband Vince to allow her time to herself. Such moments now pass more quickly, generally erased by Michelle's enthusiastic stories about her school activities or the ceaseless demands of two-year-old Brandon.

However, unsettling reminders of the cruelty of the world are still present. Last August, on Renee's birthday, Annette answered her phone to hear the voice of an adult female who asked, "May I speak with Renee?" The caller then laughed and hung up.

Detective Sue Dietrich admits that she suffered from a lingering depression that remained with her for months after Goode's conviction and even briefly considered leaving police work despite the fact that the Brazoria County 100 Club honored her as the Law Enforcement Officer of the Year. The case took an emotional toll she had not expected. Adding to her melancholy was the death of her father just months after the trial. In time, however, the old vigor returned and today she serves as police chief of Tiki Island, Texas, teaches a night criminal-justice class at the local junior college, and looks forward to those too-infrequent weekends when her youngest son returns from college for a brief visit.

After nine months of waiting, she finally saw a doctor about the lump in her breast and learned that it was a fibrocystic mass that proved to be benign.

One evening, not long ago, she accompanied friends to a country-western club and was momentarily stunned when she turned to face a young man who had asked if she might like to dance. For a moment all the old fear and anger and frustration returned as she looked into the face of the man she had helped send to prison. But after a second look, she realized that the cocky half-grin belonged not to Shane Goode but to his brother Dennis. Sue declined his offer and soon said good-bye to her friends, explaining that she'd decided to cut her evening short.

The Goode family remains bitter. Only days after the verdict, Donald Goode contacted the company that had written the life insurance policy on Renee, pointing out that he was listed as the secondary beneficiary and was therefore entitled to the $50,000 payoff. He also contacted the Texas Rangers to angrily criticize the Alvin Police and Brazoria County D.A.'s office. He asked them to reinvestigate the case against his son who he remains convinced is innocent.

Neither the insurance company nor the Rangers provided Goode with any satisfaction.

Meanwhile, Shane remains in prison, awaiting results of the routine appeal filed by Skip Cornelius. It was just a short time after he arrived to begin serving his sentence that he received an envelope in the mail which had no return address. Postmarked from Houston, it had no message. Inside were a half dozen photographs of Renee.

The Harris County Medical Examiner's office has recently come under fire from the local media. *Houston Press* reporter Steve Mc-Vicker has published a series of articles detailing botched postmortems, illegal tissue-harvesting, double-dipping by staff pathologists, and lack of supervision by county officials.

Dr. Jachimczyk and Cecil Wingo have both retired and the search is now underway for a new chief medical examiner. Among a list of potential candidates that began to circulate was Dr. William Anderson. Meanwhile, Wingo currently serves as the acting police chief in nearby Dickinson and has hinted that he would welcome the job on a permanent basis.

In Dallas, Dr. Linda Norton continues her forensic work, constantly urging colleagues to bear in mind the importance of thorough autopsies of children. At times, she says, when the work gets to her, she escapes Dallas for coastal getaways where she can scuba dive and wind surf. Being near the water, she says, allows her to forget, if only for a long weekend, the Shane Goodes of the world.

A final note: The greatest frustration of the nonfiction writer is not being able to neatly tie all loose ends. While the novelist can bend characters and events in such a manner that resolves every question, leaving the reader totally satisfied, those of us who chronicle actual events, attempting as best we can to hold fast to truth and fact, are not dealt such luxury.

What happened in the darkened room of the Goode home on that January 1994 night is the question that will forever haunt many of those you've read about in this book. As it will me. The speculations you've read are those of trained experts, not mine.

There will, I'm sure, be critics quick to point out that in telling the story I fell short of an obligation to better explain what drove Goode to commit such an unspeakable crime. Certainly those of us who have known the angst of financial hardship find it impossible to believe money worries alone were Shane's motive for murder. There had to be other demons at work, but I cannot describe them, any more than can those who dealt with him far more intimately. I am resigned to the fact that there are things for which there are no adequate explanations.

I do, however, know this: Real life is a maze of mysteries and unanswered questions. And in some darkened corridor there is an evil, real and menacing, that threatens us all.

It is sad and frightening, and the greatest truth this story has to offer.

About the Author

CARLTON STOWERS is the author of more than two dozen nonfiction books, including the Edgar Award–winning *Careless Whispers*, the Pulitzer Prize–nominated *Innocence Lost,* and *Open Secrets* and *Sins of the Son.* He has also written two books for children—*A Hero Named George* and *Hard Lessons*—which are used by elementary schools as part of their drug-and-gang-prevention programs. Stowers and his wife, Pat, live in Cedar Hill, Texas.